W9-AQE-494

THE MANDARINS

THE MANDARINS

THE CIRCULATION OF

ELITES IN CHINA, 1600-1900

BY ROBERT M. MARSH

THE FREE PRESS OF GLENCOE
A DIVISION OF THE CROWELL-COLLIER PUBLISHING COMPANY

Printed in the United States of America

For information, address:
The Free Press of Glencoe
A DIVISION OF THE
CROWELL-COLLIER PUBLISHING COMPANY
640 Fifth Avenue, New York 19, N. Y.

DESIGNED BY SIDNEY SOLOMON

Library of Congress Catalog Card Number 60-10899

DEDICATED TO
THE REVIVAL OF THE
SOCIOLOGICAL STUDY OF HISTORY

FOREWORD

THE MOST striking feature of this important work by Dr. Marsh is, I think, that it is a contribution to two fields of scholarship, sinology and sociology. And because it is at once a contribution to two fields, it is a better contribution to each. The historico-empirical data provide an excellent comparative case for a number of areas of specialized sociological interest, notably the interests in the family, formal organization, occupations and professions, and social stratification and mobility. On the other hand, both the explicit theoretical perspectives provided by these sociological fields, and the systematic empirical and statistical requirements of contemporary sociology perhaps deepen the sinologist's understanding of the Ch'ing period in Chinese history and of other related periods as well.

As a sociologist, I cannot, obviously, appraise the precise degree of Dr. Marsh's contribution to sinology. I have been more than assured, however, by specialists in that field with whom I worked conjointly in the supervision of an earlier version of this work that the contribution is considerable. As a sociologist, I can say, however, that Dr. Marsh's book will be of widespread interest and great value in our field. I have already said that it is important as a comparative case for the fields of the family, formal organization, occupations and professions, and social stratification and mobility. I want to add that its comparative relevance should bring it to the eager attention of nearly all sociologists, since for them historical and other comparative works are functional alternatives to controlled experimentation as a means of testing and refining sociological theory. Regardless of their particular substantive content, all comparative works of scholarship have a certain generalized interest for sociologists who seek to enlarge the scope of systematic theory in their field, and thus increase its essential scientific character.

Dr. Marsh's book, then, is a very readable, substantively engaging, and theoretically creative addition to sinological and sociological knowledge. I enthusiastically commend it to a wide circle of readers.

BERNARD BARBER

Barnard College
Columbia University

PREFACE

CHINA HAD its own version of the Horatio Alger myth, whereby the poor but talented boy from a humble family could succeed, by a combination of "pluck and luck," in reaching high social position. As in American society, Chinese values stated that "government ministers and generals are not born in office"; "sons shall not necessarily remain in the same social stratum as their fathers; it is legitimate for anyone to seek to better his station in life." My purpose in this book is to determine the extent to which these "open-class" values were operative in the recruitment and advancement of government officials in traditional China. I shall also attempt to explain the career patterns of these officials—the exalted mandarins—by the use of sociological theory and methods, and with the help of an understanding of Chinese history.

I wish to gratefully acknowledge the contributions which several individuals and institutions have made to my work. My greatest intellectual debts are to my teachers in the Graduate Faculty at Columbia University: William J.

Goode, whose theoretical insights and abiding interest in Chinese social structure have always been a spur to my effort; C. Martin Wilbur, whose analysis of Chinese history is, at so many points, sociologically exciting; and Bernard Barber, whose excellent systematization of the theory and the comparative data in the field of social stratification helped to define some of the central points in the argument of this study.

My obligation to Robert K. Merton is perhaps less apparent in this study than I should like it to be, but it is nonetheless real and pervasive. I am grateful to Robert S. Lynd for his encouragement throughout my graduate study, especially when difficulties confronted me. I should also like to thank Professor L. C. Goodrich for essential bibliographical and other guidance. The staffs of the following Chinese libraries gave generously of their time and have greatly assisted me in my research: Columbia, Harvard, the University of California at Berkeley, the Library of Congress, Tokyo University and the Toyo Bunko, Japan, and the Academia Sinica, Taiwan.

To the Ford Foundation I must express my deep gratitude for financial and other assistance which enabled me to carry out research both in this country and in Taiwan and Japan between 1956 and 1958. The views expressed here are my own, of course, and not necessarily those of the Ford Foundation.

My wife, Susan Han Marsh, has helped me in innumerable ways and deserves much of the credit for the completion of this study.

The author thanks the following publishers and copyright holders for their permission to excerpt and reprint selections used in this book:

The Macmillan Company for American rights and George Allen and Unwin Ltd. for foreign rights to *Yuan Mei,* by Arthur Waley.

Professors Reinhard Bendix and Seymour M. Lipset for permission to quote from their article, "Social Status and Social Structure," *British Journal of Sociology*, Vol. II No. 3, page 248.

The University of California Press for permission to quote from *Social Mobility in Industrial Society*, by Seymour M. Lipset and Rienhard Bendix, page 236.

The Free Press of Glencoe, Illinois for permission to quote from *Recent Trends in Occupational Mobility*, by Natalie Rogoff, page 31, and *The Social System*, by Talcott Parsons, page 161.

Harcourt, Brace and Company, Inc. for permission to quote from *Social Stratification*, by Bernard Barber, pages 361 and 379.

The President and Fellows of Harvard College for permission to quote from *Imperialism and Social Classes*, by Joseph Schumpeter, pages 113 and 123.

Harvard University Press for permission to quote from *The Family Revolution in Modern China*, by Marion J. Levy, Jr., pages 222-223 and 498.

The Johns Hopkins Press for permission to quote from *The Government of China, 1644-1911*, by Hsieh Pao-chao, pages 104, 110, 117 and 125, and *The Origin of Manchu Rule in China*, by Franz Michael, page 107.

Messrs. Frank W. Notestein, Chi-ming Chiao and John Lossing Buck for permission to quote from *Land Utilization in China*, pages 385 and 386.

Mrs. Margaret P. Redfield for permission to quote from *Chinese Thought and Institutions*, edited by John K. Fairbank, page 245. The rights for this book, published by the University of Chicago Press, were held by Professor Robert Redfield, and are now held by his widow, Margaret P. Redfield.

Sands and Company Ltd. for permission to quote from *China*, by Harold Gorst, pages 124 and 127.

The United States Government Printing Office for permission to quote from *Eminent Chinese of the Ch'ing Period, 1644-1912*, edited by Arthur W. Hummel, pages iii, 526, 191, 260 and 534.

The Wenner-Gren Foundation for Anthropological Research for permission to quote from *The Common Descent Group in China and its Functions*, by Hu Hsien-chin, page 88.

Yale University Press for permission to quote from *Oriental Despotism*, by Karl A. Wittfogel, pages 354 and 350.

The permission granted by the above publishers and coyright holders covers world rights in the English language for the Free Press edition of this book.

ROBERT MORTIMER MARSH

CONTENTS

FOREWORD vii

PREFACE ix

LIST OF TABLES xv

1. Introduction 1
2. The Determinants of the Amount of Elite Mobility 13
3. Chinese Social Stratification, 1600-1900 33
4. Earlier Research on Chinese Elite Mobility 71
5. Methodology 84
6. Bureaucratic *vs.* Extra-Bureaucratic Determinants of Official Advancement (1) 114
7. Bureaucratic *vs.* Extra-Bureaucratic Determinants of Official Advancement (2) 154
8. Summary, Conclusions, and Future Research 186

APPENDIX I. 572 Officials in *Eminent Chinese of the Ch'ing Period,* Classified by Manchu, Chinese Official, or Chinese Commoner Family Background 195

APPENDIX II. Supplement to Family Background Data for the Chinese Sample 201

APPENDIX III. The Formal Hierarchy of the Ch'ing Bureaucracy 206

NOTES 237

GLOSSARY 243

BIBLIOGRAPHY 259

INDEX 291

LIST OF TABLES

1. Relation of Crop Area of Farm to Fertility of Married Women in China, 45 Years Old or Over, 1929-31 17
2. Hierarchy of Degrees (Military and Civil) in Ming and Ch'ing Dynasties 55
3. Legal Salary Range for Civil and Military Officials 63
4. Relation between Family Background and Level of "Gentry" Entered, 1796-1908 80
5. Relation between Family Background and Degree-Attainment, Ming and Ch'ing Dynasties 82
6. Biographical Emphasis in Ming and Ch'ing Dynastic Histories 87
7. Frequency Distribution of Length of Career of 572 Ch'ing Officials 98
8. Biographical Categories of 572 Officials in Seven Major Ming and Ch'ing Dynasty Collections 101
9. Biographical Categories of 572 Officials in the Eminent Chinese of the Ch'ing Period 102
10. Highest Bureaucratic Rank Reached During Careers, 572 Ch'ing Officials 104

11. Relation between Highest Bureaucratic Rank Reached and Reason for Biographical Distinction of 572 Officials 105

12. Stratum Position of Family of Orientation for 572 Ch'ing Officials: Marginal Totals 111

13. Relation between Banner Membership and Official Advancement (by Highest Rank Attained Career) 120

14. Relation between Banner Membership and Official Advancement (by Length of Incumbency) 121

15. Stratum Position of Family of Orientation of 572 Officials 123

16. Relation between Family Stratum Position and Chin-Shih Degree Attainment 125

17. Relation between Family Stratum Position and Age at the Chin-Shih Degree 127

18. Relation between Intellectual Family Background and Age of Chin-Shih for Commoners 128

19. Combined Influence of Official and Intellectual Family Background upon Age at Attainment of Chin-Shih 129

20. Family Stratum Position of Officials Advancing by "Regular" and "Irregular" Mobility Paths 132

21. Relation between Family Stratum Position and Official Advancement 133

22. Relation between Family Stratum Position and Rate of Promotion 135

23. Validity of the Official vs. Commoner Differentiation According to Highest Rank Attained 136

24. Relation between Family Stratum Position and Length of Incumbency 138

25. Relation between Rank Attained and Recruitment Path Taken 139

26. Relation between Length of Incumbency and Recruitment Path Taken 140

27. Role of the Examination System in Official Advancement 143

28. Advancement of Manchu and of Chinese Commoner Regular Path Officials 144

29. Relation between Recruitment Path Taken and Highest Rank Attained When Family Position Is Held Constant (1) 145

30. Relation between Recruitment Path Taken and Later Advancement When Family Position Is Held Constant (2) 147

31. Official Tradition in Family of 454 Non-Manchu Officials 155

32. Relation between Strength of Official Family Tradition and Advancement (by Highest Rank Attained) 156

33. Relation between Strength of Official Family Tradition and Advancement (by Length of Incumbency) 157

34. Number of Successive Generations in Office 159

35. Total Number of Generations in Office 160

36. Amount of Chinese Elite Mobility, by 30-Year Periods, 1500-1900 (Relation between Status of Father and of Official-Son) 161

37. Relation between the Dynastic Cycle and the Amount of Mobility, 1590-1900 (According to Relation between Status of Father and Official-Son) 163

38. Relation between Family Stratum Position and Seniority Accumulated 165

39. Relation between Seniority and Advancement in Office (Highest Rank Attained and Number of Officials by Total Years in Office) 166

40. Relation between Seniority and Advancement in Office (Median Length of Incumbency and Number of Officials by Total Years in Office) 167

41. Relation between Seniority and Advancement, When Family Position Is Held Constant 168

42. Relation between Family Position and Advancement When Seniority Is Held Constant 169

43. Rate of Promotion among "Regular" and "Irregular" Path Chinese Commoners' Sons 172

THE
MANDARINS

CHAPTER 1 INTRODUCTION

IN CONTEMPORARY American society there is no one occupation or career which, *far more* than all others, assures one of the greatest rewards the society has to offer. Prestige, influence, wealth, and other rewards are somewhat *dispersed* among several of the professions, government service, business leadership, and politics. In China during the Ch'ing period (seventeenth through nineteenth centuries), on the other hand, the highest worldly rewards of the society were all integrated into *one* ideal career pattern—office in the imperial governmental bureaucracy. "The world cheats those who hold no office," wrote the T'ang dynasty poet-official, Po Chü-i. The supreme status of officials was based upon several factors: they were closely associated with the Emperor, the "Son of Heaven," as administrators of his Realm; their prestige and authority were second only to his and to that of a small group of nobility; official appointment and advancement presupposed, at least for many of them, the most extensive preparatory education of any career in the society, an education consisting wholly of the highly revered classics and humanistic orientation; they maintained and transmitted the core values of the culture; they had the highest earning power and wealth in the society, aside from the Imperial court itself. Office (*lu*)* ranked with longevity (*shou*) and male issue (*fu*) as central values of the culture. We may indeed speak of officials as the elite of traditional China.

> He had a black gauze cap and green silk gown,
> A jasper ring on his cap and a purple belt;
> His socks were white as snow,
> His shoes like rosy clouds;
> He'd a lordly look and natural dignity.
> A man like that, if not a god,
> Must at least be a high official or a ruler of men.[1]

A significant aspect of this one elite career model in China was that, legally, recruitment to it was open to virtually all males in the society, on an achievement basis. In this sense, China had its own version of the Horatio Alger myth, whereby the poor but talented boy from humble family background could succeed, by a combination of "pluck and luck," in attaining the highest reaches of officialdom. The public examination system was to the Chinese a major symbol of this competitive achievement. Given these two facts—at stake in the examination competition was the chance of entering the one ideal career, and recruitment to this career was legally open to all—there was an intense and widespread interest in the outcome of each of these examinations, even on the part of masses of Chinese who would never themselves participate:

> The public attention at the approach of the triennial examinations is as intense in China as the interest of the English people in the elections. Thousands assemble in the cities, and men of all descriptions collect to profit by such an extraordinary concourse of people. . . . As soon as the results are known, the country from one end to the other resounds with the names of the successful

* See Glossary for Chinese characters.

> candidates. A list is immediately published, and circulated in every city; even the peasants look at them eagerly, and read them attentively. The parents and relations of the sons of fortune receive congratulations, and patch up papers on their houses, to inform the public of the great fortune which has fallen to their lot. [Gutzlaff, 1838, II, 350-51.]

Or, as another writer put it, the names of the metropolitan graduates "became household words for the time being in every town and hamlet over . . . China" (Giles, 1882, p. 253). An eighteenth-century Chinese official recalled the impression made on him as a youth by men successful in the examination system: "If I heard that the guest had won a degree, I gazed up at him as though he were a king of peaks; all the family would come to peep and wonder, clacking their tongues at this prodigious sight" (Waley, 1956, p. 86). Between 1646 and 1904, 112 examinations for the *chin-shih*, or highest degree, were held, and 26,747 men took the degree (Fang, 1941). Many times this number of men received lower degrees in the examination system during this period.

China did not have a caste system; it was not entirely irrational for a commoner—even a peasant commoner—to seek to become an official. Many elements of Chinese culture encouraged the view that this goal was a legitimate objective for all "men of talent" (*jen-ts'ai*). Ideally speaking, office and its rewards were to devolve upon the wise, the virtuous, and the talented. There were numerous stories about the "model epoch" of Chinese antiquity and legend-history, when these "men of talent," although of rustic background and not connected with large, influential families (*hao-tsu*), could nevertheless secure official appointment (Yang, 1956, p. 119). Among Confucius' own disciples were men of humble origin; as a memorial to the throne in 1822 pointed out: "Many of the sages and worthies of antiquity rose from the midst of fish and salt, and markets and public wells" (that is, the rabble) (Gutzlaff, 1838, II, 354). The philosopher Hsün-tzu (third century B.C.) advocated that the rise and fall of men and families be based upon merit and virtue. "Ministers and generals are not born in office" was a folk belief often invoked to spur youth on to official ambition. Aphorisms and tales were buttressed by scattered actual cases of mobility, dear to the memory of the people of a locality. This ideological component of achievement was an important factor in Chinese society (Ch'ü, 1957, pp. 238-39, 243). There were, of course, elements in the culture which favored aristocracy and the monopoly of office within the same families for generations. My point is only that there were available many values and beliefs which sanctioned and even encouraged aspirations for upward mobility.

It is for these reasons that numerous observers have detected a strong achievement component among the Chinese: "Differing . . . from the coolie of Hindustan, the Chinese is ignorant of the blighting effects of caste, and is as strongly bent on raising himself to a higher position as he is on acquiring wealth" (Lane-Poole, 1894, I, 176).

Traditional China also had a set of institutionalized norms which defined the *means* by which men were to reach out for this goal of official status. We may distinguish between the *preferred* means, the *permitted* means, and the *proscribed* means of becoming an official. The preferred means, as we have already suggested, was through the several levels of the competitive examinations, which the Chinese referred to as "the ladder to the clouds" (*pu-pu ch'ing-yün*). This method involved long years of memorization and mastery of the ancient classics, the dynastic histories, commentaries, poetry, and a highly rigid form of essay-composition called the "eight-legged" essay (*pa-ku wen*), in which form candidates had to compose their answers to questions in the examinations. Interspersed through these years of study were the successive examinations at the district (*hsien*), prefectural (*fu*), provincial, metropolitan, and palace levels. Given the number of hurdles in this preferred method of mobility, it is little wonder that candidates worked furiously for years, often abandoning general study and reading, not to mention many social activities, in order to concentrate on the required material.

> The richer classes . . . take into their houses private tutors, who have already taken their degrees, and are therefore enabled to direct the pupils in adopting the proper mode to obtain the same honours. Poorer students either endeavor to obtain the requisite knowledge from books, by close application, or repair to one of the public seminaries, of which there are several, in the principal cities of larger districts. [Gutzlaff, 1838, II, 347.]

Among the *permitted* but not preferred means of seeking office were (*a*) rising from the lowest ranks of the civil or military bureaucracy without taking degrees in the examination system, and (*b*) purchase. (There is some evidence that purchase to some extent displaced the examinations as the *preferred* means of mobility during the latter part of the nineteenth century [Hsü Ta-ling, 1950].) Still other means of entering the bureaucracy, such as usurpation of office through organized rebellion, were *proscribed* by the legitimate reigning dynasty.

The important point in the present context concerns the *parallels* between Chinese and American societies. Formally, both societies have value-systems which state, "Sons shall not necessarily remain in the same social stratum as their fathers; it is *legitimate* for *anyone* to seek to better his station in life." But whereas in both societies all males were able, in principle, to compete for the highest occupational goals, not all males had the same *access* to the requirements of mobility—money, leisure, family influence, tutors, and the like. In China, peasants' sons competed at a decided disadvantage with officials' sons. This made the examination system and the other channels of mobility focal points of anxiety, tension, and social strain. The culturally sanctioned goal was open to all comers, while the actual opportunities for success through the institutionally prescribed means depended, to some extent at least, on one's family background. Another source of psychological strains and tensions was the fact that the examination system was bureaucratically administered on the basis of competition between individuals; thus, not even the sons of officials could be sure of success. There were several types of responses to this stressful competitive situation which were common to both societies. We may label these responses, following Merton, as *conformity, innovation, ritualism, retreatism,* and *rebellion* (Merton, 1957, pp. 139 ff.). Merton has dealt with these responses in the context of American society; we shall here suggest briefly some of the forms these reactions took in Chinese society during the period with which we are concerned, i.e., 1600-1900.

To the extent that Chinese sought office only through the institutionally preferred means—the examinations—and to the extent that they enforced conformity to these same standards on the part of their examiners, we may label their response as one of conformity. Candidates in the examination system have been described as having "the combustibility of German *burschen,*" for "if the chancellor proves partial, or does not carefully examine the essays, the students have often risen up against him in open rebellion and forced him to yield to their wishes" (Gutzlaff, 1838, II, 353). One official remarked, "When the lists go up much is heard of the candidates' resentment" (Waley, 1956, p. 56). The 1721 *chin-shih* examination revived a supposedly T'ang dynasty (618-907 A.D.) practice, whereby the *general reputation* of candidates was given more weight than their actual replies in the examination. " 'When the results were announced, the unsuccessful candidates . . . organized an angry demonstration, holding up [the Chief Examiner's] carriage in the street and blocking up his gate with tiles and stones, so that he could not drive in.' The Emperor K'ang Hsi dissapproved of [the examiner's] methods, and ordered Prince Yung to go through the papers of the unsuccessful candidates." In this way, the norm of impartiality was reinstated (Waley, 1956, p. 59). To cite another aspect of extreme conformity, the intensity with which many candidates threw themselves into the competition sometimes resulted in death from exhaustion during the examination.

A different situation existed when candidates sought the goal of official success by making *innovations* in the means, that is, by resorting to *illegitimate means* of attaining their goal. This was done by cheating in the examinations, by having another person take the examination in one's stead, by bribing the examiners, and by numerous other devices. Once, an underground tunnel was discovered, running under the cubicles where the candidates sat in isolation for several days to write their essays, and serving as a means of smuggling correct essays in and out! Extreme precautions against these innovations had to be taken by those in charge of the examinations. But the emperor could also manipulate the examinations in such a way as to reward or punish whole provinces. "When the emperor wishes to punish a province for some crime committed by the people, he suspends the customary examination, and nothing appears more ignominious than such degradation. But the gracious monarch more frequently grants an additional examinatoin" (Gutzlaff, 1838, II, 353).

Another type of adaptation to the discrepancy between the goal and the differential access to its realization was *ritualism*. Highly motivated candidates who failed again and again kept coming back, in many cases even unto old age. In these cases, the desire for success through the institutionalized means was so strong that repeated failure could not extinguish it, and the consequence was *over-conformity* to the means. There were also numerous cases of another kind of ritualism, where men who had taken lower degrees but not the higher ones which could qualify them for office continued to eke out a miserable livelihood as scholars and tutors. This ritualism had the function of preserving the appearance that one was still "in the race," an appearance that would have been lost had he turned to the more lucrative but less prestigeful occupations, such as commerce.

Retreatism was a response of other Chinese who failed to compete successfully in the examinations. These individuals gave up *both* the goal and the means of attaining the goal; they retired from "the world of dust," and became hermits, monks, and recluses. In more recent times, other Chinese have become alienated from both the goal and the means of the traditional achievement system. But instead of reacting by retreatism, they have taken the path of covert or overt *rebellion*. One thinks, in this connection, of those who became authors of works which sharply satirized and otherwise attacked this traditional system of officialdom and examinations—men like Wu Ching-tzu, Wu Wo-yao, Li Pao-chia, and Liu E.[2] Still other rebels, frustrated by this system, sought to substitute new means and new goals through overt rebellion, as in the case of the Taiping Rebellion of the mid-nineteenth century.[3]

The tension so characteristic of this competitive achievement system is well summed up in a poem Yüan Mei addressed in 1768 to his revered examiner in the *chin-shih* examination of thirty years previously, Teng Shih-min:

> What agony it was thirty years ago
> At Peking, waiting for the lists to appear . . . !
> I met someone who told me I had passed;
> I was bowled over by this thunderclap of joy and surprise,
> I thought it was a mistake, thought it was only a dream;
> I was in a sorry state of doubt and dread.
> Yet it was true; that staunch master Teng . . . ,
> Had written that my name was to figure on the list,
> Had rescued me out of my dark abyss . . . .
> Parents, however much they love a child,
> Have not the power to place him among the chosen few.
> Only the examiner can bring the youth to notice,
> And out of darkness carry them up to Heaven.
> [Waley, 1956, p. 24.]

Had the goal of an official career not been held out as a legitimate expectation for *all comers*, some of the above responses might not have occurred as frequently or intensely as they did. In suggesting Chinese parallels to Merton's analysis, we are not able to show which groups of candidates took which type of response. This is an important step, but is beyond the scope of this study. The general hypothesis, however, would be that those individuals subjected most fully to the discrepancies between goals and means, e.g., the underprivileged strata, would be those most likely to respond in ways other than conformity.

Thus far, we have tried to suggest certain resemblances between the achievement orientation of Chinese and American societies. Both societies are stratified, that is, they are divided into social strata between which exist institutionalized inequalities; in both societies social recruitment for the highest positions was formally open to virtually all males, on an achievement basis.

But what was the actual, as aside from the ideal, pattern of intergenerational mobility in traditional China? The purpose of this study is to attempt to determine the extent to which these "open-class" values were institutionalized and operative, and to attempt to analyze and explain our findings in terms of sociological concepts and hypotheses, and with the help of an understanding of Chinese history.

In somewhat more technical language, our dependent variable is elite mobility, as observed in Chinese society between 1600 and 1900. Elite mobility may be defined, in a preliminary way, as the social movement of individuals or groups who ascend into, occupy, or descend from the most highly valued occupational or other social roles in a society.

Stated very briefly, theory and earlier research[4] (which we shall discuss in Chapter II) suggest that the following factors are the major determinants of the processes and amounts of elite mobility:

(1) Size of elite, "elite demand," or "opportunity structure." Pre-industrial societies such as traditional China have a smaller proportion of elite positions in their working force than do industrial societies.

(2) Fertility rates. Pre-industrial elites are more likely to reproduce their numbers in the population than are industrial elites.

(3) Stratum position of the family into which one is born:

a. prestige of occupation,
b. degree of authority and power,
c. legal position,
d. economic position.

These positions are ascribed to the individual and influence his access to the elite.

(4) Stratum position of the family one marries into; its position in each of the hierarchies in (3). This shows the extent of marrying "up" or "down," as this in turn affects elite mobility.

(5) Amount of downward mobility in the society, due to the inability and/or the unwillingness of elite sons to maintain their fathers' positions.

(6) Inheritance patterns. Are they such as to dissipate or maintain the economic bases of elite position from one generation to the next?

(7) Degree to which elite mobility occurs within a context of formal bureaucratic norms:

a. extent to which the recruitment of elites is universalistic,
b. extent to which official advancement is determined by universal rules of seniority and merit.

(8) Values and norms affecting mobility:

a. formal, official, ideological norms concerning the possibility and desirability of upward mobility in the society, *b.* informal norms and beliefs of different strata, subcultures, etc., with respect to upward mobility in the society.

(9) Extent to which given members of the society have the intelligence and motivation to enter the elite (in order to enhance self-esteem, to improve the position of the immediate family, the wider kin group, etc.).

In subsequent chapters we shall use these factors in attempting to answer such questions as: What determined differences in official advancement in the Chinese bureaucracy? Did bureaucratic factors such as seniority influence Chinese officials' advancement more than such extra-bureaucratic factors as family background? Did it matter whether a Chinese official took the preferred path (the examination competition) or other paths, to office?

The Consequences of Mobility. This study concerns mainly the patterns of elite mobility in Chinese society, and the factors that explain these mobility patterns. The significance of this type of research may not be fully apparent at first. One may ask, what difference does it make how much mobility there is? Is it not more important to study what individuals and groups produce, believe, etc., than to inquire so elaborately into their class and family background? It is well to point out that different amounts and processes of social mobility *do* have important consequences both for individual behavior and for society; the study of the circulation of elites is no mere intellectual exercise. One can show that many of the events and developments of history were shaped, in part at least, by whether the actors involved were improving, declining, or remaining stationary in their social position. Mannheim argued that self-made men are keener than men of ascribed, inherited status, and are therefore better suited to times of social change. He also suggested that if self-made men over-assimilate the traits of the old elite, the society would forfeit some of its resources for change and adaptation. (Mannheim, 1950, p. 105.)

The circulation of elites has been shown to have significant consequences in the political realm. For example, in a society with considerable upward and downward mobility, the political and economic solidarity of the classes involved tends to be weakened, whether it be the working class or the elite. In America, the ideology of individual opportunity and achievement appears to have made the working class and the labor movement weaker than their European counterparts, where the ideology of collective mobility is more important. It has been found, for American society, that individuals who move up or down the social scale are more likely than those who remain stationary (as from father's to son's generation) to be politically apathetic and to abstain from voting. Students of Chinese history should be quite aware of the significance of the *issue* of *how much* and *what kinds* of social mobility and circulation of elites there should be; there was a long tradition of commentary and decision on these matters. Ch'en Yin-k'o has stressed the conflict between the aristocracy and the "new men" trained in the examination system in the T'ang dynasty. The search for "men of talent" to fill government posts went on through the centuries, with some spokesmen insisting that the best place to find such men was among the well-born, and others proposing various schemes for broadening the opportunities of men from the various provinces, ethnic groups, etc. (Kracke, 1957). Nor is it likely that the ups and downs of the dynastic cycle throughout Chinese history were entirely unrelated to the opportunities for social mobility (see Chapter VII of this study).

CHAPTER 2 THE DETERMINANTS OF THE AMOUNT OF ELITE MOBILITY

WHAT ARE the facts of elite mobility and the circulation of elites in China between 1600 and 1900 which call for explanation? First, there are the facts of *intra-generational* mobility; second, the facts of *inter-generational* mobility. As to the first, in our analysis of the career lines of a sample of 572 governmental officials we shall observe the following kinds of differences: (*a*) these officials differed in the way they were recruited to the bureaucracy—some took the preferred path, the examination system; others entered through alternative means, such as purchase; (*b*) they differed as to whether they achieved the highest degree in the examination system (*chin-shih*) or not; (*c*) there were considerable age differences among those who took the *chin-shih* degree. These 572 officials also differed as to: (*d*) the highest rank they reached in the bureaucratic hierarchy during their careers; (*e*) the length of time they held high-rank posts; and (*f*) their rate of promotion, the proportion of their total career which they spent in high-rank posts. We must attempt, in this part of our study, to account for these several differences in Chinese intra-generational mobility. As to the facts of inter-generational mobility, we must explain why the families in our sample differed with respect to the number of successive generations who held office.

Our analysis of the circulation of elites in China, then, will proceed along two lines: first, the *career patterns* of officials—their recruitment and official advancement; second, the degree to which elite families rose and fell, or maintained their elite status, over two or more generations.

We may now turn to sociological theory and earlier research, to see how they shed light on the above problems. We shall examine each of the determinants of social mobility which we introduced at the end of Chapter I.

Size of the Elite. The individuals in our Chinese elite sample are distributed through a three-hundred-year period, from about 1600 to 1900. It is possible that some of the above facts of mobility might be explained by changes in the *size* of the Chinese elite during these three centuries. An expansion in the number of official posts would enable more men to enter the elite and advance in the bureaucracy. Chang Chung-li (1953, 1955) has estimated that the elite constituted approximately 2 per cent of the total population of China in the nineteenth century. In the 1880's, when China's population was officially recorded as between 350 million and 400 million individuals, or about 70 million households (*hu*), Chang estimates the distribution indicated in the accompanying table. Chang estimates that the average size of elite households was five individuals. Thus, the 1,500,000 elite individuals, plus the members of their immediate families, amounted to 7,500,000 people, or approximately 2 per cent of the total population of China. No Chinese population estimates are based upon modern censuses and may therefore be widely in error.

Of the 1.5 million individuals in the elite in late nineteenth-century China, 86 per cent were "lower" or local elite (licentiates, *sheng-yüan*), and the remaining 14 per cent were "upper elite," i.e., officials, holders of official titles, and degree-holders who were eligible for office—*chin-shih*, *chü-jen*, and *kung-sheng*. (*Sheng-yüan* were not, as such, eligible for office.) Of all the elite, only 2 per cent were actually in office; the other 12 per cent eligible for office were not appointed; the remaining 86 per cent of the elite were not eligible for office, but, rather, performed local leadership roles as teachers, landowners, merchants, and fulfilled other "gentry functions" (see Chapter III).

Stratum	*Number of Households*	*Percentage of Total Population*
Elite (officials and degree-holders)	1,500,000	2
Farmers, peasants	56,000,000	80
All others: merchants, artisans, etc.	12,500,000	18
Total	70,000,000	100

If there were variations in the amount of elite mobility in China between 1600 and 1900, this could have resulted from (*a*) changes in the demand for elite, e.g., an expansion of elite positions in relation to the rest of the working force, and/or from (*b*) all other factors: fertility rates, less discrimination against commoners' sons, etc. In principle, it would be valuable to distinguish that aspect of mobility due to demand factors from those aspects of mobility due to all other factors (cf. Rogoff, 1953). Unfortunately, at the present time, we cannot estimate with any accuracy whether the 2 per cent figure for the elite had changed since the seventeenth or eighteenth centuries. The status of Ch'ing population statistics is currently a matter of considerable debate among historians and demographers; this fact makes it impossible to estimate the extent to which changes in the amount of mobility in our sample are due to changes in the demand for elite. While there are some rough indications that the absolute size of the Chinese elite grew between 1600 and 1900 (Chang, 1955, pp. 111-13), it is unlikely that this increase was proportionate to the growth of the population as a whole. The size of the Chinese elite, then, at best probably remained a constant proportion of the growing population; it may have even declined in relation to the total population or working force. Given the uncertain state of our knowledge in this area, we cannot attempt to explain changes in the amount of mobility on the basis of changes in elite demand or opportunity structure.

Fertility Rates. A second factor which may account for the amount of elite mobility in a society is class differences in fertility. If the elite more than reproduces its numbers in the population, it can, conceivably, fill all the elite openings from among itself, thus preventing the ascent of lower-strata individuals. If, on the other hand, the elite fails to reproduce its numbers, then lower-strata individuals must rise to fill these elite openings. The writer knows of no reliable data on fertility for the Ch'ing period. For what it is worth, we cite the findings of some studies done in China between the two World Wars. Buck (1937, pp. 384-86) collected data on 10,700 wives in 101 rural localities for the period 1929-31. He found (see Table 1) that fertility increased slightly with economic status, as measured by the size of the crop area of the farm.

Lamson (1935) summarized his own and others' findings drawn from a series of small samples of urban communities during the period from the 1910's to the early 1930's. His data show a more markedly direct association between fertility and economic status.

Buck summarizes these findings: "the central fact is that the differences in the fertility of different economic groups

Table 1—Relation of Crop Area of Farm to Fertility of Married Women in China, 45 Years Old or Over, 1929-31

Size of Farm*	Total Number Children Born per 1,000 Wives	Number of Wives
Very large	5510	2946
Large	5350	2284
Medium large	5280	1845
Medium	5060	1697
Small	5030	1514
Total	5288 (average)	10,286

*Note that the sample over-represents large farms and under-represents small farms.

are much less important in China's rural population than they are in the West. To the extent that they do exist, they are, like those found by Lamson for urban communities, in the opposite direction" (p. 384). Put very simply, it appears that while in China the higher socio-economic strata had *more* children than the lower economic strata, in modern American society the higher socio-economic strata had *fewer* children than the lower economic strata. The higher status and wealthier families in general had more surviving offspring than did the lower status and poorer families; the former group may have married younger than the latter. These and other factors made for a *direct* relationship between socio-economic status and family size. This being so, we cannot explain the amount of elite mobility in China between 1600 and 1900 on the basis of the failure of the elite to reproduce itself. Whatever upward mobility there was (non-elite sons becoming elite) occurred *despite* the fact that members of the elite typically had one or more sons who could potentially succeed them.

Sample	NUMBER OF CHILDREN PER 1,000 MOTHERS Living	Dead	Total
438 upper-class mothers, aged 40-44	4570	1680	6250
1,000 lower-class mothers, age 40 or over	2300	2400	4700

[Lamson, 1935, p. 312, Table 3.]

Stratum Position of Family of Orientation. The position of the family into which one is born is a crucial determinant of one's mobility in any society. China, like the United States, was a stratified society; the position one's family held in this system of stratification influenced his chances for elite mobility and official advancement. Since this concept of "stratum position of family of orientation" occupies a central place in our analysis of Chinese elite mobility, we had better develop it at some length. We shall first present a theory of stratification and then show the role of the family in stratification.

A *Theory of Stratification.* Every complex society has those who lead and those who are led; some who command great prestige and authority and others little; the wealthy, the not-so-wealthy, and the poor. How are we to explain the near-universality of this fact?[1] The fundamental reasons for stratification in society seem to be as follows:[2] Every social system has a division of labor, a differentiation of roles which are functionally essential for the maintenance of the system. In common-sense terms, a society in which everyone fulfills exactly the same function is inconceivable. These functionally important and differentiated roles become the major social roles—e.g., occupations—of the individuals in the society.

Such roles as the political, economic, military, and religious are functionally important in all societies, but their relative evaluation within each society varies from society to society. It appears that these roles are evaluated on the basis of the degree of knowledge and/or responsibility which their successful performance demands. Those roles requiring either an extensive body of ideas and skills, or the control over a large number of other people's roles, or both, tend to be evaluated more highly by the members of a society than roles requiring fewer ideas, skills, and smaller spans of control.

Along these axes of knowledge and responsibility, then, (*a*) the members of a society make invidious distinctions as to the functionally important and differentiated roles of their society, and (*b*) they may extend their invidious distinctions even to the *individuals* performing the roles. The essence of men's orientation to their own and other men's roles and functions is *evaluative*.

The values by which men evaluate these major social roles tend to be integrated into common value systems, except at times of radical social change; they do not vary at random from individual to individual. These rankings tend to be patterned, shared by all or most of the members of the society.

We have argued that social stratification is a product of social differentiation and of the evaluation of these functionally important roles by the members of the society. We have also argued that, no matter what the *relative* evaluation within a society of such universally functional roles as the political, economic, religious, and military, *within* each of these categories of roles, those roles calling for greater knowledge and responsibility will be ranked higher in the society than those involving less knowledge and responsibility.

Finally, in this theory "social stratification" is identified as that structure of institutionalized inequality in which men are ranked higher and lower on the basis of the normative evaluation accorded to their major social roles by members of the society, and rewarded differentially in terms of this ranking.

Social stratification, in this sense, is only one form of stratification in societies. Other processes and systems of stratification are, only in the limiting case, perfectly correlated with the system of social stratification. For example, economic stratification—the differentiation of the sources and amounts of income, and of consumption patterns in a society—always varies more or less independently of the ranking of men's major social roles. In societies which stress legal criteria of stratification, men who are legally in similar categories may or may not be similar in their economic position or their social ranking. Similarly, the stratification of power and authority may or may not correlate with the foregoing dimensions of stratification in a given society. Chapter III is devoted to an analysis of the historical facts of stratification in China during the period 1600 to 1900, with special reference to the interrelationships between social, legal, economic, and authority stratification.

We may now state more fully the relation of this basic theory of stratification to our dependent variable, elite mobility. Mobility is part of the dynamic side of social stratification. While social stratification concerns the *structure* of differential rankings of major roles, mobility concerns the processes and amounts of *movement* within the structure.

In this study, we are interested in vertical rather than horizontal mobility. Vertical mobility is specifically *upward* or *downward* movement between less and more highly evaluated roles within the system of stratification. According to this definition, movement between two occupational roles which are *equally* evaluated by the society involves horizontal but not vertical mobility. Horizontal mobility is, of course, a datum in the analysis of vertical mobility. There is, presumably, more horizontal than vertical mobility in any society. In Rogoff's study, for example, 60 to 75 per cent of the sons had occupations different from those of the fathers, but most of this mobility was horizontal, not vertical (Rogoff, 1953). Here, our data are limited to vertical mobility.

Further, we are here interested in that type of vertical mobility which involves only a small fraction of the population of a society, i.e., *elite* rather than mass mobility. From the basic theory of stratification, it follows that the elite roles at stake in elite vertical mobility are roles which are the *most highly valued* in a given society, those roles which involve the greatest knowledge and responsibility. The number of roles is not the essential criterion in elite mobility. Certain highly specialized but relatively low-ranking roles also involve only a small fraction of the population. Although elite mobility typically involves only a relatively few people, the criterion is the highly valued roles at stake, not the number of people. The term "elite" has been used to refer both to the individuals who occupy these high positions and also to the positions themselves. Thus, there have been studies of "the power elite," "the Nazi elite," "the elite and the upper class," the "industrial elite," etc. In using the term elite, we do not imply "power elite," "ruling class," or similar notions that a monopoly of power is consciously shared and manipulated by the elite individuals *as a group* (Mills, 1956; see also Janowitz, 1954). The proof of this assertion is beyond the scope of this study. The aspects of the study of elites with which we are concerned are their intra-generational recruitment and advancement and their inter-generational mobility. We shall use the terms "elite mobility" and "the circulation of the elites" interchangeably to refer to these aspects.

Now we must analyze the relation of the family to this system of stratification and mobility. A considerable body of social thought, sociological theory, and research argues that equality of opportunity is incompatible with any strong, positive solidarity of the family system in a society, and that the strain toward aristocracy or status ascription is, at least in part, a result of the solidarity which issues from the family as an institution. As Schumpeter put it:

> The individual belongs to a given class neither by choice, nor by any other action, nor by innate qualities—in sum, his class membership is not individual at all. It stems from his membership in a given clan or lineage. The family, not the physical person, is the true unit of class and class theory. [1955, p 113.]

In much the same terms, Parsons writes: "So long . . . as there is a solidary kinship unit, it is impossible for the wives and children of those high and low in the occupational system to be equally treated, regardless of their personal achievements" (1951, p. 161).

To state this more systematically: First, in every known society, at birth, and before an individual's capacities in the direction of *achieved* statuses can be known, his initial stratum position is *ascribed* on the basis of the stratum position of his family of orientation. Second, in the extreme case, an individual's stratum position at birth is also a sufficient criterion of his stratum position *throughout his life*. Third, at the opposite extreme, the stratum position of one's family of orientation would be completely irrelevant to one's own stratum postion in adulthood; one's adult stratum position would be determined by other than kinship factors. Fourth, between these two extremes are all empirical societies.

Fifth, in all societies there is at least a *tendency* toward the ascription of stratum position throughout life on the basis of the stratum position of one's family of orientation, for the following reasons: (*a*) the family is a solidary unit, based upon biological union, common residence, and the function of socializing the young; (*b*) diffuse, affective ties are required among family members if the family is to be effective in its socialization functions; (*c*) parents in different strata cannot help socializing their children to be like themselves because given parents have insufficient contact with other role-models; (*d*) one has a lifelong identification with the family. The solidary nature of kinship accounts for its ascriptive tendency, and the ascriptive tendency explains why the family has important consequences for mobility. "Children of the more highly placed come to have differential advantages, by virtue of their ascribed kinship status, not shared by those lower down" (Parsons, 1951, p. 161).

The individual is born into a given family, which consists of whatever in the society is the effective initial kinship unit. In American society this unit is, typically, only one's parents and siblings. In China between 1600 and 1900, several factors made the initial effective kinship unit not only one's parents and siblings, but also the generations of one's paternal grandparents and great-grandparents. We shall speak of any and all of these forebears and relatives as the *family of orientation* of the elite individuals in our sample, realizing that these effective kinship units are not the same in American and Chinese societies.

Each individual's family of orientation has a certain *stratum position,* that is, it is ranked higher or lower according to its social status, economic status, legal status, authority, etc. Each family has certain "life chances" in relation to whichever of the above aspects of stratification—economic, legal, etc.—are emphasized in a given society. Stratum position is used here as a summary measure of the over-all rank of a family. The individual shares this stratum position with his family of orientation, at least until adulthood. The *difference* between the stratum position of an elite individual's family of orientation and his own (adult) elite stratum position will be spoken of as his vertical mobility.

Finally, that aggregate of families of orientation with an approximately equal stratum position in the system of stratification will be called a *stratum.* The individual shares a common stratum position with his family of orientation; all the families with an approximately equal stratum position form a stratum; the system of stratification of a society consists of two or more strata. We shall differentiate our Chinese elite sample into three major strata: Manchus; Chinese from official and degree-holding families; and Chinese from commoner families. (The reasons for this classification of strata are given in subsequent chapters.)

A word of explanation is in order as to why we use the concept of "stratum" instead of the concept of "class." The writer is among those who deplore the trend in recent sociology to make "class" and "stratum" interchangeable categories. The term "class" has been much misused. Warner, for example (1941, 1942), asserted that he had rejected Marx; in fact, Warner's concept and analysis of class bore almost no resemblance to Marx's. The "classical" concept of class as formulated by Marx was *not* a theory of stratification; it was a tool for explaining *changes* in total societies (Dahrendorf, 1959). By "class" Marx did not refer to what we in this study call "stratum," namely, layers in a hierarchical system differentiated by gradual distinctions in prestige, income, influence, etc. Rather, for Marx, "The analysis of social class is concerned with an assessment of the chances that common economic conditions and common experiences of a group will lead to organized action" (Lipset and Bendix, 1951, p. 248).

We shall use "stratum" rather than "class" in this study, then, first because it is more applicable to China in the 1600-1900 period. Marx linked class phenomena to the industrial revolution and the emergence of new conditions—the shifting of the basis of property from landowning and trade to *capital*, and the emergence of two new classes, the bourgeoisie and the proletariat—which conditions were absent from China in the period of this study. Second, what was characteristic of Ch'ing China was a system of *strata*, with institutionalized inequalities in status, prestige, income, and the like. It is this phenomenon with which we are concerned.

Our first major hypothesis, then, will be: *differences in official advancement observed among our sample of officials of the Ch'ing period* (ca. 1600-1900) *are a result of differences in the stratum position of their families of orientation.* In Chapter III it will be shown that, during the Ch'ing period, the Manchus formed the highest stratum in the system of stratification, Chinese from official and degree-holding families the next highest stratum, and Chinese from commoner families the lowest stratum. Therefore, we shall hypothesize that Manchus had the greatest official advancement, Chinese from official degree-holding families next most, and Chinese from commoner families least. (Since the sons of Manchus and of Chinese official families were *born* into a high stratum position, even if they became officials they cannot be said to have been *upward mobile*. Commoners' sons who became officials, on the other hand, did realize upward mobility. It is when we focus upon *intra-generational* or career mobility that it is legitimate to say of all men who reached a given high rank in the bureaucracy that they had great *official advancement*, regardless of the stratum into which they had been born. An official from a Manchu or an official family who reached high bureaucratic rank cannot be said to have been markedly upward mobile, according to our definition, but can be said to have had great official advancement.) At the end of this chapter we shall state all the hypotheses to be tested in this study.

Hypergamy, Hypogamy, and Endogamy. Every individual who marries is, during his lifetime, a member of two distinct kin groups—the family he is born into and the family he himself creates, consisting of himself, his spouse, and their children. The latter family is referred to as his *family of procreation*. If one's adult stratum position is higher than that of his family of orientation, this may be due to his having married "up." Therefore, in the analysis of elite mobility or official advancement, it is well to pay attention to the stratum position both of the family one is born into and also of the family one marries into. Most marriages in any society are between stratum equals rather than between individuals of unequal stratum position. Unfortunately, in this study we have data only on the stratum position of the family of orientation of our Chinese elite; we have no systematic data on the effect of hypergamy or hypogamy (marrying "up" or "down," respectively) on elite mobility and official advancement.

Downward Mobility. Another factor which influences the amount of elite mobility is the amount of downward mobility. Even if the size of the elite fails to expand, and even though the elite fully reproduces its numbers, if a certain proportion of the sons of the elite are either not motivated or not able to enter and maintain elite positions, the result will again be an increase in the amount of upward and downward mobility.

There is evidence that the facts of Chinese elite mobility were, to some extent, the result of downward mobility. Proverbs attested to this: "A man can account for himself, but how can he account for his descendants?"; "prosperity has its reverses," and the like. Francis L. K. Hsu has shown, on the basis of biographical sources, that relatively few clans enjoyed prominence, especially political prominence, over two or three consecutive generations, and that between 75 per cent and 94 per cent of the biographies in three district gazeteers show prominence lasting not more than three successive generations (1948, pp. 305 ff.). The data of the present study, to be presented in Chapter VII, definitely support this conclusion concerning downward mobility. There were many reasons for the downward mobility of members of the Chinese elite. One was the summary punishment of high officials, whose political prominence made their positions the more hazardous to maintain. In other cases, the sons of the elite were simply incapable of maintaining the family's elite position—the son of a golden or silver parent may have an admixture of brass and iron, as Plato put it. Again, the sons of elite families sometimes preferred to consume their inherited wealth in luxury and idleness and to avoid the rigors of an official career. Such sons often lacked the incentive of poverty and were not brought up to cultivate and display austere probity after the manner of the best role-models of Classical China. China was, in this respect, similar to English landed families: ". . . families had risen only to fall again. For one that survived a score were destroyed, overtaken by those natural disasters which beset families—failure of heirs, wanton extravagance, reckless loyalty, sheer bad luck" (Plumb, 1956, quoted in Barber, 1957, p. 379). For these and other reasons, there was downward mobility in China. Therefore, it is clear that another source of the inter-generational upward mobility observable in our Chinese sample was this pattern of downward mobility.

Inheritance Patterns. The extent to which elite families are able to maintain their position is also related to the patterns of inheritance in a society. Consider two elite individuals, one in Ch'ing China, the other in modern America. The areas of investment are much more varied in capitalist America than in China, where, until the nineteenth century, investment in land was the preferred type. The American, with his greater testamentary freedom, could bequeath all his wealth to one son, thereby keeping intact his total nest egg. Did not the Chinese pattern of mandatory equal inheritance for all sons make for a splintering of landholdings within a few generations, thereby dissipating the economic bases of elite position to a greater extent than in American society? The writer is on somewhat unsure ground here, but would tentatively assert that this was not the case. "Arrived" elite individuals in the two societies seem to have acted more alike than dissimilarly. The splintering effect of equal inheritance in China was slightest precisely at the elite level: the eldest son of the deceased elite individual would become head of the household; the other sons would continue to live together in the same extended household and to share the income from the family estate. As long as the family was prosperous, it did not tend to divide the property and break up. Property division and the taking-up of separate land was more a sign of downward mobility or a declining economic situation than of "arrived" elite position. There was no pattern comparable to the American practice of executing the will immediately after the father's death—to do this would have been a disgraceful violation of filial piety. If, two or more generations later, the household was already declining or disintegrating, then the branch families might divide the remaining property and split up. For these reasons, we shall assume in this study that the factor of inheritance patterns did not in itself make for considerable downward mobility among Chinese elite families; other factors, which we suggested above, were more important sources of downward mobility.

Formal Bureaucratic Norms. The mobility of the Chinese elite which we shall attempt to explain in this study occurred in a *bureaucratic context.* The 572 individuals in our Chinese elite sample had careers as appointed, salaried, largely non-aristocratic and non-hereditary officials, and were recruited to a considerable extent from the examination system. Career advancement in a bureaucracy is organized in "a system of 'promotions,' according to seniority or to achievement or both" (Weber, 1947, p. 334). This suggests the hypothesis that *differences in official advancement among these officials were the result of the operation of formal bureaucratic rules, especially seniority and/or merit* (performance, achievement). An earlier hypothesis stated that official advancement was a function of *extra-bureaucratic* influences, e.g., differences in the stratum position of the family of orientation. We shall analyze the influence of both these factors upon official advancement in this study, to see whether one was more strongly related to advancement than the other. One hypothesis asserts that advancement was *bureaucratically determined*, that is, determined by impartially administered formal rules relating to one's official performance and to one's inclusion with other officials having the same amount of seniority or the same civil service grade. The other hypothesis states that advancement was determined *extra-bureaucratically*, by the carry-over of the stratum position of one's family of orientation.

To the extent that our analysis of the Chinese elite supports the former rather than the latter hypothesis, we shall have grounds for regarding Chinese elite mobility as bureaucratically determined. Of the two types of bureaucratic determinants of advancement—seniority and merit—we have data for our Chinese sample only on seniority, and our hypotheses on bureaucratic influences will be limited to the influence of seniority.

Values and Norms Which Affect Mobility. We may distinguish two extreme types of value-systems as they bear on social mobility. One is the "open-class" type which strongly approves of upward mobility. At the other extreme is the "closed society" or "caste" type of norms and values, with a strong disapproval of upward mobility. All concrete societies have some *combination* of these two extreme views toward mobility. In Chapter I we argued that Chinese society between 1600 and 1900, like twentieth-century American society, tended more to the "open-class" than to the "caste" type. Both societies had value-systems which stated that "sons shall not necessarily remain in the same stratum position as their fathers." Both societies also had "caste" elements. Many American whites apply open-class norms to the mobility of their own group and caste norms to the mobility of Negroes. Small communities are likely to have more caste-type norms than large cities (Hollingshead, 1949). In China, as we pointed out in Chapter I, norms discouraging mobility existed alongside norms which approved of mobility; but the latter norms seem to have been emphasized more fully. In principle, we might account for some of the mobility differences *within* China on the basis of differences in norms toward mobility; in fact, we have no data on variations in norms within China as they affected the mobility patterns of the officials in our sample.

Intelligence and Motivation. The final factors which theory and earlier research suggest as determinants of elite mobility are differences in intelligence and in the motivation to succeed. It is, of course, difficult to isolate the effect of "native intelligence" from the effect of stratum position and educational attainment, so closely are these intertwined. However, Lipset and Bendix conclude that "the discrepancy between the distribution of intelligence in a given generation of youth and the distribution of social positions in the parental generation is a major dynamic factor affecting mobility in all societies in which educational achievement or other qualities associated with intelligence play an important role in status placement" (1959, p. 236). It is likely that this statement can be applied to China.

Similarly, in both Chinese and American societies it is likely that lower-stratum boys whose parents had high expectations for them and who urged them to achieve upward mobility were more likely to attain elite positions, other things being equal, than were those lower-stratum boys whose family and early socialization emphasized "accepting one's lot in life." Parental expectations and other factors made for motivational differences which in turn influenced the official advancement and mobility of elites.

Unfortunately, we cannot test hypotheses on the effect of intelligence and motivation upon elite mobility; we lack systematic evidence regarding these factors for our Chinese elite sample.

Summary of Hypotheses. Of the several factors which theory suggests as possible determinants of elite mobility, several have been excluded in the present study; others have been accepted as hypotheses to be tested in this study. Of the first group, we lack data on differences within our sample in the variables of: (*a*) inheritance patterns, (*b*) values and norms affecting mobility, (*c*) changes in the proportion of the Chinese working force in the elite, (*d*) hypergamy or hypogamy, (*e*) performance or merit, (*f*) intelligence and motivation. Future research must attempt to discover which, if any, of these variables correlate with differences in official advancement and elite mobility.

The hypotheses which can be tested with our data are as follows:

I. The general hypothesis of *Extra-Bureaucratic* Determinants of Official Recruitment and Advancement

A. Bureaucratic recruitment path taken is a function of the stratum position of family of orientation:

1. Chinese from official families are more likely than Chinese from commoner families to (*a*) take the preferred path (the examination system); (*b*) receive the *chin-shih* degree.

2. Manchus and Chinese from official families who take the *chin-shih* are likely to do so at a younger age than Chinese from commoner families.

B. Official advancement within the Ch'ing bureaucracy is a function of the stratum position of family of orientation:

1. Manchu officials are more likely than Chinese from official families, and the latter more likely than Chinese from commoner families, to:

(*a*) reach given high-rank posts during their career,
(*b*) have a high rate of promotion,
(*c*) have longer incumbency in given high-rank posts,
(*d*) accumulate longer seniority.

II. The *alternative* general hypothesis of *Bureaucratic* Determinants of Official Recruitment and Advancement

A. Official advancement within the Ch'ing bureaucracy was a function of impersonal, formal bureaucratic rules:

1. Officials recruited through the preferred "regular" path (examinations) are more likely than officials recruited through the "irregular" path to:

(*a*) reach given high-rank posts,
(*b*) have a high rate of promotion,
(*c*) have a longer incumbency in given high-rank posts.

2. Official advancement (highest rank reached and length of incumbency in high-rank posts) is a function of the amount of seniority accumulated.

We shall, then, test hypotheses concerning the *relative influence* of (*a*) bureaucratic factors—recruitment path taken and seniority, and (*b*) extra-bureaucratic factors—the stratum position of the family of orientation, upon (*c*) official advancement—highest rank reached and length of incumbency. These hypotheses will be tested in Chapters VI and VII.

In this chapter, we have drawn upon sociological theory and research as a source of ideas which may help us understand and explain certain aspects of Chinese stratification and elite mobility in the 1600-1900 period. In the next chapter, we shall further consider this problem in the light of historical data from the Ch'ing period. It is hoped that our knowledge based on the concepts and hypotheses of sociology will be illuminated by the facts and interpretations of history, and vice versa.

CHAPTER 3 CHINESE SOCIAL STRATIFICATION, 1600-1900

ANY ADEQUATE social history of stratification in China between 1600 and 1900 would have to discuss an enormous number of concrete factors involved in stratification, e.g., merchant guilds, misappropriation of public funds by officials, landownership and tenancy, secret societies, the government monopolies, the position of local elders and headmen, the "dynastic cycle," the prohibitions against official cliques and all popular assemblies, in addition to the regional variation of all these factors within Chinese society.

Were our discussion primarily descriptive, rather than oriented toward the testing of hypotheses, it would be necessary to analyze intensively all of the above—and many other—concrete factors. For our purposes, it is sufficient to isolate those elements of stratification which influenced the stratum position of the families of orientation of our Chinese sample.

The elements we shall treat in this chapter are: social-evaluational, legal, and economic stratification, the dynastic cycle, and the impact of Manchu rule.

Social Stratification

We begin our analysis with these problems, raised by the theory of stratification we outlined in Chapter II: What were the main social-occupational roles on which stratum position was based in China? What was the functional significance of each of these roles? What was the evaluation of these roles? We shall attempt to explain the differential ranking of these major occupational roles by reference to their functions.

The crudest approximation to a classification of all functionally significant roles is the traditional Chinese distinction, stated in *Mencius*, between mental and manual labor (*lao-hsin* and *lao-li*), corresponding to the distinction between the rulers and the ruled.[1] Of the whole population, only the imperial family, the officials, degree-holders, and scholars eschewed manual labor, according to this view. Their function was to rule. Ruling was more highly evaluated than performing manual labor.

A less crude traditional Chinese classification of occupations was that of the "four people" (*ssu-min*): scholars, farmers, artisans, and merchants (*shih nung kung shang*). In this list, "scholars" included officials and teachers. Below these four strata were the military (*ping*). In this view, farmers were ranked above everyone except scholars because the government regarded agriculture as its root (*pen*)—that on which it depended—rather than, e.g., trade and a market economy, or military conquest.

Both these traditional Chinese classifications give important clues to the stratification of occupations, but neither is adequate for the purpose of empirical sociological analysis. As our discussion proceeds, it will become clear that the first of these classifications obscures the complex stratification *within* the ruled group, and that the second one is more an indication of Chinese ideological criteria of stratification than an empirical account of prestige ranking.

The classification we shall use in this study stems from recent research on Chinese society, particularly that of K. A. Wittfogel, Chi Ch'ao-ting, Ch'ü T'ung-tsu, W. Eberhard, and Chang Chung-li. A major theme in this research has been that Chinese officialdom and "gentry" held the highest position in the traditional system of stratification because of the functions they performed for the system as a whole. Other roles in the society, such as those of peasants and merchants, were less significant and were not as highly valued by the members of the society. In the present analysis, we shall divide all the functionally significant, valued roles into three levels of prestige ranking: high, medium, and low. More levels of prestige evaluation than these three could be distinguished, but for our purposes this threefold division is adequate.

Highly-Valued Roles. The highest-valued functionally significant roles in traditional Chinese society were those of the Emperor, the imperial family, the nobility, and the officials in the imperial bureaucracy. The functions fulfilled by these roles were mainly *integrative*. For one thing, the local village in China was not a self-sufficient, self-contained community (Fukutake, 1946, pp. 180-222, 476-89). Villages were interdependent in many ways. Problems of irrigation, protection against floods and other natural calamities, economic interchange, social interaction such as residential migration and extra-local marriage, etc., all required types of integration and regulation above the village level. The normative expectations of one village were not necessarily those of another; "the problem of order"—the possibility of a war of all against all—was involved.[2] The crucial integrative function of these most highly valued roles, then, was administrative. Performance of these roles gave to all Chinese a membership in a larger State, with benefits ranging from hydraulic control to a political-religious world-view.

By thus producing a relatively unified Empire, the Emperor and the bureaucracy functioned to suppress feudalism. If we define feudalism in political terms, as a system in which the essential relation is not that between subject and ruler, or state and citizen, but between lord and vassal, then China was clearly non-feudal. More precisely, feudalism is a system in which "each individual is identified as responsible to some particular individual higher than himself in the hierarchy and related to others outside of that direct line by virtue of his overlord's relation to them" (Levy, 1955, p. 498). For clear evidence of a feudal society in China, it is necessary to go back at least 2,000 years (Ch'ü, 1937; Bodde, 1956). Another aspect of feudalism, closed social classes, was also not characteristic of Ch'ing China: the system administered by the Emperor and the officials gave at least formal possibilities for achievement, as against ascription, to almost the entire population. The Asian scholars who see Ch'ing China as "semi-feudal" focus more on economic than on political phenomena—for example, the *de facto* serflike position of masses of peasants vis-a-vis landlords and officials in bad times (Hozumi, 1940; Li Hsün, 1957).

Medium-Valued Roles. The functions of the above bureaucratic roles were largely confined to high-level system problems, e.g., tax collections and maintaining peace and order. A *hsien*—comparable in size to an American county—could have a population of several hundred thousand, yet a single *hsien* magistrate was typically in charge of the administration of the entire area. The busy round of the *hsien* magistrate cannot have been too different from that of a

Prefect, and we have a description of the latter's duties in a poem by Yüan Mei, one of the officials in our sample:

> Morning after morning at the fifth watch I climb into my carriage;
> I must pay my respects to those above me, meet them, see them off,
> Answer the questions of their clients and guests while time flies away.
> The inner wall of Nanking is sixty leagues round,
> To do the whole circuit of the town is about a day's job.
> When at last I manage to get home the lamps are beginning to be lit; . . .
> Gasping with hunger, yet holding out, I put my papers in order;
> Just on the verge of reaching a decision I go back again to the start.
> I am haunted by the fear that further delay may do harm to my people;
> Yet I know that when I hurry I make a lot of mistakes.
> The tangled threads are straightened out; at last I am leaving my office
> When a young Bachelor turns up, and wants to show me an essay:
> "Knowing that your worship was previously employed in the Han-lin Academy
> I felt I should not be doing my duty if I did not pay my respects."

Still other tasks arose, far into the night: "Owing to the negligence of the gaolers, several prisoners have escaped; the public granary-keepers have allowed an inch of rot to spread over the corn, and finally, when Yüan Mei has at last got to bed and is fast asleep, there is a knock at the door, and someone announces that a fire has broken out. 'The Prefect's attendance is urgently requested' " (Waley, 1956, pp. 39-40). There is the further fact that frequent transfers made the local official virtually a stranger in the *hsien*. The handling of *hsien*-level system-problems therefore required an intermediate leadership elite, whose roles would complement those of the official bureaucracy. With about 1,500 *hsien* in China, on the basis of Chang's estimates of the size of the elite (1953, 1955) we may say that there were, on the average, about 700 elite individuals per *hsien* during the first half of the nineteenth century and about 950 elite individuals per *hsien* in the latter part of the nineteenth century.

Chang (1955, pp. 54-70; 212) has classified these important local leadership roles as "traditional gentry functions," such as raising funds for financing and operating irrigation, granaries, and other public works, and for government expenses; arbitration in settling local disputes; organizing and commanding local defense corps; acting as intermediaries between the government and the people; maintaining temples; performing ideological functions in ceremonies; and philanthropy, both in establishing charity organizations and in individual almsgiving. Another "gentry function" was to finance and lecture in academies (*shu-yüan*); indeed, the higher degree-holders (*chin-shih*, *chü-jen*, *kung-sheng*, and *chien-sheng*) contributed heavily to the financing of these academies, and all but monopolized the lecturer positions in them (Chang, pp. 63, 64, 217). The performance of these and other functions was a crucial sustaining mechanism for the society as a whole.

These intermediately valued roles were filled, first by degree-holders not in office, the local literati, and second, by those who assumed these roles because their income provided both the necessary leisure and the excess capital. The latter group often did not hold degrees, but were large landowners or wealthy merchants, such as those merchants in close contact with officials in the government monopolies. The motivation to get degrees and office among this latter group was usually strong, but the point is that holding degrees was not an essential qualification for membership in this group whose roles were evaluated as lower only than those of officialdom.

A given landowner or wealthy merchant could hold disparate positions: however high he might be in the system of economic stratification, if our analysis is correct, his social status or prestige would be evaluated as *low* until he became involved in the above local leadership functions, at which time his social status would correlate more highly with his economic status. If our analysis is correct, it would also follow that his social status would never approach perfect correlation with his economic status until he, or a kinsman, achieved government office. This would be especially true of the extremely wealthy landowners and merchants. This incongruity between the economic status and prestige evaluation of wealthy landlords and merchants was clearly functional for the society: it motivated those who had the economic surplus to direct their leisure and their capital into system-problems, instead of exclusively into more private uses. Also, the achievement of high social status through the performance of local leadership roles had the latent function of investing wealthy men's loyalties in the status quo, thereby channeling their influence into non-deviant lines. This pattern retarded the development of capitalism during the Ch'ing period. (Weber, 1951, 103, 199, 227, 244-247; Teng and Fairbank, 1954, 108-18; Feuerwerker, 1958.)

Here, then, are some of the functions of the traditional Chinese system of stratification, at the middle level of evaluation of occupational roles. The system offered higher social evaluation to all those who participated in local leadership roles. Those who participated by virtue of degrees in the examination system were already largely committed to the system because of the ideological indoctrination of the examination system through which they had so arduously passed. Those who participated by virtue of wealth rather than ideological training were discouraged from using their economically derived influence in any politically deviant way: to do so would have been highly irrational, for it would have meant investing economically in a system which one was politically attempting to alter. It should be noted that, under certain conditions, people of high economic status *do* attempt to politically alter the system, as in the case of the New Deal program of Franklin D. Roosevelt. This whole problem of "class traitors," or upper-stratum individuals who identify with the interests of the lower strata, calls for more attention by researchers than it has so far received.

Before turning to those occupational roles which were evaluated as relatively low, an important terminological problem must be confronted. In sinological literature the group performing these local leadership roles of which we have been speaking is usually referred to as the "gentry" (Fei, 1946; Levy, 1949; Chang, 1956). Though it is sometimes recognized that the English gentry were unlike the Chinese local elite, the term still continues to be applied to China.

"Gentry" is usually a translation of the Chinese term *shen-shih*. One connotation of "gentry"—property in land, country squires—applies more to England than to China; several other connotations of "gentry" do not apply at all to China. In the families of the English gentry, all the land and most of the money passed to the eldest son; Chinese family property was equally divided among all the sons rather than descending by primogeniture. This meant that, in England, gentry rank was hereditary, at least for the eldest son. In China, on the other hand, *shen-shih* were degree-holders in the Confucian examination system, and each generation anew was inseparably connected with this examination competition; none of the sons could inherit his *shen-shih* rank apart from his personal achievement in this competition. It is true that the younger sons of the English gentry might achieve gentry rank later in life, after making their own fortune away from home, in law or business, and then investing it in land, but *their* oldest son would then inherit gentry rank, whereas the Chinese son could not inherit his father's *shen-shih* status. This is undoubtedly the reason why Tawney and others assert that there was no development of squires in China comparable to England. Again, while English squires were usually at least modestly well-off, by virtue of landed property, in China many degree-holders had to teach for a living, instead of being independent scholars. It was said that poverty was the common condition of the scholar. As a Western observer put it:

> Of the successful candidates for literary degrees the merest fraction obtain employment as their number is always vastly in excess of the appointments to be distributed. Consequently there is an enormous class composed of those unemployed and disappointed literati. . . . These elegant and accomplished scholars are driven into all kinds of shifts in order to pick up a livelihood. [Gorst, 1899, pp. 124, 127.]

This is also the reason why Weber (1951, p. 112) and others have identified the literati in China as a *status group*, having honor and deference in common, rather than as an economic class, having wealth as a common characteristic.

Since "gentry" conveys these several misleading connotations,[3] the writer proposes that the more neutral term, "local elite," be substituted for it. In this study, "local elite" will refer to that group whose local leadership roles brought them middle-level evaluation in the traditional Chinese system of social stratification.

Lowly-Valued Roles. The vast majority of the Chinese population were peasant-farmers, who produced the basic medium of wealth in the society, grain, on small, intensively cultivated patches of land. Within this large group, whose roles we shall collectively define as low in evaluation, there were clearly great variations in prestige evaluation. For example, proprietors employing farm labor who were not their own kin were more highly ranked than tenant farmers, whose labor was wholly a family endeavor. Our justification in lumping together all these gradations is that all these roles were ranked lower than local leadership roles. They involved less knowledge and less responsibility: few among this vast group were literate; few had any responsibility aside from their families and local village life. A considerable economic burden often fell on this large segment of the population, a fact which has received much attention in recent mainland Chinese scholarship. Members of this lowly-valued segment of the population were economically exploited by the highly- and medium-valued segments: they were conscripted for the *corvée*, while the higher groups often succeeded in legally or extra-legally avoiding conscription; the burden of taxation payments on crops fell on them; and they were made to pay exorbitant rents and interest rates.

The majority of merchants and businessmen were in the lowly-valued group. There were important differences in wealth and prestige among merchants. At the highest level were the merchants connected with the great government salt and iron monopolies; in the middle level were those who owned stores and manufactories in towns and cities; at the bottom were the small peddlers (*hsiao-fan*). To the extent that these highest- and middle-level merchants were *also* able to participate in the local leadership roles mentioned above, they would be ranked higher than if they performed only merchant roles.

Artisans, similarly, were mostly ranked in the low group. Many artisans were at the same time small farmers or merchants. A common combination would be farmer and weaver of cloth and baskets.

Even the above relatively lowly-valued roles were more highly valued than the group of so-called "mean" occupations (the *chien-min*). This relatively small group included boat people, prostitutes, actors, domestic slaves, etc. We shall analyze this group more fully below, in connection with the legal criteria of stratification in the Ch'ing period. This group was ranked at the very bottom, both legally and in social evaluation.

Historical Dynamics of Stratification

Both the system of social stratification we have discussed above and the system of legal stratification we shall discuss below were influenced by the particular historical dynamics of the period 1600-1900 in China. In this section we shall briefly trace the interaction between stratification and two of these historical processes: the dynastic cycle and the conquest and rule of China by the Manchus. An analysis of Manchu-Chinese relations will also point up some aspects of the stratification of authority in Ch'ing China.

The Dynastic Cycle. Through their long history, the Chinese have been ruled not by one dynasty, but by a succession of different dynasties. A given dynasty was considered as deserving the political loyalty of all the subjects—for our purposes, conformity to the system of stratification—so long as it still had the "Mandate of Heaven." When did a dynasty lose the Mandate? The test was pragmatic: extreme duress for the people, along with symbolic omens and portents, meant that the dynasty had lost its Mandate and *could be legitimately overthrown* in favor of a new dynasty. History was a record of the rise and fall of dynasties, of a continuous cycle of social stability and instability. The Chinese have been called the most rebellious but the least revolutionary of peoples: even the overthrow of a dynasty did not legitimize a basic, revolutionary change in the system of stratification; it signaled, rather, a *return* to a traditional, ideal *status quo ante,* which had been outraged in the downward swing of the dynastic cycle.

What were the correlates of this cycle? First, it was, in addition to the ritualistic change of ruling Houses, a socioeconomic cycle. Typically, the "fall" of a dynasty was associated with the impairment of the peasant-agrarian base on which Chinese society rested. Inherent in this process were such interrelated patterns as official corruption, the draining of the Imperial Treasury through lavish court expenditures, the rise of the land tax, the concentration of land ownership, and the progressive impoverishment of the peasantry (Wang, 1936; Wittfogel, 1935). Second, the early period of a dynasty, and, in some cases, the beginning of a new reign within a dynasty, was marked by socio-economic and other reforms.

These generalizations apply to the fall of the Ming and the rise of the Manchu Ch'ing Dynasty (seventeenth century), to the great era of Ch'ing order, prosperity, and expansion (eighteenth century), and to the decline and fall of the Ch'ing (nineteenth and early twentieth centuries).

Here we shall analyze only one aspect of the dynastic cycle during this three-hundred-year period: the ethnic stratification between Manchus and Han Chinese. From a theoretical point of view, ethnic factors are not themselves primary criteria of stratification. This follows from the theory sketched above, which states that the primary criterion of social stratification is the differential evaluation of functionally significant social roles. In this sense, ethnic factors are secondary criteria, like wealth. Ethnic differences may or may not correlate with the stratification of functional roles in any given society. In Ch'ing China, ethnic differences between Manchus and Han Chinese *did* correlate highly with social and other elements of stratification, and for this reason we must analyze the relationships between the Manchu conquerors and their Han Chinese subjects.

Relations between Manchus and Chinese. Ethnic factors were more consequential for stratification during the Ch'ing period than they had been during the Ming dynasty (1368-1644). The Ming had been a native Chinese ruling house, with the surname of Chu; the Manchus came to the throne as aliens, regarded by the Chinese as "barbarians." Manchu language was Altaic; Chinese, Sinitic. The Manchus originated from a Tungus border tribe, the Nü-chen, and were thus related to the founders of the earlier conquest dynasty of Chin (A.D. 1115-1234). The Manchus were mounted archers, skilled horsemen and virile warriors. The particular group of Nü-chen people who became the core of Manchu power during the Ch'ing period were the Chien-chou Nü-chen, who had come originally from the Sungari River Valley, northeast of China proper. Under the Ming dynasty, the Nü-chen tribes became a vassal state, enjoying the privilege of feudal suzerainity which the Chinese emperors had bestowed upon them. During the Ming period, the Manchus had come into contact with the settled Chinese communities in Liaotung—the old Chinese part of what is now known as Manchuria. As a result of this contact, a certain amount of assimilation went on among the Manchus: they added to their old tribalism, with its hereditary nobility, new elements such as greater use of agriculture and life in walled towns. But, in the eyes of many Chinese within the Great Wall, the Manchus remained an alien ethnic group, an "out-group." This fact of ethnic differences between the ruling dynasty and the ruled Chinese populace had at least two important consequences for stratification. The first of these consequences was that Chinese had to decide between political loyalty and alienation vis-à-vis the Manchus. The Manchu invaders took Peking in 1644, but until 1683 the retreating Ming rulers and their loyalist followers continued to reassert their pre-eminent right over the Manchus to the throne. Nor did all alienation from the Manchus and all resistance to their rule ever die out, even after the official submission of the Ming. Until the very end of the Ch'ing dynasty there were Ming loyalists, particularly in secret societies in South China. The particular importance of this alienation for our study is that many Chinese who would have aspired to a career in the governmental bureaucracy retired or avoided an official career. Research is needed on the problem of the social origins of Chinese who accepted Manchu rule versus those Chinese who were disaffected and alienated from Manchu rule. We need to know whether, and for how long, this alienation altered the social composition of Chinese officialdom.

Second, the fact that the Manchus were an alien dynasty

of conquest influenced the stratification of authority between Manchus and Chinese within the bureaucracy. We shall document two aspects of this: (*a*) the way in which Manchus exploited their authority in the central bureaucracy; (*b*) the ways in which Manchu authority and privilege were limited. Defining the limits of influence is a necessary task in any analysis. Because influence is always reciprocal, it tends to be limited, however unequal its distribution may be among the individuals or groups involved.

We may make several broad comparisons between the early Ch'ing and the late Ch'ing periods, as a means of analyzing the extent and the limits of Manchu bureaucratic authority.

(1) More of the Chinese elite were alienated from the Manchus in the early than in the late Ch'ing. During the Ch'ing period, the Manchus slowly won the support of the Chinese elite, both in the bureaucracy and at the local leadership level. The Taiping Rebellion (1850-64) threatened both Manchus and Chinese scholar-officials with a common enemy and made them realize the identity of their interests in the face of any drastic change.

(2) Manchus became more and more sinicized as the Ch'ing period wore on. As early as 1580-1640 they had remodeled certain elements of their own system in conformity with the Chinese model—they made a transition from a tribal despotism and feudalism to a Chinese type of bureaucratic superstructure (Michael, 1942; Ma, 1956, pp. 333-52). But this early political and economic acculturation had been deliberate on the part of the Manchus; what they resisted were such types of acculturation as forsaking the horse and the military skills in favor of literature and a sedentary life. Thus, in the early Ch'ing period, the Manchus attempted either to prevent or to limit further sinicization. For example, about 1636 the Manchu emperor T'ai Tsung (Abahai) admonished

the Manchurian nobility never to forget the old art of mounted archery:

> It was a memorable scene when he gathered his princes, beiles and Manchu dignitaries around him and ordered a notable to read to the assembly from the history of the Chin, the kin of the Manchus. . . . the edict . . . warned [the] people not to imitate Chinese names and manners, to conserve the old straightness and simplicity and not to become extravagant and luxurious. After the reading T'ai Tsung spoke of the warning example of the history of the Chin, who did not heed their emperor's advice. They gave up mounted archery for wine and women, and their empire was destroyed. [Michael, 1942, 107.]

Manchu-Chinese intermarriage was rigidly banned, and the Manchus were encouraged to believe in their superiority over the Chinese. Nurhaci, founder of the Ch'ing dynasty, asserted that the Manchus had been feudal nobles, proud seigneurs and vassals, and were therefore higher in standing than the ancestor of the Ming dynasty, a mere monk. The Ch'ien Lung Emperor in the eighteenth century proposed the same ideology: none of the ethnically Chinese dynasties could have the authority of the Mongol Yüan dynasty or the Manchu Ch'ing dynasty, because the former had been founded by Chinese *commoners,* whereas the latter two had been founded by noble vassals (Michael, 1942, p. 119). However, by the last half of the nineteenth century the Manchus had become more like the Chinese than any of the earlier Tartar conquest dynasties (Wittfogel and Feng, 1949, Introduction). Intermarriage was still banned, but nevertheless occurred. The use of Manchu, even as a secondary official language, had all but disappeared; the Manchus themselves had virtually forgotten it (Wright, 1957, p. 53). This trend is well illustrated by Yüan Mei's observations in the late eighteenth century: "Nowadays the Manchus are much more cultivated than the Chinese. Even their military men all write poetry." He cited the case of K'uei-lun, a Manchu General, then commanding in Fukien, who practiced the art of "fingertip" painting and wrote elegant verse inscriptions on his pictures (Waley, 1956, p. 28).

(3) In the early Ch'ing period, apart from holding some offices on the provincial level, the Manchus had remained in Peking and in the more or less isolated military garrisons in a few key locations. They had had castelike privileges over the Chinese. By the mid-nineteenth century, on the other hand, the authority of the rank-and-file Manchus had so declined (Kanda, 1948, pp. 271-96), due to poverty, inadequate stipends, conspicuous consumption, and population increase that, in 1861, edicts allowed Manchu Bannermen to participate in Chinese village life, to choose their occupation freely, and to compete in the examination system (Wright, 1957, p. 54). But once they left their special Banner garrisons and entered Chinese local life, the Manchus were to be under the jurisdiction of Chinese magistrates.

(4) In the early Ch'ing, the proportion of Manchu to Chinese officials was far greater than the proportion of Manchus to Chinese in the population as a whole. In the later Ch'ing period, there was a higher proportion of Chinese in office. During the first century of Ch'ing rule, for every Manchu official there were only 1.5 Chinese officials (i.e., about forty Manchus to sixty Chinese). During the second century of the Ch'ing period, there were two Chinese for every Manchu official, and in the last sixty years of the dynasty, there were about three Chinese for every Manchu in office (Hsieh, 1925, p. 297). Even this lowest proportion of Manchus in office far over-represented the actual proportion of Manchus in the Chinese population. Meadows in 1847 was struck by the "very unfair proportion of Manchus employed in office" (Meadows, 1847, p. 195). But at least there was a tendency toward recruiting a larger proportion of Chinese into officialdom.

Because a higher proportion of all Manchus than of all

Chinese could be officials, it was also true that competition was much less keen among the Manchus than among the Chinese. The Manchus' literary examinations for office were either wholly dispensed with, or made much less difficult, and were also conducted according to a different system. In the metropolitan *chin-shih* examinations, for example, Manchu Bannermen competed among themselves, not with the Chinese, and the successful candidates were listed in separate Chinese and Manchu groups.

There is anecdotal evidence that Manchu special privilege rested even less upon ability as the dynastic period wore on. Thus, Feng-shen-chi-lun, 1763-1807, although a grandson of Emperor Kao-tsung, "was a typical Manchu nobleman of the period who, though degenerate and incompetent, held important posts" (Hummel, 1943, I, 260).

(5) There is at least anecdotal evidence that punishment was meted out impartially to Manchu and Chinese officials. A Chinese official, Liu T'ung-hsun, who served in the bureaucracy between 1724 and 1773, "was sent several times to try officials accused of corruption, and usually his verdict won imperial approval, even though death sentences were meted out to several Manchus in high position" (Hummel, I, 534).

We have seen some of the ways in which the Manchus made an impact upon Chinese stratification, particularly at the elite level. But we have also seen that a process of co-optation[4]—the actual and ostensible sharing of authority between Manchus and Chinese—went on apace throughout the Ch'ing period, in such areas as Manchu sinicization, Chinese participation and recruitment, Manchu decline, and impartial bureaucratic punishments. This process of co-optation precluded any one-way influence of Manchus upon Chinese; it made this influence progressively a reciprocal one.

The incursion of the Manchus during the Ch'ing period resulted in their superimposition upon the earlier Chinese system of stratification. The over-all structure was not inverted or transformed; it remained, as in Ming times (as we shall see below): (Manchus, Bannermen), Chinese officials, Chinese local elite, Chinese commoners, outcastes, in that order. But the top positions—officialdom—were now divided between Chinese and their alien conquerors; yet not so equally divided that the *essentials* of political and military power were forfeited by the Manchus during their rule. Chinese could still rise in the system, but to do so, they had to compete with Manchus.

Legal Criteria of Stratification

In the Ch'ing period, there were at least three different legal categories of people which carried invidious distinctions relevant to stratification. These three categories of people were: (1) the Elite (*kuei*), officials, holders of ranks, titles, and degrees; (2) the Commoners (*liang*), the mass of the population in the "respectable" occupations; and 3) the outcast or pariah occupations (*chien*). These were traditional terms, though their meaning had changed during different dynastic periods. While the complex historical development of the legal criteria of stratification cannot be gone into here, we may summarize one line of this development as follows: In feudal China (before Ch'in times, pre-246 B.C.), law was the tool of the feudal aristocrats (*kuei*), who placed themselves outside the law by distinguishing law (*fa*) from propriety (*li*) and by asserting that, while the people must obey the law, the only code binding on them, the nobility, was the code of propriety. Then, during the Ch'in dynasty, the Legalists (*fa-chia*) destroyed this legal monopoly of the aristocrats and nobility: the legal code became the Emperor's; *all* subjects—including the nobility—were to conform to it. However, the institutionalization of this universalistic pattern broke down somewhat in later dynastic periods, as Confucianism replaced Legalism as the government's official policy: the officials and the local elite groups, while not succeeding in placing themselves *beyond the law* entirely again, nevertheless attained a *legal position of special privilege* vis-à-vis the common people (Ch'ü, 1937). In this section, we shall be concerned with this special legal privilege enjoyed by officials and local elite during the Ch'ing. We shall refer to the Imperial Clansmen and nobility, the officials and Bannermen, as *Elite of the Realm,* and reserve the term *local elite* for the degree-holders and others who performed leadership roles on the local level. A member of the Elite of the Realm would usually also be a member of the local elite, but the reverse would not be necessarily true.

We may cite Ch'ing Dynasty sumptuary laws as a preliminary example of invidious legal distinctions among officials, commoners, and other strata in Chinese society. The *Ta-Ch'ing lü-li* specifies:

> The houses, apartments, carriages, dresses, furniture, and other articles used by the officers of the government, and by the people in general, shall be conformable to the established rules and gradations. Accordingly, the individual who possesses any such articles for use, contrary to these rules and gradations, shall, if an officer of the government, be punished with 100 blows, deposed from his office, and rendered incapable of future service; if a private individual is guilty of this offense, the master of the family in which the article is used shall be punished with 50 blows. [Staunton, 1810, p. 185.]

Ch'ü T'ung-tsu has commented on these legal restrictions on the style of life of the several strata:

> The officials, together with their family members, had a style of life quite different from that of commoners. . . . The style of life was not conditioned economically, as is the situation in modern capitalist society. Instead, it was regulated legally under sumptuary laws. The official class was . . . unthreatened by any propertied class. The sumptuary laws served to minimize or limit the exercise of economic power to such an extent that wealth alone did not guarantee the right to consume. [Ch'ü, 1957, p. 245.]

In Ch'ing times, there was no longer any sumptuary law prejudicial to merchants (Ch'ü, 1957, p. 248). Wealthier merchants often enjoyed the same style of life as that of the official-elite. The legal criteria and distinctions we shall analyze below were not all-important; they interacted with wealth, landownership, education, ancestry, and local position in determining stratification during the Ch'ing period.

The Elite. Of this group, Ch'ing law specified some statuses which were directly inheritable from generation to generation and others which were not directly hereditary. (Those not directly inheritable might still be achieved by the next generation, e.g., officials' descendents might themselves gain appointment to office.)

Chief among those whose position was hereditary were those included, since T'ang dynasty times (A.D. 618-907), in the "Eight Privileged groups" (*pa-i*). By our period (late Ming and Ch'ing), according to Sir George Staunton, only two of these eight groups had any existence in practice: those of imperial blood (*i-ch'in*) and those of nobility (*i-kuei*). The privilege of imperial blood was extended to all the relatives of the Emperor descended from the same ancestor, i.e., Princes of the Blood (*wang*), first to eighth degree; to all those of the Emperor's mother and grandmother within four degrees of consanguinity; to all those relatives of the Empress, within three degrees; and to all those relatives of the consort of the Heir Apparent within two degrees.[5]

Also included among the Elite of the Realm whose position was hereditary were consorts of the imperial princesses, Nobles of the imperial lineage of the ninth through the twelfth ranks, children of the Princes of the Blood, their princesses, consorts, and concubines; Imperial Clansmen, i.e., descendents of the acknowledged founder of the Ch'ing dynasty, Nurhaci; collateral relatives, i.e., descendents from the collateral line of the Emperor Hsien Tsu (Nurhaci), and the "Eight Great Families" (*pa-ta-chia*). The founders of the

Eight Great Families were eight Manchu princes: Daisan, Dorgon, Dodo, Haoge, Jirgalang, Boggodo, Lekedehun, and Yoto, in that order of rank. These men lived between 1583 and 1723, and their descendents, after 1778, enjoyed the right of "perpetual inheritance."

Although the foregoing (and some of the following) imperial titles (*Tsung-shih chüeh-hao*) were directly inheritable, many of them were not "perpetually inheritable." Many titles were transmitted in a descending scale: e.g., the son of a Beile or Prince of the Blood of the third degree became a Beile or Prince of the Blood of the fourth degree.

Others than those related by blood or marriage to the imperial family were also members of the Elite of the Realm whose titles and ranks were directly inheritable for a specified number of generations. These were the nobility (*i-kuei*). They were: Dukes (*kung*), Marquises (*hou*), Earls (*po*), Viscounts (*tzu*), Barons (*nan*), and the four minor hereditary titles: *Ch'ing-ch'e-tu-wei, Ch'i-tu-wei, Yün-ch'i-wei,* and *En-ch'i-wei.*

This entire group of the imperial family and nobility, of course, comprised only an infinitesimal fraction of the total population. They were unequivocally at the apex of the traditional Chinese system of legal stratification. During most of the period here under analysis, the absolute monarchy functioned to secure for this group heavily disproportionate advantages in authority, power, wealth, prestige, and leisure. The Emperor had merely to visit the southern provinces, as he did in 1751, and a severe economic dislocation resulted.

> Much of the grain usually sent to Peking had to be retained in the south, as the Emperor and Dowager Empress arrived with a horde of officials and attendants. It was difficult to estimate how much these human locusts would consume and constant adjustments and readjustments had to be made. In the decree announcing the tour, the Emperor had of course made the usual promise that the arrangements for his reception would be on a modest scale and would inflict no burden on his people. But local officials regarded this clause as a mere conventional

> formula, and were not willing to run the risk of being impeached for disloyalty. Triumphal arches had to be erected, the embankments of the Grand Canal had to be repaired or rebuilt in order to accommodate safely the vast crowds that would assemble to watch the Royal Barges pass, temporary palaces had to be erected all along the route. All this necessitated impounding vast numbers of peasants at a time of year when their labour was urgently needed in the fields. Prices, of course, leapt up, and we find the Treasury calmly anticipating inflation and minting extra currency. . . . Nor was it only the Exchequer and the population at large that suffered. Influential individuals whose houses the Emperor signified his intention of visiting were often on such occasions reduced to beggary by the expense of entertaining him. [Waley, 1956, pp. 54-55.]

The second major segment of the Elite of the Realm was formed by Manchu, Mongol, and Chinese Bannermen—the military organization created by the Manchus—and by the imperial bureaucracy. Political office was, in most cases, not formally hereditary. Membership in this segment of the Elite of the Realm went to all civil (*wen*) and military (*wu*) officials who had appointments within the "nine-rank" (*chiu-p'in*) hierarchy, in posts in the capital or in the provinces. Collectively, officials were called *chin-shen*, or *shih-huan*.

Members of the imperial family and nobility with the rank of Duke, Marquis, and Earl took precedence over even the highest of these government officials who did not possess such hereditary titles in addition to their official rank. Viscounts were equivalent to officials of the first rank; barons to officials of the second rank; *Ch'ing-ch'e-tu-wei* to those of the third rank; *Ch'i-tu-wei* to the fourth rank; *Yün-ch'i-wei* to the fifth rank; and *En-ch'i-wei* equivalent to officials of the seventh rank.[6]

The stratification within officialdom in the Ch'ing period is presented in connection with the Formal Hierarchy of this civil and military bureaucracy in Appendix III.

Before turning to a lower stratum of this legally privileged elite group—the local elite, the *shen-shih*, or degree-holders—we may note, first, that high evaluation in the system of *social* stratification corresponded very closely to elite *legal* status. The two groups were virtually identical. Second, by being officials or titled, many landlords attained *shih-ta-fu* position; had they not had these offices or titles, both their legal and their social status would have been lower. The *shih-ta-fu* position was a legal buffer, a protective coating for landlords (T'ao Hsi-sheng, 1954).

Below officialdom, but still within the elite legal category, were the literati, the degree-holders, variously called *shen-shih, hsiang-shen, shen-chin, chin-ch'i, shih-tzu.* The several levels within this group are summarized in Table 2.

Table 2—Hierarchy of Degrees (Military and Civil) in Ming and Ch'ing Dynasties*

1. *Chin-shih*—through Palace and Metropolitan Examinations
2. *Chü-jen*—through provincial examination.
3. *Kung-sheng* (Senior Licentiate)—through provincial examination. Sub-types, e.g., *kung-sheng* through:
   a. Noteworthy accomplishments
   b. Special selection
   c. Imperial favor
   d. Seniority
   e. Supplementary list
   f. Purchase
4. *Chien-sheng* (Student in the Imperial Academy)—through:
   a. Imperial favor
   b. Inheritance
   c. Virtue or noteworthy accomplishments
   d. Purchase
5. *Sheng-yüan* or *Hsiu ts'ai* (Bachelor or Licentiate)—through prefectural examination. Sub-types:
   a. Those on stipend
   b. "Additional Bachelors"
   c. "Supplementary Bachelors"
6. *Yin-sheng* (Government student by inheritance)
7. *T'ung-sheng* (Junior student)

* Adapted from Chang Chung-li, *The Chinese Gentry*, p. 9, *passim*, and from W. F. Mayers, *The Chinese Government* (3d ed.; Shanghai, 1897). Chang has one of the most complete treatments of this complex examination and degree system available in English. In Chinese, see Ch'i Ju-shan, *Chun-kuo-ti k'o-ming* (China's Examination System) (Taipei: Chung-kuo hsin-wen ch'u-pan kung-ssu, 1956).

An important legal distinction within this degree structure was between (1) those who held only the lowest degrees in the examination system, licentiates (*sheng-yüan*) and *chien-sheng,* and (2) those with higher degrees (*chin-shih, chü-jen, kung-sheng*). The latter were eligible for office, while the former were not.

On the other hand, all levels of degree-holders had certain legal privileges denied to commoners:

> Les Bacheliers jouissent du privelège d'être exempts de toute fonction servile ou *yao-i,* et de n'être passibles ni de la flagellation, ni de la bastonnade, ni du fouet *pien-ta.* Par *yao-i,* on entend toute espece de service ou corvée que le peuple a coutume de rendre aux mandarins, a raison par example de leurs voyages, de constructions, etc. [Zi, 1894, p. 10.]

One of the points at which there was the clearest discrepancy between legal and social stratification concerned the relatives of degree-holders, particularly relatives outside their immediate family. Chang Chung-li argues that, in terms of strict legal criteria, all the kin of a degree-holder except his nuclear family were considered *commoners* (below the elite group). He admits, however, that these more distant relatives were successful as "hangers-ons" in that they had a *socially* more privileged position than those with no kinsmen whatever among the degree-holders. In Chang's own words:

> When I made the distinction between "gentry" and their kinsmen "hangers-on" I had in mind primarily the legal definition of "*shen-shih*" or "*shen-chin*" whose privileges and functions theoretically could not be usurped by their "hangers-on." There is no specific term in Chinese for the "hangers-on" I spoke of. It is really my personal impression from the sources I have covered . . . that a distinction should be made of them from the rest of the "commoners" in Chinese society. That is, I had the notion that this group of gentry kinsmen had socially a more advantageous position than the other non-gentry members of society and sometimes performed some of the gentry functions; yet one should recognize that when the chips were down they were treated as commoners before the law. This explains why, when one's brother was already a gentry member, one should

> still strive to become a gentry member oneself. If a gentry member's uncle did not have a gentry title or degree, he would be known as the uncle of gentry so-and-so or honored as an elder . . . . , but he could not be called a gentry member himself. He would command due respect and position but only because of his kinsman's gentry position. [Chang Chung-li, letter to the author, February 4, 1957].

Discrepancies of this sort between legal and social stratification were not unique to China; they may also be found in medieval Western feudalism and in early modern Western "estate" society (Barber, 1957, pp. 55-57).

Commoners. The vast majority of the Chinese population were legally classed as commoners (*liang*). We prefer the term commoners to "the masses," since the referents of the latter term in sociological literature have been (1) an industrial proletariat or (2) a mass communications audience. Both of these referents are obviously inapplicable to pre-twentieth-century China. The legal category of commoner corresponded approximately to the group whose major occupations were evaluated as low in the system of social stratification (*p'ing-min, chung-to, shu-jen, pu-i, pai-hsing, ch'i-min,* etc.). The legal commoners were those in the "respectable" occupations, as opposed to those in outcast or pariah occupations (*chien*). They were those not possessing degrees, offices, hereditary ranks, titles, or honors. They were, therefore, those without privilege and high rank, in contrast to those positively privileged (the elite) and to those negatively privileged or discriminated against (the outcast occupations).

Legally, merchants were much better off during the Ch'ing period than they had been in some earlier periods in Chinese history. They were classed as among the "respectable" occupations; accordingly, they and their descendents could take examinations and enter office. A category of *shang-chi* (merchant status) was created for the salt merchants of Chekiang in 1600.[7] Salt merchants were particularly favored by the Manchu government and became the aristocracy of the merchants. Their children, by being listed in the *shang-chi*, were given special quotas, a privilege which better enabled them to become degree-holders and officials (Ho, 1954, p. 155). Ordinarily, one's native place determined where he could take the government examination. Those on this salt-merchant list were exempt from having to take the examinations in a place determined by their native district; they could go before the provincial level in the examination system after they had passed the examination given specially for them by the Salt Controller (*Yen-yün-shih* or *Yen-fa-tao*). This special category was found in Chihli (Tientsin), Kiangsu (Yangchow), Chekiang (Hangchow), Shantung (Chi-nan or Tsinan), Shansi (Chiehchow), and Kwangtung (Canton).

Pariah or Mean People. That minority of the population whose occupation was regarded as pariah were classed in the lowest of the three major legal categories. The legal criteria operative here were not exclusively occupational or instrumental, however. People in these occupations were also regarded as *morally* sullied, in contrast to the elite and the commoners, whose ancestry was seen as "pure" (*ch'ing-pai*). As will be seen below, members of this lowest legal stratum were often defined as the descendents of various *socially deviant* groups within the Chinese population, e.g., criminals and their families and unassimilated conquered peoples. Because of their occupations, these pariah groups were devalued on instrumental grounds; they were also devalued on moral grounds, for being "impure" people. This reinforcement of purely instrumental evaluation by moral evaluation facilitated the social control of these deviant groups.

As we noted above, members of this lowest legal stratum were *negatively* privileged: so long as they held special occupations, they were barred from intermarriage with commoners; from taking the government examinations, however literate they might be; from purchasing office, however wealthy they might be. They were punished by law more heavily than commoners, for the same crime. They were denied the right to upward mobility into the bureaucracy, so long as they held these "improper" occupations.

The *Ta-Ch'ing hui-tien shih-li* carries a detailed list of these occupations.[8] Included were: prostitutes, actors, lictors, i.e., lowly *yamen* assistants (sometimes given the epithet "the rats under the altar"), odd-jobbers (*ku-kung-jen*), domestic and other kinds of slaves (*nu-pi*), and, in the early Ch'ing period, such groups as the musicians (*yüeh-hu*) of Shansi, the "beggars" (*kai-hu*) of Kiangnan, the boat people (*tanka* or *tan-chia*) and fishermen (*chiu-hsing yü-hu*) of Canton and Chekiang, servants (*pan-tang, shih-p'u*) in Anhwei, etc.

Some of the members of these pariah occupations had downward mobile ancestors who, in earlier times, had been convicted of such crimes as rebellion, robbery, murder, etc. Accessories to these crimes as well as their families were included in the punishment, which had consisted in being lowered from the status of commoners to that of pariah or outcast. This group whose downward mobility was legally imposed was called the "fallen people" (*to-min*). Another group included in this pariah stratum were the conquered but unassimilated "barbarians," such as the *Man* of Kwangtung and Fukien.

Slaves (*nu-pi*), mostly domestic slaves (*chia-nu*), were drawn from several sources into the outcast stratum.[9] Some were born of slaves (*chia-sheng-nu, chia-ch'an-tzu*), others were bought, as when commoners sold themselves into slavery; slaves could be resold to another master; meritorious officials were given criminals as slaves; criminals could also be sold as slaves to commoners. A common source was that, when one became an official, many commoners would throw themselves into his service as slaves. Debtors could become slaves. Included within domestic slaves were also cooks, palanquin-bearers, etc. In the Ch'ing period there were also some new types of slaves, such as the bondservants (*pao-i*) of the

Inner Divisions of the Manchu Banners (Cheng, 1946, pp. 59-80).

There were invidious distinctions even among slaves. Those in the lifelong employment contract with a rich family, not subject to sale to another family, had higher status (*chang-sui*) than other types of slaves (Sano, 1947-48, pp. 62-63).

Strictly speaking, some of these legal statuses within the pariah or "mean" people category did not form a caste. There were some possibilities for upward mobility into the higher legal categories. Some domestic slaves could purchase emancipation (*shu-shen*), others could be freed by their masters without paying a fee. If a master killed his slaves, the families of these slaves could be freed. According to the principles of "pureness after three (four) generations" (*san-tai*, or *ssu-tai ch'ing-pai yüan-tse*), the descendents of the emancipated became, legally, commoners (*liang*) (Sano, pp. 76-77).

During the reign of the Yung-cheng Emperor (1723-35), the emancipation of many groups of slaves and outcasts was decreed; their occupation and legal status were changed to those of the commoners. It is doubtful, however, whether these official decrees allowing legal mobility succeeded in changing attitudes. The boat people of Canton (*t'an-hu*), although allowed to cultivate land instead of having to fish, were still discriminated against. According to a Western observer a whole century after these Yung-cheng edicts: "Poor people on shore still consider it degrading to marry with them" (Morrison, 1817, p. 69). Lü Ssu-mien also notes that these edicts making various "mean" people free commoners did not gain full social acceptance (Lü, 1954, I, 80).

Economic Stratification

There are several theoretical bases from which economic stratification can be analyzed.[10] For the Marxist, the ownership versus non-ownership of the means of production is the basis of economic stratification. Lipset and Bendix (1959, pp. 272-75) adopt the economist's distinction between the status of individuals as "producers" and their status as "consumers," and point out that the amount of one's income is not necessarily a good indicator of his consumption status, or style of life. For the purposes of this study, we shall define economic stratification as the ranking of individuals as higher or lower in terms of the *source* and the *amount* of their regular income. These criteria are secondary, not primary, criteria of stratification. This is because wealth and property *per se* are not essential qualifications for high stratificational position. Rather, source and amount of income are a possible *reward* for filling highly evaluated roles, or a *means* of attaining highly evaluated roles and high position in the system of social stratification. (Cf. Barber, 1957, pp. 50-54, *et passim.*)

The Sources of Income in the Ch'ing Period. The most highly ranked source of income was *office-holding*. Officials' sources of income can be divided into the legal and the extra-legal, and the former can be divided further into: (*a*) salary in taels silver; (*b*) salary in piculs of rice; (*c*) "yang-lien," extra salary to "nourish honesty" among officials; and (*d*) administrative expenses (*kung-fei*). Extra-legal official income came in the form of gifts and the lucrative "squeeze," by which local officials collected for themselves a certain fraction of the money and/or grain from the land tax of the area they administered. Some of this extra-legal income was tacitly sanctioned by the dynasty as a supplement to the inadequate legal income of officials.

A second source of income was rent, collected by landlords from the peasant farmers. Absentee landlordism was more prevalent in central China than in North China. Income from various private enterprises was a third source. Included here were income from commerce and mercantile activities; interest from loans and pawnshops; and profit from handicraft production, mostly on a very small scale. The local elite derived income from two additional sources: professional services (teaching, serving as secretaries to officials, holding academic subsidies, e.g., students on government stipends) and what has been referred to above, following Chang Chung-li, as "gentry services" (i.e., income from promotion and management of public works projects, management of local defense corps, of relief and welfare institutions, of government-sponsored agencies, such as likin bureaus, of clan organizations, etc.).

The major source of income for the bulk of the population was, of course, none of the above, but rather farming and other primary extractive occupations, such as fishing. According to the traditional Chinese theory of land tenure, land was divided into two layers: the surface and the subsoil. The possessor of the subsoil was the *title holder* of the land; if he possessed the subsoil but not the surface, he was an *absentee landlord*. Only if he possessed both the subsoil and the surface rights was he the *full owner*. Those who possessed only the surface without the subsoil were termed *tenants* (Fei, 1939, p. 177). One can distinguish the following economic strata: absentee landlords; landlords who were themselves also cultivators; owner-cultivators; part owner-cultivators and part tenant-farmers; tenants; tenants who were concurrently hired laborers; hired agricultural laborers, who lacked land, agricultural implements of their own, and cash.

The Amount of Regular Income in the Ch'ing Period. For the elite segment of the Ch'ing population, the most extensive study of the amount of income is that of Chang Chung-li (1953). Chang's estimates of income distribution apply only to the 1880's, and the limitations of his data and method make it necessary to accept his estimates with caution. With these reservations in mind, we may proceed to analyze the distribution of income in late Ch'ing China.

The amount of legal income for officials of the various ranks is stated in Table 3.

Table 3—Legal Salary Range for Civil and Military Officials

CIVIL OFFICIALS

Rank	Taels*	Rice (in shih, or piculs), metropolitan officials	Yang-Lien
	TYPES OF SALARY		
1	180	90	
2	150	75	(Governor-General, 2a,
3	130	65	13,000 to 20,000 taels)
4	105	52	(Circuit Intendant, 4a,
5	80	40	8,000 to 16,000 taels)
6	60	30	
7	45	22	(District Magistrate, 7a,
8	40	20	400 to 2257 taels)
9a	33	16	
9b	33	15	

MILITARY OFFICIALS

Rank	Taels	Perquisites	Yang-Lien
	TYPES OF SALARY		
1	81	524	
2a	67	444	(Brigadier-General, 2a,
2b	53	324	1,500 taels)
3a	39	204	
3b	39	192	
4	27	114	
5	18	72	(Second Captain, 5b,
6	14	33	200 taels)
7	12	23	

* The exchange rate between the Hai-Kuan (customs) Tael and the U. S. dollar during the 1880's was 1 Tael = $1.28 (C. Yang, 1931, p. 151).

What stands out most here, perhaps, is not the range of salary in taels or rice from the highest to the lowest rank, but the disparity between these amounts and the amount of "yang-lien" income, that is, income given to officials as a reward for honesty and probity. But this disparity is nothing in comparison with the disparity between the legal and extra-legal income of the 2,000 officials in key local posts, especially district magistrates. Chang estimates that, while there were variations in extra-legal income depending on the location of the posts, the average *hsien* or district magistrate was able to squeeze approximately 30,000 taels annually from the local taxes. This would give district magistrates an extra-legal income about thirty times larger than their legal income. The great mass of officials—those in metropolitan and non-key regional posts—were only able to squeeze about 1,000 taels in extra-legal income. This made the average extra-legal income for officials as a whole about ten times greater than their legal income, according to Chang. Thus, we have the following average distribution of income for officialdom as a whole:

	Percentage of Income
1. From official salary (taels and rice)	1
2. From "Yang Lien" or honesty rewards	5
3. From administrative allowances	1
Total legal sources	7
4 Extra-legal income	93
Total	100

As a nineteenth-century Western observer summed it up:

> An official's salary as magistrate of a district is miserably small; three hundred dollars perhaps, with an allowance of three times as much to "encourage probity." Notwithstanding this suggestive inducement he ekes out his income by irregular methods, some of which are sanctioned by custom and some practiced though not sanctioned. [Martin, 1896, p. 332.]

One of the best indications of the great income one could derive from an official career is provided by the purchase system:

> The price of a circuit intendant, the highest office in the province purchasable, was worth 30,000 taels. The salary of a circuit intendant was 105 taels a year with two or three thousand taels of allowance for the same period. It would take the purchaser at least ten years to gain back the capital were he to earn it legitimately and honestly. Unprofitable as it might appear, the rank and file of the "waiting officials" who qualified by purchase suddenly increased so that . . . the [Tao-kuang Emperor] found it necessary to make up another price list for the purchase of the privilege of getting an appointment before the regular turn came. [Hsieh, 1925, p. 110.]

Officials commonly amassed a fortune; rare was he who did not. Perhaps the most dramatic case of official financial aggrandizement during the Ch'ing period was that of an official in our sample, the Grand Secretary Ho-shen (1750-99). With a legitimate salary of 180 taels a year, Ho-shen mustered a fortune of 80 million taels in movable property alone!

Let us turn now to several of Chang's estimates regarding the income of the total elite group in late nineteenth-century China. The total number of elite in this period was 1,500,000 individuals; assuming an average elite family to be five individuals, the size of the elite and their families was 7,500,000, or 2 per cent of the total population. Of the 1,500,000 elite individuals, 14 per cent were "upper elite," that is, officials, holders of official titles, and higher degree-holders, eligible for office (*chin-shih, chü-jen,* and *kung-sheng*). The remaining 86 per cent were "lower elite," that is, licentiates (*sheng-yüan*), imperial students through purchase (*li kung-sheng*), and Imperial Collegians (*chien-sheng*). These 1,500,000 elite individuals can also be divided into "regular" elite—those who had achieved degrees through the examination competitions—and "irregular" elite—those who had purchased their elite position. Of the total elite group, 64 per cent were "regular" elite and the remaining 36 per cent "irregular" elite. We may now analyze the amount and distribution of income among these segments of the elite.

First, Chang estimates that, after taxes, 32 per cent of all elite income for the 1,500,000 elite individuals was from rents, 22 per cent was from entrepreneurial activity and interest on loans, while the remaining 46 per cent was from official, professional, and "gentry" services. That the largest source of elite income was from *services* performed as officials, teachers, and local "gentry" leaders, and not from land rents, shows, according to Chang, that the Chinese elite were *not* predominantly a landed gentry. It is more correct to speak of the upper elite as a landed gentry, for Chang shows that perhaps 45 per cent of the total income for an average official or higher degree-holder was from rents. It is inaccurate to regard the lower elite as a landed gentry, for, according to Chang, only 23 per cent of their total income came from rents, while the bulk of their income came from "gentry services" (39 per cent) and from professional services (21 per cent).

Second, there is evidence that the over-all income of regular and irregular elite individuals did not differ markedly (Chang, 1953, pp. 482-83). They received about an equal amount from office, from rents, and from "gentry services" on the local level. While the regular elite had a larger income from professional services, such as teaching, than the irregular elite, the latter made up for this difference by having a larger income than the former group from mercantile pursuits. (These statements refer, of course, to the late nineteenth century.)

Third, how were the several sources of elite income distributed between "upper" and "lower" elite? Chang's estimates show that 75 per cent of all income from rent which went to the elite went to the upper elite, while the remaining 25 per cent of rent income went to the lower elite. The upper elite also received a larger proportion of the entrepreneurial income (67 per cent as against 33 per cent for the lower elite). The upper elite, by definition, received all the income from office, since only they were eligible to hold office. As to the remaining two sources of elite income—professional services and "gentry" services—the bulk of it went to the *lower* gentry: 91 per cent of all income from professional services and 82 per cent of all income from gentry services. It is important to realize that the upper elite received a disproportionate amount of all elite income. Chang's data suggest that the 14 per cent of the elite who were "upper elite" received 60 per cent of the total amount of elite income from all sources. The upper elite and their immediate families, numbering 1 million individuals, received a yearly total income of 363 taels per capita, which was more than four times higher than the average per capita income for all elite, namely, 84 taels per year. The lower elite and their families, numbering 6.5 million individuals, had an annual per capita income of 37 taels, that is, slightly less than one-half the average income of all elite (84 taels), and about one-tenth the income of the upper elite. However, the income of even the lower elite was probably seven times greater than the average per capita income for all commoners in late Ch'ing China.

Fourth, Chang also attempts to estimate China's Gross National Product for the 1880's (pp. 447-50). This is defined as "the aggregate of the values of products originating in all branches of economic activity, plus net income from abroad." Without going into details on this, we may note Chang's calculation that, of the total Gross National Product (roughly 2,700,000,000 taels), about 23 per cent of it went to the 2 per cent of the population who were in the elite. The other 98 per cent of the population received 77 per cent of the Gross Product. The per capita income of the elite 2 per cent was 84 taels, in contrast to a per capita income of 6 taels for the other 98 per cent of the population (p. 475). The difference between the elite and the commoners in *disposable* income (i.e., after taxes) was even greater than this 84:6 ratio because, as we have already noted, the elite were able to evade taxes more readily than the commoners. The "great households" (*ta-hu*), made up of members of the elite, were extremely influential in local affairs; they were able to evade taxes because few officials dared to challenge their entrenched position. Altogether, according to Chang, 265 million taels were collected annually in governmental and semi-official tax levies. This burden was shouldered by the landowners. Since about 25 per cent of the land was owned by absentee landlords and members of the elite, if the tax burden were proportionate, we would expect that about one-fourth of the taxes would be paid by this elite group. In fact, commoners had to pay taxes at a rate of two to five times per *mou* of land larger than that paid by the elite. Consequently, the actual tax ratio between commoners and elite, instead of being 3:1, was, even conservatively speaking, 6:1, respectively. Thus the per capital *disposable* income may have been on the order of 4.5 taels for commoners as against 75 taels for the elite, a ratio of nearly 17:1 (Chang, p. 477). This suggests the extreme disparity of income distribution in Chinese society and shows the rather close correlation between legal, social, and economic stratification.

Although our study is primarily concerned with the elite 2 per cent of the Chinese population, we should say a bit more about economic stratification among the 98 per cent of the population who were commoners from a legal standpoint. Numerous studies have shown that (*a*) a majority of Chinese farmers were peasant proprietors, owner-cultivators, rather than tenant-farmers, but that (*b*), nevertheless, there was considerable concentration of landownership, with most cultivators owning only small plots of land while a few owners possessed huge holdings. The most satisfactory data we have were obtained during the twentieth century, from the Japanese-sponsored South Manchurian Railway research in North China, and from several Chinese field surveys. With caution, these can be applied to the Ch'ing period. Sano (1947, II, 34-35) summarizes these data as follows:

Stratum	Percentage of All Households	Percentage of All Cultivated Land Owned
Landlords and rich peasants	10	60
Middle peasants	20	20
Poor peasants	70	20
Total	100	100

In 1934-35, Nationalist government statistics showed that for eighty-nine districts (*hsien*) scattered through eleven provinces, 1,545 families of large landlords owned an average of 2,030 *mou* of land per family. On the other hand, 752,865 peasant families in these districts owned an average of 15.8 *mou* of land, which was 1/128.5 of the average holding for the large landlords. (Institute of Pacific Relations, 1939, p. 3.) In South China, about 1930, the landlords, comprising from 2 to 4 per cent of the population, owned from 30 per cent to 50 per cent of the land, on which they collected rent. At the other extreme, the approximately 70 per cent of the population who were poor peasants owned about 25 per cent of the land, on the average (p. 4). Tawney (1932, pp. 54-77) and others have described the disadvantages suffered by the peasants in their business dealings as a result of their low position in the system of economic stratification. The farmer could not command the best price for his produce because, since transportation of crops was prohibitively expensive, he had to sell on the local market, and was therefore prey to the local monopolist. Because the farmer lacked reserve funds, he had to sell immediately after harvest, when prices were falling. When the farmer sought credit, he was exploited by the moneylender; 25 per cent interest rates were not considered exorbitant; interest rates of even 60 per cent were not uncommon. Tenant farmers in Shansi had to pay 60 per cent of their grain harvest as rent, and had to pay it during the winter or else they would not be allowed to plant in the spring. This again drove the farmer to the moneylender, who was often his landlord. (Institute of Pacific Relations, 1939, p. 19.) Given the slow turnover in agricultural production—the time from sowing until harvest—credit was essential for the farmer. Next to drought, it was the inability to meet the claims of the moneylender which, at least in parts of China, was the main cause of the downward economic mobility and ruin of peasant families.

Summary

We have analyzed some of the social, legal, and economic elements and historical dynamics of stratification in the Ch'ing period. The purpose of this analysis was to show the background of the elite mobility which is the main focus of this study. It was in this structure of stratification that elite mobility occurred. Before analyzing our own mobility data, we shall review, in the next chapter, earlier empirical research on elite mobility in the Ch'ing period.

CHAPTER 4 EARLIER RESEARCH ON CHINESE ELITE MOBILITY

MORE IS KNOWN sociologically about Western than about Chinese elite mobility. There are several reasons for this. Traditionally, those with most access to the raw data on elite mobility in China—scholar-officials—either had a purely administrative orientation toward these data, or else they made no use of it in research because they were given to humanistic studies: philosophy, classics, history, and belles lettres. Later, foreign scholarship on China—Sinology—largely followed this textual, philological bent of the traditional indigenous scholarship. Studies of officials usually centered upon their memorials and other writings, or on the mobility of only individuals or small groups of officials.

As social history developed, both Chinese and foreign scholars from time to time asserted generalizations regarding Chinese elite mobility. But their assertions were rarely backed up with any systematic data, presented either in tabular form or otherwise; supporting evidence was usually anecdotal, in the form of "illustrative" cases. Though some of these scholars may have gathered systematic data on mobility, since they did not publish it along with their analytical operations, we cannot take their conclusions for granted.

There are several empirical studies of special aspects of stratification and mobility for earlier periods of Chinese history.[1] Though they are significant as earlier social history, we cannot rely on them for conclusions about mobility in the Ch'ing period simply because there is good evidence that Chinese social structure was not altogether static. We know that during Ming and Ch'ing times (1368-1912) there were several important institutional changes, with obvious consequences for mobility. First, we have already discussed, in Chapter III, the Manchu invasion, Manchu-Chinese relations within the bureaucracy during the phases of the 1600-1900 dynastic cycle, and the fact that merchants were no longer prohibited from seeking mobility into officialdom. Ho Ping-ti has shown that a group of about 300 transport and factory merchant families produced 139 *chin-shih* and 208 *chü-jen* degree-holders, between 1646 and 1802 (1954, p. 165).

Second, the objective chances for bureaucratic mobility also increased during this period because the extent to which men were given bureaucratic appointment on the basis of *direct* inheritance of their father's official status declined in favor of a relatively more universalistic basis of appointment. In the biographies of Chinese officials which I have consulted, I saw much more often the phrase, "his forebears were products of the examination system, and were unsullied [by business, soldiery, etc.] from generation to generation" (*chia-shih chia-k'o ch'ing-pai hsiang-shan*), than the phrase "appointed to office by virtue of his father's services" (*yung fu-yin pu-kuan*). Of the several methods of recruiting officials, those which most favored the descendants of officials

—direct inheritance (*hsi-chüeh*) and the *yin* privilege—had been more commonly used before Ming and Ch'ing times. "The Ming and Ch'ing emperors reduced the *yin* prerogative to a shadow of its former self" (Wittfogel, 1957, p. 350). After 1467, only one son, grandson, or male collateral of only the officials in the top three ranks could use the *yin* privilege to enter the bureaucracy. Furthermore, *yin* beneficiaries could themselves attain only a minor position in the central government, or the post of Prefect in the provincial administration, unless they passed the civil service examinations apart from their *yin* privilege. The effect of these limitations on direct inheritance was to enhance the opportunities of those rising through the more universalistic examination system, for there were fewer *yin* candidates to compete with for appointment (Wittfogel and Feng, 1949, p. 463). Furthermore, as Pulleyblank has noted (1953), even though many examination products were the sons of officials and degree-holders, the fact that they prepared for and competed in the examination system at all, instead of relying on birth alone, indicates the inroads of universalistic achievement patterns in Chinese society.

Recruitment became heavily organized by the examination system and, especially during the latter part of the Ch'ing period, by the purchase system. While recruitment could still favor the sons of the elite becoming elite, there is evidence that upward mobility could and did take place through the examination system and purchase: men without official family backgrounds were, to some degree, recruited by these two methods during Ming and Ch'ing times (Ho, 1959). These and other institutional changes introduced factors whose effect on mobility must be studied afresh.

Most recently, there has been a burst of Chinese Marxist studies of stratification and mobility in China.[2] Much of this research is polemical rather than objective. Where traditional dynastic historians grouped those who led and participated in anti-dynastic uprisings as "bandits," Marxist scholars tend to see these generals and rebel leaders as leaders of "peasant, anti-feudal revolutions," notwithstanding the fact that most, if not all of these leaders, were not oriented toward a new alignment of classes so much as toward imperial dynastic designs of their own. Another deficiency of this research is that, despite the claim of "scientific" socialism, old-fashioned moralizing abounds. For example, cases are piled up to show the extortion of the "evil" officials from "the people." Although Weber wrote a generation ago, and knew the data less well, his analysis of official corruption was far more penetrating than the essentially moralistic approach shared, in this instance, by Marxists and traditional Chinese and Sinological observers. Weber saw that it was not the "squeeze" as such, but the *highly variable* total quantity of this pocketing of fees by officials, from year to year, that constituted the real problem for the central treasury. The "drain" varied greatly from year to year, and was therefore unpredictable for the government, because each official's extortion was a function of highly idiosyncratic factors: his family needs, the cost of getting office in the first place, the degree of wealth of the area of the official's jurisdiction, etc. (Weber, 1951, pp. 57-59).

We turn now to the few pioneering attempts at systematic empirical analysis of Ch'ing elite mobility. As early as 1894 Etienne Zi published data on the subsequent official mobility of 324 men who, between 1646 and 1894, had received the *chin-shih* degree with high honors (*chuang-yüan, pang-yen,* and *t'an-hua*) (Zi, 1894, pp. 219-41). These honors went to 321 Chinese and three Bannermen, two of whom were Chinese and one Mongol. However, when offices and ranks held were analyzed—as indices of the authority and mobility of this group—it was found that these factors did not correlate with intellectual attainment at all: the Manchus dominated the authority structure. In 1893, Zi pointed out, the highest offices were held by 350 Chinese and 398 Bannermen, of whom 318 were Manchus. This roughly fifty-fifty distribution was drastically out of proportion to the minority that the Manchus were in the total population.

Zi's data also show that, (*a*) of these 324 top-ranking graduates throughout the Ch'ing period, 27 per cent reached posts in the two highest civil service ranks (*cheng i-p'in* through *tsung erh-p'in*), and another 24 per cent reached middle-rank posts, between the third and the sixth ranks; (*b*) on the other hand, fully 34 per cent of this group of 324 appear to have had no significant official career at all: Zi does not list them as having any post in the bureaucracy. We may assume that the majority of these men had never taken office, or retired early, or died, or remained in very low posts. Zi's study thus indicates a far from perfect correlation between intellectual attainment and later official career advancement; in fact, it shows that ethnic factors were more highly associated with authority and official advancement than was intellectual attainment.

In 1947, P'an Kuang-tan published a study of ninety-one prominent clans of Chia-hsing (Kashing), Chekiang, during the Ming and Ch'ing periods. Most of these clans had at least one degree-holder, including fifty-eight men who had received the *chin-shih* with high honors (*wei-k'o*). P'an concluded that at least three factors were highly correlated with the vertical mobility (*hsing t'i sheng shuai*) of these clans over generations: residential mobility (*i-hsi*), marriage (*hun-yin*), and longevity (*shou*). Forty-four of these prominent clans had histories of establishing new homes outside Chia-hsing Prefecture; but they did not give up their ancestral home in Chia-hsing. By having two homes, these clans had greater adaptability and control over the exigencies of social conditions: in settled and peaceful times, they could undertake new enterprises in new regions and exploit the situation; in adverse times, they could withdraw to their more secure residence.

By residential mobility and wise marriage choices, several of these clans remained prominent for eight or nine generations. Wise marriage choice at times involved marrying outside the region, or even taking as wife or concubines females whose presumed hereditary capacities were superior, though their social status was low. (P'an is noted in China in connection with eugenics, and he stressed hereditary factors in maintaining prominent clans [Ying, 1956, pp. 79-83].) The effect of longevity is obvious: if a male died without issue, or if all the male issue of a clan in a given generation died young, the clan itself would die out. In addition to showing the effect of residential mobility, marriage and longevity, P'an's study is also valuable for its inclusion of popular "explanations" of clan mobility, such as geomancy (*feng-shui*) and mobility as "a reward for accumulated virtue."

In the last analysis, P'an saw the mobility of prominent clans as a function, not so much of any of the foregoing factors, as of such "external" factors as social disorders and natural disasters. Thus, he asserted that Kiangsu and Chekiang provinces more frequently had prominent families, not primarily because of *conscious efforts* at residential mobility and marriage connections, but because these provinces had more peaceful and settled conditions than other regions.

In 1947, P'an Kuang-tan and Fei Hsiao-t'ung published a study of social mobility and the examination system. They point out that there is as yet no conclusive empirical demonstration of either of two extreme views: that the examination system functioned as a mobility ladder for lower status individuals, or, on the other hand, that its products were predominantly of high status background.

P'an and Fei's data were 915 published examination papers of degree candidates successful between 1662 and the last Ch'ing reign period. Included were both the "vermillion seal" examination papers (*chu-chüan*) of metropolitan graduates and the "ink-seal" examination papers (*mo-chüan*) of provincial-level graduates. P'an and Fei drew the following conclusions: mobility in the examination system went disproportionately to those from degree-holding families of orientation; to those from absentee-landlord city-dwelling families; and to those from independent peasant families in rural areas. Conversely, those without degree-holding members among their four previous paternal generations, as well as those from tenant-farmer families, were extremely unlikely to be among those who passed the examinations.

As to rural-urban differences, of the 758 candidates whose papers had this information, 398, or 53 per cent, were from cities (*ch'eng-shih*), 41 per cent from rural areas (*hsiang*), and 6 per cent from intermediate areas, towns (*chen*), defined in Ch'ing times as places with 50,000 or more people. P'an and Fei analyze this material in terms similar to Taussig and Joslyn's "productivity ratios" (1932, pp. 84-91), by which the latter authors compared the occupations of the fathers of their sample of business-leader sons with the total number of married males in the respective occupational strata at the time of the median year of birth of the sons. P'an and Fei use the same logic, even though their measure is less refined. They point out that the 90 per cent of the Chinese population which was rural produced 44 per cent of their sample of examination candidates. This indicates that cities were proportionately more productive of successful candidates than were rural areas. However, the proportion of city versus country candidates varied with the proportion of absentee landlords versus independent owner-cultivators in a given region. Thus, Kiangsu, with a high development of absentee landlordism—i.e., landlords lived in cities, more or less off rents from their rural holdings—had the highest percentage (75 per cent) of city examination candidates, in this sample. All these conclusions refer, of course, only to those in this sample who passed the examinations, not necessarily to those in office. Conversely, Shantung, Shansi, and Honan, with relatively more owner-cultivators, had a lower percentage of city and a higher percentage of rural candidates who were successful.

As to family background factors, 609, or 67 per cent, of the 915 candidates' fathers were degree-holders. Of the remaining 33 per cent of the candidates, all but 14 per cent had at least one degree-holding grandfather, great-grandfather, or great-great-grandfather. The authors argue that these facts show how narrow was the road for commoners' descendents who sought mobility through the examinations.

Can we conclude with P'an and Fei that the examination system was not a significant mechanism for upward mobility into the elite during the Ch'ing period? During the period covered by their sample, many thousands of men took degrees in the various levels of the examination system: we have no way of knowing how representative this sample of 915 men is of the larger population. These 915 men had their examination papers specially printed for their relatives and friends, and this may constitute a serious bias. Here, however, an interesting methodological point arises: The study by Ho Ping-ti (1959), which we shall review below, with a much larger Ch'ing sample than that of P'an and Fei, shows a remarkably *similar* pattern of upward mobility. P'an and Fei show that only 14 per cent of their sample were from commoner families; Ho shows that only 19 per cent of the *chin-shih* graduates in his Ch'ing sample were from commoner families. The two samples, despite their differences in size and representativeness, support each other to a considerable extent in showing a rather small degree of upward mobility in the Ch'ing examinations.

The research of the anthropologist Francis L. K. Hsu, although dealing with social mobility throughout Chinese history and not containing conclusions specifically on Ch'ing mobility, should be noted. Using the Chinese biographical dictionary, *Li-tai ming-jen nien-li pei-chuan tsung-piao* (Chiang Liang-fu, 1937), he tabulated the names, native place, and dates of birth of 2,897 individuals who bore one of thirty different surnames. These included five of the commonest surnames in China. Of the total, 24 per cent of those with the same surname and same birthplace were not born within a range of fifteen to sixty years of each other, and were not considered as cases of *continuous prominence* in the same family over two or more generations. Another 48 per cent of the total had the same surname but were of different birthplaces, and were regarded as non-kin (in much the same way, for example, as a New York City Brown and a Dallas Brown would be assumed to be unrelated, except perhaps distantly). This meant, according to Hsu, that only the remaining 24 per cent of the total could be cases of *continuous prominence* over two or more generations in the same family—these were the individuals with the same surname, the same birthplace, and who were born within a fifteen- to sixty-year range of each other. Hsu's general conclusion, based on this and other data, is that "intellectual and especially political prominence rarely endured *continuously* for more than two generations in any given family, particularly along direct lineal descent" (1948, pp. 305, 309; 1949).

It is clear that Hsu's analysis is limited to the question of inter-generational social mobility rather than to intra-generational, or career, mobility. Also, he deals with the very generalized factor of "prominence," instead of differentiating between types of prominence, such as official, artistic, intellectual, and the like. Such a differentiation might show significant mobility differences among the several types of prominence.

Another study of Ch'ing elite mobility which deserves our attention is that of Chang Chung-li (1955). On the basis of over 5,000 biographies of nineteenth-century Chinese who passed one or more levels of the examination system and thereby entered either the "lower gentry" or the "upper gentry," Chang concluded (Part IV) that there was a pattern during the century of "high and increasing mobility." Chang shows that, for the period 1796-1908, about 35 per cent of his sample of men who entered the "gentry" (*shen-shih*) stratum by virtue of getting degrees were "newcomers." That is, this 35 per cent had no degree-holders or officials among their fathers, grandfathers, and great-grandfathers. The other 65 per cent did, and were termed men from "established gentry" family backgrounds. Again, we see that the "productivity ratio" of the small elite stratum was many times that of its size, in comparison to the mass of commoners.

Did the "gentry" from established gentry families also monopolize the upper levels of the gentry degree hierarchy, leaving most of the newcomers in the lower levels of the gentry? Chang's data bear on this question also.

Table 4 shows that, for Chang's sample of 2,146 degree-holders, there is no relationship between family background in degree status and whether one reached the lower or the

Table 4—Relation between Family Background and Level of "Gentry" Entered, 1796-1908*

	FAMILY BACKGROUND				
	Newcomer		Estab. Gentry		
Level Reached	Number	Per Cent	Number	Per Cent	Total
"Upper gentry" (Officials and degree-holders above *sheng-yüan*)	541	73	1,015	72	1,556
"Lower gentry" (Licentiates or *sheng-yüan*)	203	27	387	28	590
Total	744	100	1,402	100	2,146

* Adapted from Chang Chung-li, *The Chinese Gentry*, Table 36, p. 222.

upper stratum *within* the "gentry" elite. On the other hand, as we have seen, the small fraction of the population who were "established gentry" produced twice as many successful new degree candidates (1,402 vs. 744 men) as did the vast majority of the population, the commoners. This table, along with other points made by Chang, has many social, political, and economic implications for elite mobility which we shall examine below, in connection with the survey analysis of our own sample of 572 Ch'ing officials.

Wittfogel's 1957 summary of his findings, if extended to the Ch'ing period, supports the hypothesis of a relatively low degree of upward mobility:

> If the Sui and T'ang emperors established the examinations, in part at least, in order to alter the social composition of the ranking officialdom, then it must be said that the system failed to achieve this purpose. The examinations . . . added a varying amount of "fresh blood" to the ranking officialdom. But this did not destroy the trend toward sociopolitical self-perpetuation, which dominated the thoughts and actions of this group. [p. 354.]

Perhaps the most extensive research, to date, on mobility through the examination system has been done by Ho Ping-ti (1959 and forthcoming). Ho tabulated the family backgrounds of all the graduates from forty-four Ming and Ch'ing dynasty *chin-shih* examinations, totaling 11,249 individuals, and also the data on 22,785 individuals taking one of the lower degrees. His principal findings are expressed in Table 5.

Ho's data show that the amount of social mobility in the examination system declined from Ming to Ch'ing times. If we limit our comments to the second and third columns, which deal with Ch'ing data only, we can conclude: First, as we have seen before, the small elite segment of the population (officials and degree-holders) produced a greatly disproportionate number of those successful in the examinations. Only 19 per cent of the *chin-shih* graduates came from legally commoner families; another 18 pr cent came from families we have termed local elite; the remainder came from the official and higher degree-holder stratum of the population. Second, the lower degrees in the examination system (*chü-jen* and *kung-sheng*) were not more accessible to commoners' sons than was the *chin-shih* degree. However, in comparison with the *chin-shih*, a slightly higher percentage of local elite sons and a slightly lower percentage of officials sons received the *chü-jen* or *kung-sheng* degree.

Table 5—Relation between Family Background and Degree-Attainment, Ming and Ch'ing Dynasties

	DEGREE ATTAINED					
	Ming Chin-shih		Ch'ing Chin-shih		Nineteenth-Century Chü-jen and Kung-sheng	
Family Background (father, grandfather, and great-grandfather)	Number	Per Cent	Number	Per Cent	Number	Per Cent
Officials or higher degree-holders	2209	50	3795	63	11,780	52
Sheng-yüan (lowest degree)	119	3	1123	18	6311	28
No officials or degree-holders	2068	47	1149	19	4694	20
	4396	100	6067	100	22,785	100

It should be clear from this review of the literature on Ch'ing elite mobility that there is anything but agreement, even on the apparently simple question of the *amount* of mobility. On the one hand, Hsu and Chang assert that there was a relatively large amount of mobility; on the other hand, Zi, P'an and Fei, Wittfogel and Ho (Ch'ing data only) seem to show that the chances were very much against commoners' sons as contrasted with the small elite segment.

In large measure, these studies of mobility through the examination system which we have reviewed may be seen as limited to the problem of elite *recruitment*, rather than dealing with recruitment as well as later official *advancement*.

Without follow-up studies of the later official careers of the men who took the examination path to their initial appointment in the bureaucracy, we shall have an inadequate account of the *over-all* process of intra-generational elite mobility. Studies which treat the graduates of a given year as a *cohort* whose careers are followed up in a kind of panel study may find that the carry-over from recruitment to later advancement is far from perfect. Degree-holders were often more numerous than the number of available official posts. Securing appointment may have been a much greater obstacle for commoners' sons than for officials' sons. One finding from the present study will illustrate the point that there were different patterns of mobility within the bureaucracy than would be expected on the basis of the examination system. My data show that while 80 per cent of the sons of official families entered officialdom through the examination competition, the other 20 per cent who did not take the examinations nevertheless held posts in the top three ranks *much longer* than did commoners' sons who *had* taken the examination path. As we shall see, it was commoners' sons who did *not* take the examinations whose official advancement more closely approximated that of the sons of official families. What I am suggesting, then, is that the examination competition may not be the most significant place to look, in studies of mobility. What is needed is the systematic analysis of *alternative* recruitment paths (examinations, purchase, rising through the ranks, military careers) and their influence, along with the influence of other factors, upon official advancement in the bureaucracy as a whole, including officials of all ranks. The present study is a modest step in this direction.

CHAPTER 5 METHODOLOGY

Chinese Biographies as Sources

OUR DATA in this study come from two types of sources, which we may term the structural and the biographical. Chapters III and IV drew most heavily upon structural social-historical sources on Chinese stratification and mobility between 1600 and 1900. In Appendix III we shall present an outline of the formal organization of the Chinese Imperial bureaucracy. This "nine-rank" hierarchy formed the context of the elite mobility of the individual officials in our sample. Sources on this hierarchy are another type of structural source.

The predominant type of source in this study, however, is the biographical. Both in quantity of data and in research time consumed, the firmest underpinnings of our study are biographical. The first question is, then, how adequate is Chinese biography as data for a study of family stratum position and elite mobility?

In the first place, Chinese biographical sources—especially biographies of government officials—exist in great quantity.

China, perhaps to a greater extent than any other society in the world, is rich in biographical data, even for fairly remote historical periods. A Chinese historiographer (Han, 1955, p. 202) has estimated that by far the largest space in the voluminous Chinese dynastic histories (*cheng-shih*) is allotted to biographies—as much as 62 per cent of the total number of volumes. The histories of the Ming and Ch'ing dynasties (*Ming-shih* and *Ch'ing-shih kao*) concern us here, and the same tendency holds true for them; 66 per cent of the volumes of the *Ming-shih* (220 out of 332 *chüan*) and 59 per cent of the volumes of the *Ch'ing-shih kao* (312 out of 536 *chüan*) are exclusively biographical. Local histories for provinces, districts, etc., also had large biographical sections.

A few remarks on dynastic histories are in order. The official histories of the Ming and Ch'ing dynasties were compiled on the basis of their respective archival sources, such as the "Veritable Records" (*Shih-lu*) of the various reign-periods of each dynasty. In conformity with tradition, these histories were compiled by historical commissions only after each dynasty's fall. The *Ming-shih* was compiled by Ch'ing scholars, after sixty years' work; the *Ch'ing History*, published as yet only in draft form (*Ch'ing-shih kao*), is the work of post-1911 historians of Republican China.

There were several biases at work in this method. The historical commissions were composed of government-approved scholars. The previous dynasty's "Veritable Records" were always censored before being printed, and facts were altered, added, and concealed in the interests of the reigning dynasty. After the completion of the history, all the archival records of the Ming dynasty were destroyed by the Ch'ing. Censorship was heavy in the Ch'ing period, and many privately written histories thought to be prejudicial to the early Manchu emperors were also destroyed. Hu Shih has summed up these biases:

> The Manchu conquest of China and the racial struggles and prejudices resulting from it greatly restricted the freedom of all historical and biographical writing that had anything to do with persons and events connected with the long conflicts between the two peoples. Court intrigue and political and partisan strife throughout the dynasty also were responsible for much of the suppression and distortion of biographical truth. The tyranny of the intellectual fashion of the age, the traditional prejudices against unorthodox thinkers, writers or artists, and dynastic or political support of schools of thought supposedly advantageous to the reigning house, led to distorted judgments in biographical literature. Numerous works were irretrievably lost through official prohibition and long neglect. Official "veritable" records were doctored and sometimes redoctored. Private works were altered and deleted in order to make publication or re-publication possible. [1943, p. iii.]

Despite this tampering with historical data and writing, the biographical data used in this study are highly reliable and accurate. This is due to several things. First, the official biographies of officials were not based principally on the "Veritable Records," which were more concerned with the person and activities of the Emperor. Officials' biographies were based on archives kept separately from those concerning the court, and were less likely to be tampered with. Second, Ch'ing censorship was not always efficient. Some banned books escaped destruction and were hidden in private homes, in Japan, and elsewhere abroad. "In recent decades, modern scholarship has done much to unearth hidden documents, establish new evidence, and rectify some of the distorted versions of earlier biographers. Unexpurgated editions of suppressed works have appeared. New biographies of once defamed personages have been produced" (Hu Shih, 1943, p. iii). Third, the "Veritable Records" we have today for Ch'ing reigns were reproduced photolithographically from the archives. They are therefore free from later editorial tampering, with the exception that the records for some of the reigns were revised even before they were committed to the archives. These *Shih-lu* remain, however, the least politically edited source we have on Ch'ing history (Wright, 1957, pp. 401-2). For biographical data, the *Ch'ing-shih kao* has many small errors, and we have consequently relied more upon other Chinese biographical collections.[1]

Let us return to the problem of the biographical emphasis in these histories. Table 6 compares the number of volumes (*chüan*) in both the Ming and the Ch'ing dynasty histories which are devoted to social-institutional treatises (*chih*) with the number given purely to biographies of individuals.

Table 6—Biographical Emphasis in Ming and Ch'ing Dynastic Histories

	NUMBER OF VOLUMES IN:	
Category	*Ming-Shih**	*Ch'ing Shih Kao†*
Social-institutional ‡	35	47
Biographical	219	315

* *Ming-shih*, po-na ed. of the Twenty-four Histories, Shanghai.
† Chao Erh-hsun *et al.* (eds.), *Ch'ing-shih kao*, 1927 ed.
‡ Ceremonies (*Li*), Examinations and Official Recruitment (*Hsüan-chü*), Bureaucracy (*Chih-kuan*), Food and Money (*Shih-huo*), Military (*Ping*), Law (*Hsing-fa*).

The explanation of the heavy emphasis on biography in the dynastic and local histories is that the orthodox Confucianists—who largely controlled the writing of these sources—viewed historical dynamics much more in terms of individuals than in terms of impersonal social and economic forces (Teng and Fairbank, 1954, pp. 125-26; Wright, 1957, pp. 43-45, 267). There are several indications of this. The "praise and blame" school of historiography (*pao-pien*) interpreted the fall of a dynasty in terms of the personal moral degeneracy of the last Emperor. The bureaucratic problem of selection and recruitment of officials (*hsüan-chü*) was traditionally conceived of as the search for individual men of talent (*jen-ts'ai*). In the nineteenth century, when the Ch'ing dynasty was threatened from within by dynastic decline and peasant rebellions, and from without by the intervention of the European Powers, this imperial search for men of talent was resorted to almost as a panacea (Teng and Fairbank, 1954, pp. 125-26, 197-98, 206-7; Wright, 1957, p. 69). Nor should this be seen as the decadence of the system; on the contrary, it was traditional for officials to conceive of reform in this way. The crucial point is that there was no corresponding support for proposals seeking *institutional* reforms, except among the revolutionary minority; the conservatives tended to continue to view the problem in terms of the *individual*, by the same standards that gave biographies of individuals such a prominent place in historical sources. Meager indeed were the planned attempts to introduce social change, during the nineteenth century, in comparison with the reliance put on recruiting individual "men of talent."

History, then, was seen as the mirror of the acts of individual Emperors, officials, and others, and it was only logical that the biographies of these individuals constituted a major portion of the annals of history.

When we turn from the question of quantity to that of the reliability of this mass of biographical data, we discover the first weakness: the individual biographies are, in fact, highly impersonal.[2] Their impersonality and their often stereotyped form resulted from the Confucian view of the individual as part of a socio-moral network. Where impersonal socio-economic forces were regarded as less important than the actions of individuals in relation to historical dynamics, in the biography of an individual, idiosyncratic, personal qualities were displaced by emphasis on his success or failure in carrying out traditional Confucian moral precepts. To bring this into sharper focus: the impact which individuals had on history was seen in terms of the Confucian sociomoral network.

Several types of omission or unreliability result from this formulaic character of Chinese biography and extend all the way from dynastic biographical collections to biographies in local histories. First, birth date is seldom given. Instead, the date the individual received his highest degree in the examination system is usually the first date given: one's private, biological birth was a less important datum than the "birth" of one's official, public career.

Preceding this date, biographies typically list four kinds of information: First, the several alternate names of the individual (*hsing, ming, tzu, pieh-tzu, hao, pieh-hao,* etc.). Second, the individual's "native place," e.g., "a man of Chia-hsing, Chekiang." This place was usually one's family seat, the location of his ancestral temple, the place where he was officially registered. Third, the individual's ancestors are listed, providing that they, in turn, fit into the Confucian code. Thus, if his ancestors had been officials, scholars, degree-holders, or had embodied traditional Confucian virtues, these facts would be listed. If an artisan or merchant, the chances of these facts being mentioned were fewer, though there were many exceptions in biographies. An important shortcoming is that landlords (*ti-chu*) are rarely mentioned as such in Chinese biographies, despite the fact that many officials' families had been landlords, and that landlords were often of higher income and more authority than merchants. Landlords, as such, had no place in the Confucian "scholars-farmers-artisans-merchants" hierarchy, although one sees the expression "to advance, take office; to retire, take farming duties" (*chin tse shih, t'ui tse wu-nung*). However, the term *wu-nung*—take farming duties—is ambiguous. Unless otherwise specified, those who *wu-nung* were not necessarily themselves tillers, or poor peasants. *Wu-nung* can also mean owning land. Many who *wu-nung* were of this type, and may have even been big landlords (*tien-lien ch'ien-mo*).

The fourth kind of information typically given in biographies are personality traits, which also tend to be Confucian moral clichés. One sees them repeatedly in these biographies, often stated in exactly the same phrases! The individual is said to have been a precocious child, gifted in literature, etc., at an early age, and to have had great filial piety. Those close to him are said to have prophesied a brilliant career for him, and he is supposed to have impressed the Emperor or some high official at his first audience with them. If he holds office in the provinces, the people are said to regard him as "father and mother," and to extol his administration. The learned official is supposed to be without personal wealth, owning nothing except a collection of books or art objects.

Lest this formulaic, impersonal aspect be thought of as too great a liability for social research, certain redeeming factors must be pointed out. *Chuan-chi* or *lieh-chuan* are only one type of biographical source; many of their impersonal qualities are compensated for in other sources. Happily, this is precisely what has been done in the biographical cyclopaedia, *Eminent Chinese of the Ch'ing Period, 1644-1912*, from which our sample of officials was drawn. For example, *nien-p'u* (chronological biographies) give birth dates and a very adequate chronology, and the "miscellaneous notes" (*pi-chi*) genre of biography carries short jottings on the personality of the individual.

Nor is the standardization of the content of *chuan-chi* or *lieh-chuan* entirely a liability. In some respects, it even facilitates the coding process in social research. For instance, data on ancestors and family of orientation usually occur at the beginning of the biography, if at all, thus making for the more efficient coding of a large sample. Also, coding comparability is much more fully realized here than in the looser forms of biographical writing. Thus, the researcher can expect to find fairly comparable types of data on bureaucratic career for all those officials who are given biographical attention.

Again, the important question for our purposes is not how much this formulaic, impersonal factor impairs biographical style *in general*, but rather, how much it specifically affects the two variables which are central in this study—stratum position of family of orientation and elite bureaucratic mobility. The adequacy of the several types of biographical sources for data on family background will be discussed in detail in the next section of this chapter; at the present, let us concentrate upon bureaucratic career data in these biographies (*chuan-chi* and *lieh-chuan*).

On what sources were biographies based, and what was the method of their compilation?[3] The parts dealing with one's official career were composed on the basis of scrupulously kept archival and official records. The first group of records was kept in the History Office in Peking (*Kuo Shih Kuan*), and were the material for the "basic biographies" (*Kuo Shih Kuan pen-chuan*). These records included the diaries of the Emperor's activities (*ch'i-chü chu*), the Record of Current Administration (*shih-cheng chi*), the Court Calendar (*jih-li*), and the "Veritable Records" of each reign.

The second major group of documents on which bureaucratic career data in biographies were based came from the Board of Civil Service, *Li Pu*. These included dossiers on officials—their successive appointments and the regular assessments of their abilities made at the autumn assizes by their superiors. They also included the "Account of Conduct" (*hsing-chuang*), prepared at the death of each official by the Department of Merit Assessments (*K'ao-kung ssu*), a branch of the Board of Civil Service.

From these documents, a fairly complete picture was derived of the entire bureaucratic career, from the date and nature of the individual's first appointment, or earliest post, through successive transfers, promotions, demotions, dismissals, leaves of absence for mourning, etc., and concluding with retirement and death dates, and final official honors and ranks.

It should be made clear that the final composition of biographies was usually in the hands of neither of these government bureaus, but rather, a friend, relative, disciple, or former subordinate of the deceased official. This person's document was merely *checked* by the above government bureaus before being included in the official history of the dynasty, or by the officials in charge of the compilation of a local history. This person's document was also used in funerary eulogies and odes, epitaphs, etc., which were in turn also included in some of the biographical collections aside from dynastic histories. For example, in the collection *Kuo-ch'ao ch'i-hsien lei-cheng* (Ch'ing Dynasty Biographies Arranged by Categories), the first biography listed for an official is usually the "Basic Biography" from the History Office; the second and successive biographies for the same official are compiled (*chuan*) by disciples and former subordinates on the basis of stone inscriptions (*shen-tao pei-ming*), or by friends, at the behest of survivors of the official (e.g., *shih-hsiao chuan-lu*). Although the material from the History Office and the Board of Civil Service yield the best data on official career mobility, these latter, private biographies are richer sources on the stratum position of one's family of orientation and on the informal aspects of his career.

The method of the present study deliberately focuses upon the more objective aspects of bureaucratic career mobility—how high an official rose, how fast, and how long he held posts at a given level, aspects which best lend themselves to measurement. In this way, we have attempted to use the best features of Chinese biographical data, and to build upon this foundation a reliable and valid analysis of official advancement.

Composition of the Chinese Sample

A difficult decision faces us at the very outset, one that must be made at least partly on arbitrary grounds. What universe or population shall be considered as "the elite" in China between 1600-1900? In Chapters I and III we argued that the most highly evaluated roles in China were those of the officials in the imperial bureaucracy. We must now choose between two alternatives: (1) By "elite" we mean *all* officials in *all* ranks of the bureaucracy; or (2) by "elite" we mean only the most *distinguished* officials, those who *excelled* in official performance, in literature, or in some other way. The writer favors alternative (1), both because it is based upon a much more objective criterion of inclusion, and also because his judgment of Ch'ing stratification tells him that even the lowest-ranking officials had relatively great prestige, and were certainly regarded by the mass of commoners as elite. But before we settle for this decision, let us examine the methodological consequences of each alternative.

In alternative (1), we must draw a sample; the population—all officialdom through three centuries—is too large to be analyzed *in toto*. A random sample of all officials could, in principle, be drawn, since official records contain at least their names and some facts on their careers. But comparable data on the factors relevant to this study—especially stratum position of family of orientation—and to other sociological problems could never be gathered, except for a biased minority of all officials. Therefore, we can never hope to draw a random sample of all officials which will yield comparable data on relevant variables and from which determinate generalizations can be made to the larger population of officials. Since, in this alternative, the sample will be non-random, we should state as fully as possible the characteristics of the sample, so that the respects in which it is non-random may be known.

In alternative (2), if the group studied included *all distinguished* officials, it would comprise a census; sampling considerations could be dispensed with, for one would have studied *everyone* defined as a distinguished official. Or the group studied might include *only distinguished* officials but not *all* distinguished officials; in this case, sampling problems would again come to the fore. The flaw in alternative (2) is, of course, that agreement among all the experts as to who should and should not be included among "distinguished officials" is rarely, if ever, reached. Research would have to wait upon these controversies over inclusion and exclusion.

In this study we shall follow alternative (1), mainly because it is our judgment that being an official at *any* level constituted an extreme achievement in Chinese society. Our definition of elite will be: all officials in the bureaucracy.

Our sample of 572 officials was drawn from the two-volume biographical dictionary, *Eminent Chinese of the Ch'ing Period, 1644-1912* (Hummel, 1943; hereafter referred to as ECCP). The title of this work is somewhat misleading. The official dates of the Ch'ing period, 1644-1912, are not inclusive of the dates of those whose biographies are included: several individuals were born in the mid-1500's and were already dead by 1644. The officials in our sample whose career began earliest were Li Ch'eng-liang, 1566; Wang Hsiang-ch'ien, 1571; Liu Ting, 1580; and T'ang Hsien-tsu, 1583. The ECCP is, then, more properly a biographical cyclopedia of Chinese (Han people), Manchus, and others living in China between the sixteenth and twentieth centuries. The ECCP is a co-operative effort of some fifty Western and Asian Sinologists, and contains altogether eight-hundred-odd biographies. It is not unlike *Who's Who in America* and other dictionaries and cyclopedias of national biography, but its average entry is longer, and, on the whole, it is more extensively documented, especially with primary sources, than are comparable biographical dictionaries on Westerners. The biographies in the ECCP were prepared between 1934 and 1942, and edited by Arthur W. Hummel, then Librarian of the Far Eastern Division of the Library of Congress.

The ECCP has been reviewed as an "outstanding achievement of American Sinology," as "far more extensive than any other work of Chinese biography in any Western language," and as "far more critical and rigorous in its use of source material than any comparable work, even in Chinese."[4] Teng and Biggerstaff (1950, p. 238) state that it is specifically superior to the Chinese biographical collection, *Biographies of Seven Hundred Notables of the Ch'ing Period* (*Ch'ing-tai ch'i-pai ming-jen chuan*) (Ts'ai, 1937). Although it is less extensive than some of the larger Chinese language collections of Ch'ing biographies, its sources go considerably beyond the sources of these earlier Chinese-language biographical collections. Not only more up-to-date Chinese and Western sources, but valuable contemporary Western and other non-Chinese language material bearing on the lives and times of these men were consulted. Furthermore, by 1934, earlier and less tampered-with texts and editions of many biographical sources had again come to light. These sources had been suppressed by the "literary inquisition" under the Ch'ien-lung Emperor, or altered by early Manchu Emperors' interest in making the first Manchu Emperors' records look more "Chinese" than they had in fact been. For example, the Ch'ien-lung Emperor revised the "Veritable Records" of the first three Ch'ing Emperors, Nurhaci, Abahai, and Fu-lin, to give his ancestors a more Chinese appearance. These suppressed sources had been either unavailable or very inaccessible at the time of the compilation of some of the Chinese-language Ch'ing biographical collections.

It was for these reasons—greater recency and reliability of primary sources, uniformly high critical standards, and accessibility—that the ECCP was made the basis for the selection of our sample.

The ECCP was not without its defects, however. For the purposes of this study, these defects were of two types: first, its unsystematic, judgmental nature *as a sample* (including its alleged bias in the direction of biographies of writers and bibliophiles; we shall attempt to defend the

ECCP against this criticism, for "Who's Who" sources often over-represent writers). Second, its specific lacunae in data on family stratum background and bureaucratic careers—variables central to this study.

Let us first consider the ECCP from the point of view of sampling methodology. In fairness, it must be realized that the ECCP was not meant to be a sample from which generalizations could be made to a larger, determinate population. Rather, it represents the informed judgment of specialists as to what individuals had "left marks on Chinese society and had obviously *made* history" (letter from A. W. Hummel to the writer, March 10, 1955). Thus, the statistical universe—the group from which those given biographies were selected—was a most indeterminate one, the parameters of which were "the making of history." Though the ECCP was not intended as a statistical sample, in the present sociological study, we shall evaluate it *as though* it were a sample.

The ECCP did impose some checks against bias. One check was that most of the individuals chosen for inclusion in the ECCP had already been the subject of biographies in the dynastic and local histories and other source books: they are men who are encountered again and again in the sources on the Ch'ing period. This provided at least a rough kind of reliability: many who had obviously made history in the Ch'ing period were accorded more frequent and more lengthy biographical notice in Chinese sources, and these the ECCP included.

What from our point of view was a second check, was unintentional in the research of the ECCP contributors and editors. This was that the ECCP entries were not originally chosen on the basis of family background, an independent variable in this study. The ECCP entries were chosen on the basis of the achievements of their careers: family background was so incidental a factor to the contributors and editors of the ECCP that, as we shall see below, many entries even ignore the Chinese data on stratum position of family of orientation.

The third check was achieved, according to Mr. Hummel, by soliciting suggestions about whom to include and about biographical contributions from a wide variety of specialists. Accordingly, the ECCP's entries represent the interests of scholars in the fields of the political, economic, social, technological, religious, philosophical, artistic, scientific, and linguistic history of the Ch'ing period. This check aimed at making the over-all inclusion a balanced one.

In this connection, we must confront a common criticism of the ECCP, namely, that it *does* give more attention to one special group than to others. It is said that there is too much emphasis on writers and bibliophiles for a general cyclopedia of this sort, that men who authored or collected books were heavily favored for inclusion, as opposed to those whose impact lay wholly outside of books.

Before meeting this criticism, we must state our own criteria of inclusion, for we do not propose to defend the ECCP *as a whole*, but rather, only those 572 biographies of officials which we have drawn for our sample in this study. The question we must deal with below is whether our sample of 572 officials has a larger proportion of writers than in fact existed among officials.

From the 800-odd original entries in the ECCP, then, we chose 572 individuals for statistical analysis in the present study. We could afford to be quite precise, within the limitations of the original. The 572 individuals chosen had in common an official career in the imperial governmental bureaucracy, during late Ming or Ch'ing times. This career had to be at least two years in duration in order for inclusion in our sample.

Let us first note (see Table 7) the frequency distribution of duration of career of this sample. This table shows that, as to length of official career, our sample is fairly evenly distributed roughly along a normal bell-shaped curve; there is, at least, no tendency toward clustering at some one point. In our sample, the officials with the shortest careers were Wang Chien, Tai Ming-shih, and Yang Kuang-hsien. The seven officials with the longest careers in our sample were Le-pao, fifty-nine years; Sung-yün, sixty years; Ch'ang-ling, *ca.* sixty years; Hsiao Yung-tsao, sixty-three years; Shih I-chih, sixty-three years; Maci, sixty-five years; and Ming-liang, sixty-seven years. These men, of course, all lived between seventy-nine and eighty-seven years.

The median length of official career for our sample is 26.2 years. The first characteristic of our sample, then, is that, although 34.3 per cent served less than twenty years, the mid-point of 26.2 years denotes a sample of individuals for whom official career was the major continuous role and status of their adult lives. These "respondents" are predominantly not "part-time" officials, or men who experienced a variety of occupational roles outside the government bureaucracy. (From

Table 7—Frequency Distribution of Length of Career of 572 Ch'ing Officials

Length of Career (in Years)*	OFFICIALS Number	Per Cent
2-7	39	6.8
8-13	73	12.8
14-19	84	14.7
20-25	87	15.2
26-31	86	15.0
32-37	79	13.8
38-43	56	9.8
44-49	40	7.0
50 and over	28	4.9
Total	572	100.0

* This is the length of career in *substantive* posts, not the years that official rank, buttons, etc., were held. Years on leave for kinship mourning are deducted from total length of career. (Officials were expected to take leaves of about 27 months at the death of each parent to satisfy the Confucian mourning ritual. In extraordinary cases where the official's services were indispensable, the Emperor could compel the official to forego this mourning period and remain at his post. Many of the officials in our sample, in fact, had several years' absence for mourning during their career.)

time to time in this study, we shall, for the sake of convenience, take the liberty of calling our 572 sample officials "respondents." This is a term often used in sociology to refer to the individuals about whom data have been gathered.)

Defining which of the careers, among the ECCP entries, should be coded as an "official career" posed many difficult problems.[5] Not all those with official *rank* or official *buttons* had an official *career*: the Canton trader, Wu Ch'ung-yüeh, held both the rank of financial commissioner and the Red Coral Button of the second rank, as rewards for his donations to the government, but he was technically not an official, and therefore does not appear in our sample. Again, members of the Manchu Imperial family and nobility were included as officials, providing, apart from their purely royal and noble ranks, they also held substantive military and/or civil ranks and posts. Ideally, then, the population from which our sample might have been drawn is: all military and civil officials holding substantive posts in the nine-rank bureaucratic hierarchy, and having careers within the period from late Ming through Ch'ing times. The parameters of this population, therefore, would be much more delimited than those represented by the original ECCP criteria of selection.

Let us now confront the criticism that the *officials* we have selected as a sample from the ECCP are disproportionately those with literary and bibliophilic interests. Although we do not know precisely how these two groups of officials—the one group productive in literary output, book collecting, etc., the other group not productive in this way—differ *in respects that will affect our analysis*, we must at least pay attention to this criticism. We cannot assume *a priori* that these two kinds of officials had similar patterns of family background and elite bureaucratic mobility.

The first reply to this criticism is that many of the ECCP entries who were primarily or solely scholars, bibliophiles, poets, teachers, editors, historians, and philosophers had not been officials and therefore were not included in our sample. (See, for example, the ECCP biographies of Chang Chin-wu, Chang Hai-p'eng, Chao I-ch'ing, Chiang Kuang-hsu, Hsu Shu-k'uei, Hsu Wen-ching, Huang P'ei-lieh, Ku Kuang-ch'i, Ma Yüeh-kuang, Mao Chin, Mo Yu-chih, Pao T'ing-po, Shao T'ing-ts'ai, and Ting Ping.) Nevertheless, our sample continues to have a large number of officials who were *also* scholars, poets, bibliophiles, etc.—men like Chao Chih-ch'ien, Ch'eng Chin-fang, Chi Chen-i, Chiao Hung, Ch'ien T'ai-chi, Ch'ou Chao-ao, Chu I-tsun, Chu Yün, Fa-shih-shan, Ho Ch'o, Hsü Ch'ien-hsüeh, and others. Are there proportionately more writers in this sample than in officialdom as a whole?

In order to give a more exact idea of how many of our sample officials were also writers, we present Table 8. This table shows under what biographical category or categories in seven leading Ming and Ch'ing dynasty collections the officials in our sample appeared.[6] The category in which one's biography appeared depended upon the particular social status or role in which one was thought to have achieved distinction. Most of these statuses and roles were very highly evaluated in Chinese society. In Table 8, the many different biographical categories in these collections will be grouped into five divisions, and the number of our respondents in each individual category will be listed.

Table 8 may be expressed in simplified form, as follows: (1) categorized as officials, 79 per cent; (2) categorized as writers, scholars, etc., 9 per cent; (3) categorized for Confucian virtues, 4 per cent; (4) categorized as Imperial family, nobility, 4 per cent; (5) not categorized in these seven collections, 4 per cent.

Table 8 indicates that the great majority of our sample officials were famous primarily *as officials*, rather than as writers and scholars, according to the criteria of these leading biographical collections. Expressed conversely, only 9 per cent of our sample of officials achieved more fame as writers and scholars than as officials.

The ECCP's own biographical categories of reasons for the inclusion of the 572 individuals in our sample give essentially the same result, although the proportion of those categorized in the ECCP as distinguished purely in their official role is smaller, in relation to the proportion of those

Table 8—Biographical Categories of 572 Officials in Seven Major Ming and Ch'ing Dynasty Collections

Biographical Category	Number of Respondents
1. Officials—civil and military	
Grand secretaries (*Tsai-fu*)	74
Ministers (*Ch'ing-erh*)	78
High officials (*Ta-ch'en*)	68
Officials in general (*Ch'ing-shih kao, Lieh-chuan* section)	44
Ministers of the boards and courts (*Pu-yuan ta-ch'en*)	5
Nine ministers of the Grand Secretariat (*Nei-ko chiu-ch'ing*)	2
Literary officials (*Tz'u-ch'en*)	30
Hanlin and Imperial supervisors (*Han-chan*)	1
Censors (*Chien-ch'en*—"admonishing officials")	6
Governors-general and governors (*Tu-fu, Chiang-ch'en*)	40
Generals (*Chiang-shuai*)	36
Officials (*Lang-shu*)	7
Officials of Two Dynasties (*Erh-ch'en*)	19
Circuit intendents (*Chien-ssu*)	8
River control officials (*Ho-ch'en*)	1
Prefects and magistrates (*Shou-ling*)	16
Model officials (lower ranks) (*Hsün-li*)	5
Official assistants (*Liao-tso*)	6
Ordinary military men (*Ts'ai-wu*)	2
Diplomats, foreign ministers (*Hsin-pan ta-ch'en*)	13
Retired officials of former dynasties (*I-i*)	1
Traitors (*Ni-ch'en, Chien-ch'en*)	13
Total	475
2. Writers, scholars, artists, etc.	
Confucianists (*Ju-lin, Ju-hsüeh*)	19
Classical scholars (*Ching-hsüeh*)	3
Belle-lettrists (*Wen-yuan, Wen-hsüeh*)	28
"Artists" and craftsmen (*I-shu, wen-i*), including physicians and geomancers	4
Total	54

Table 8—Biographical Categories of 572 Officials in Seven Major Ming and Ch'ing Dynasty Collections (Cont'd.)

3. Those embodying Confucian virtues, etc.	
The loyal (*Chung-i, Chung-chieh*)	18
The filial (*Hsiao-i, Hsiao-yu, Hsiao-shu*)	1
Those who carried out good deeds (*Cho-hsing, Chen-chieh, Ju-hsing*)	6
Hermits (*Yin-i*)	1
Total	26
4. Imperial family and nobility	
Princes of the Blood (*Chu-wang*)	18
Imperial household princes and nobility (*Tsung-shih wang-kung*)	7
Total	25
5. No biographical category	
Not included in these seven collections	24
Total number of the five categories	604*

* This total is larger than the number of respondents (572) because some were included under more than one biographical category.

included as famous partly or wholly for literary reasons. Table 9 presents the breakdown of this same sample of 572 officials in the categories by which the ECCP identified them.

Table 9 reduces our assurance that the great majority of our sample officials were famous primarily as officials: here, only 48 per cent, rather than 79 per cent, were included as

Table 9—Biographical Categories of 572 Officials in the Eminent Chinese of the Ch'ing Period

	OFFICIALS	
Biographical Category	*Number*	*Per Cent*
Imperial family and nobility (Manchus)	27	5
Only officials (civil and military)	273	48
Official *and* scholars, writers, etc.	145	25
Only scholars, writers, etc.	102	18
Others*	10	2
No category	15	2
Total	572	100

* Scholar and military, military and calligrapher, pirate, politician and literary man, martyr, military and literary man, executed, and first Chinese graduate from an American university.

officials, apart from literary activities. On the other hand, 43 per cent were included in the ECCP either partly or wholly because of their fame as writers, scholars, and the like.

We have here, then, two versions of biographical categorization of the same 572 individuals, one version based on traditional Chinese biographical collections, the other version based on modern Asian-Western biographical scholarship. Since these versions conflict somewhat in the weight they give to the literary and scholarly distinction of these individuals, on which are we to put the greater reliance? In the writer's opinion, as regards the matter of biographical categorization, the ECCP version should be taken more seriously, for this simple reason: in categorizing the individual entries, the ECCP biographers were less bound by traditional conventions; they were more free to judge each biographical entry on its own merits and to assess the reasons for the individual's distinction in the perspective of time.

We are left, then, with the burden of the original criticism: despite the ECCP compilers' attempts to balance the entries in terms of widely divergent roles and statuses, the officials in our sample are, to a large extent, those who were also famous as writers, etc. At least 18 per cent of this group even had careers as writers and scholars which overshadowed their bureaucratic careers. A great many officials on whom there *are* biographical data are not represented in the ECCP sample.

There are, however, two other considerations which lessen the burden of this criticism. First, our sample is not so unrepresentative as might be thought, in view of the fact that it was *typical*, particularly for civil officials (*wen-kuan*), to be active also as writers, scholars, calligraphers, etc., and therefore to leave literary remains (*wen-chi*, etc.). This was inevitable, given the heavily humanistic education of those officials who had entered the bureaucracy through the examination system. It is also inevitable, given the fact that any history of any nation necessarily over-represents those who leave documents written by them or about them.

In the second place, by including in our sample those individuals whose distinction lay partly or wholly outside their official careers—in literature, scholarship, etc.—we increase the degree to which our sample is representative of *lower-level* officials. If we eliminated from our sample those successful in extra-official roles, the group remaining in the sample would be officials in the highest-rank posts, virtually to the exclusion of any lower-ranking officials.

Table 10 shows the differences in bureaucratic advancement among the 572 officials in our sample, i.e., the level in the nine-rank hierarchy which our respondents differentially reached at the highest point in their careers.

Table 10—Highest Bureaucratic Rank Reached During Careers, 572 Ch'ing Officials*

	OFFICIALS	
Highest Rank Reached	*Number*	*Per Cent*
Rank 1 (*Cheng, tsung i-p'in*)	298	52
Rank 2-3 (*Cheng, tsung erh, san p'in*)	137	24
Rank 4-9 (*Cheng, tsung ssu-chiu p'in*)	137	24
Total	572	100

* For an outline of this nine-rank hierarchy, see Appendix III of this study, on the Formal Structure of the Ch'ing Bureaucracy.

Altogether, then, 76 per cent of our sample rose to posts in the three highest ranks; only 24 per cent spent their entire career in posts between the fourth and ninth ranks. This distribution obviously is an inversion of the normal pyramidal structure of a bureaucracy. (An exception to this normal pyramidal structure may be found in American university faculties, where there are more full professors than instructors.)

It is at this point that the group of writers and scholars in our sample may be used to our analytical advantage. There is a roughly inverse correlation between high official advancement (defined here as reaching posts in the highest three ranks) and being distinguished for such extra-official roles as writer and scholar. Table 11 shows this correlation.

Table 11—Relation between Highest Bureaucratic Rank Reached and Reason for Biographical Distinction of 572 Officials

	HIGHEST RANK REACHED			
	3B Rank or Higher		Never above 4A Rank	
Reason for Distinction	Number	Per Cent	Number	Per Cent
Categorized as officials only	305	70	16	12
Categorized as writers, scholars, etc.	130	30	121	88
Total	435	100	137	100

$P < 0.001$ $\quad T_b = 0.25$ $\quad \sqrt{T_b} = 0.50$

(For a discussion of statistical methods in this study, see the end of this chapter.)

From this table it appears that upper-level officials—those above the fourth rank—were more likely to be famous *as* officials than as writers, at least as far as biographical categorization is concerned. Lower-level officials—those between the fourth and ninth rank—on the other hand, were more likely to achieve distinction as writers than as officials, providing that they achieved distinction at all. Of the upper group of officials, 70 per cent were categorized in the biographical collections only as officials; of the lower group of officials, 88 per cent were categorized as writers, etc., in addition to or rather than as purely officials. This difference is statistically significant at the 0.001 level, with a correlation ($\sqrt{T_b}$) of 0.5.

In this sense, then, we may use to our advantage the group of officials who were also noted as writers and the like. This literary group gives our sample a slightly greater representativeness for lower-level officials, men like T'ang Hsien-tsu, whose success as an official was indifferent—he never rose above lower-rank posts—but whose literary or other success was considerable. This feature of our sample is similar to the Taussig and Joslyn American sample, and may be used to the same advantage: "leaders of lesser ranks are also represented, and represented in sufficient numbers to make possible a comparison between the several grades in respect to occupational origins and conditions of environment" (Taussig and Joslyn, 1932, p. 40).

To conclude this discussion of sampling bias, let us conceive of all Chinese officialdom in terms of four groups: (1) those distinguished both as officials and as writers, scholars, etc.; (2) those distinguished as officials but not as writers, etc., although they may, like Yü-ch'ien, have left a literary collection; (3) those distinguished as writers, etc., but not as officials; (4) those officials who were distinguished neither as officials nor as writers, etc.

We have seen that our sample contains groups (1), (2), and (3); in the last analysis, group (4)—by far the largest group in officialdom—is not represented in our sample. Another group of officials not represented here are those who held high office even though their careers were commonplace.

Our sample, then, over-represents high officials, and, among lower officials, those famous as writers and scholars. In this respect, it is like previous Sinological studies of Chinese officialdom. For example, the Ch'ing section of Wittfogel's sample (1938, pp. 11-12) was drawn from the biographical source titled *Ch'ing-shih wai-chuan* and was limited almost wholly to high-ranking officials. In studies of this sort, there are no determinate bases for statistical generalization from the sample to *any* larger population of officials.

Ideally, the testing of hypotheses requires random sample data, if conclusions from the sample are to be made with stated degrees of probability. Since our sample is not a probability sample, we cannot, in any strict sense, test our hypotheses. We can only assert that our findings hold for the sample in which they were tested. Our data can support, qualify, or invalidate our hypotheses only with respect to our own sample.

These sampling problems have also been encountered in

American studies of elite mobility. Warner and Abegglen, with a 47.6 per cent mail return, note that smaller business firms and mining were under-represented in their sample, while manufacturing and financial enterprises were both over-represented (Warner and Abegglen, 1955, p. 236). Mills was handicapped by the criteria of inclusion for businessmen in the *Dictionary of American Biography*: some businessmen were included for reasons having little to do with their business achievements; others were ineligible no matter how eminent they were in the business world of their day (Mills, 1945, p. 20). Finally, Miller dealt with what amounts to a *census* of all the presidents and board chairmen of the largest corporations in four fields of business. But his census covers only 190 individuals (Miller, 1949).

In the last analysis, then, our sample is of value because it contains data on the family background and on the vertical elite mobility of a group, some of whom were distinguished as officials, others distinguished as non-officials and relatively low as officials, and others falling between these types. Sampling bias is somewhat compensated here by the fact that our sample provides genuine empirical variation in both family stratum position and in elite mobility, and thereby lends itself to systematic limited testing of our hypotheses.

Measurement of the Independent Variable: Family Stratum Position

We have confronted one criticism of the ECCP, the fact that it is a judgmental or purposive sample, including the charge that it has a literary-bibliophilic bias. We turn now to the ECCP's second shortcoming, from our point of view: its specific lacunae in data on stratum position of family of orientation for the 572 officials in our sample.

Although the ECCP was the source from which our sample was selected, a great range of Chinese primary sources of biographical relevance had to be consulted, especially for family background data, but also for career mobility in the bureaucracy. Here, the point making the ECCP in itself inadequate for our analytic purposes was simply a difference in emphasis: in some cases where Chinese sources had indicated the stratum position of the respondent's father, grandfather, etc., ECCP did not see fit to include these data. The impression given by ECCP in these cases was that no social origins data existed for these respondents. Since it is known that a man's ancestors' achievements and distinctions, if there were such, were usually listed in his own biography, it can be assumed tentatively that many of those respondents with no mention of ancestors, aside, perhaps, from their names, tended to have somewhat *lower* social origins. It was thus crucial to exhaust as many as possible of the biographical sources outside the ECCP to ascertain whether those without social origins data in ECCP actually had no social origins data in any of the available Chinese primary biographical sources.

1. Standard biographies
   a. Indexes to biographical collections
   b. Individual collections of biographies
   c. Biographies in local histories
2. Chronological biographies (*nien-p'u*)
3. Genealogies (*chia-p'u, tsung-p'u, tsu-p'u*)
4. Biographies in literary collections (*wen-chi, ho-chi*)
5. Government examination lists for various years
   a. Metropolitan graduates
   b. Provincial graduates
   c. Other examination lists

(See Bibliography of this study for a more complete citation.)

This was the major research step of this study: it involved not merely checking for omissions in the ECCP entries, but also ordering data on the variable termed "stratum position of family of orientation." Thus, when we present our marginal totals, and claim that eighty-nine respondents, or 15 per cent of the sample, are without any family background data, such an assertion holds true for the following sources:

It cannot be overemphasized that cross-checks among the above sources were essential. No single source could be relied on for family background data; some sources had omissions for a given respondent's social origins which another source provided, but for another respondent, the former sources might provide data which the latter omitted.

On the basis of these sources, forty-four officials in our sample were classified as coming from higher stratum family backgrounds than had been indicated in the ECCP. Appendix II gives the details on the stratum position of these forty-four men's families. We found no cases of officials coming from *lower* stratum families than indicated in the ECCP.

There was a special problem in measuring the stratum position of the family of orientation of the individuals in our sample. This was to determine whether the official ranks, posts, titles, and honors held by immediate ancestors (typically, one's father, grandfather, and great-grandfather) could have been operative in the period of the lives of our respondents. Did one's immediate forebears hold rank, etc., during one's own childhood, youth, or official career? Or, were the ranks listed for these forebears only accorded to them *posthumously*, or after the respondent's own career was underway or over, and perhaps *because* of the career attainments of the respondent?[7] In the former case, one's family of orientation had one or another kind of actual *advantage* in the system of stratification, and this advantage could operate, through status ascription, to increase the advancement of our respondents. In the latter case, such advantages existed only after one's career was underway or completed.

The Ch'ing dynasty followed Ming precedents here, as in so many other institutional practices. It bestowed *feng-kao*, by which the immediate ancestors and relatives of meritorious officials received (*i-feng*) official ranks, titles, and honors (*feng-tseng i, erh, san tai*). The typical pattern was that, at the death of a distinguished official, he and his immediate forebears would be honored posthumously. The sources usually indicate clearly the nature of the bestowal of these honors. On the one hand, such-and-such specified ancestors and relatives are said in the biography to have been honored (*kuei*) *because* of the respondent. In this case, one or more of the following verbs will introduce the actual official ranks, titles, etc.: *kao-tseng, kao-feng, i-tseng, i-feng, chin-tseng, chin-feng, ch'ih-tz'u,* and *li-feng.*[8] In these cases, there is no evidence that the respondent's forebears possessed positional advantages in the system of stratification; rather, they were dependent upon the respondent for their recognition. Our analysis, on the contrary, focuses upon the dependence of the respondent for status upon his immediate forebears and family of orientation.

On the other hand, the sources indicated that some respondents' families had actually held official posts, ranks, etc., quite independently of the respondent. For example, the biography of Liang Shih-cheng explicitly states that his father was selected to be a district education official (8B rank) and was "not honored on account of the son, Shih-cheng" (*Kuo-ch'ao ch'i-hsien lei-cheng,* 23/6a). In general, the verbs or phrases, *li-shou, kao-shou,* and *yüan-jen* indicated that the ancestors or relatives in question had held official rank, etc., independently of the respondent.

The totals we arrived at for our sample are given in Table 12.

Measurement of Chinese Official Advancement

Until now, we have been concerned with the measurement of the independent variable, family background. Also necessary is a brief statement on the methods of measuring the dependent variable, official advancement. We shall measure differences in official advancement among our sample of

Table 12—Stratum Position of Family of Orientation for 572 Ch'ing Officials: Marginal Totals

Family Position	OFFICIALS Number	Per Cent
Manchus: Imperial family, nobility, officials	102	18
Manchus: No indication of above high position, but Bannerman	16	3
Chinese: Official families, including Bannerman	253	44
Chinese: Local elite, degree-holders	31	5
Chinese: All commoners	170	30
Total	572	100

572 officials by ascertaining (*a*) the highest rank within the nine-rank Chinese bureaucratic hierarchy which each individual reached during his career, and (*b*) how many years he held posts in specified high ranks. As cutting-points for rank reached, we chose: (1) those who never rose above the fourth rank (*ssu-p'in*)—officials who always held posts between ranks four and nine; (2) those who reached third- and second-rank posts, but not first- or highest-rank posts; (3) those who reached first-rank posts, the highest in the Empire. (For the posts in these several ranks, see Appendix III.) Officials in the highest three ranks (*i-p'in* through *san-p'in*) were "great officials" (*ta-yüan*), for whom civil service laws were only loosely applied, except for a few very important stipulations. Officials in ranks four through nine were much more strictly subject to the laws of the Board of Civil Service. In addition to this justification for our cutting-points, there was also the fact that only officials in the three highest ranks were allowed to recommend men for official appointment (Hsieh, 1925, pp. 99-104).

No index used in measurement is perfect. Here, there were several faults. The rank of the posts one held determined one's official salary, both in money (taels [*feng-yin*]) and in rice (*feng-mi*) (*Ch'ing-ch'ao t'ung-tien*, 71/7170-7171), and also certain symbolic distinctions, such as official costumes, insignias, buttons, etc. To a lesser extent, rank correlated with the *prestige* of one's post. Rank did not necessarily correlate with authority and power, however. Within the same rank, different posts had different degrees of authority and power. For example, all the Presidents of the Six Boards (*Liu-pu*) were ranked as 1B (*Tsung i-p'in*), but the Presidents of the Boards of Civil Service (*Li-pu*), Revenue (*Hu-pu*), and Punishments (*Hsing-pu*) had more power than the President of the Board of Rites (*Li-pu*). The matter was further complicated by the fact that many officials held concurrent posts (*chien-jen*), and these were sometimes of slightly different rank.

The use of rank (*p'in-chi*) as the measure of elite mobility is justified, however, by the fact that a movement from rank 5B to 5A or from 4A to 3B, etc., was recognized by all *as a promotion.* As early in the Ch'ing period as 1652, Asitan, a Manchu official in our sample, memorialized the throne "on the necessity of codifying the nine-rank system . . . of rating official posts in order to avoid confusion in promotion and degradation" (ECCP, I, 13). Hsieh reports:

> . . . without a special edict of the emperor, half a rank at a time was the common promotion or demotion; one full rank at a time would immediately become the gossip of the mandarin circle. . . . The Government was jealously strict as to this rule: their favorite way of getting around it was, not to make big jumps, but to take little jumps with extremely great frequency. [1925, pp. 117, 125.]

Statistical Methods

Because of the non-random nature of our sample, the conclusions we shall draw represent probable tendencies rather than proved facts which can be generalized to a determinate larger population. This does not mean that our analysis must be only elementary. In the first place, two of our variables—age at which the *chin-shih* degree was attained and official advancement, measured in terms of rank reached, etc.—are quantitative. Rank reached in the nine-rank hierarchy, number of years in high posts, rate of promotion, and age are equal-interval measures. Our other variables are qualitative, and include both continuous variables (stratum position of family of orientation) and discontinuous variables (recruitment path taken and whether or not the *chin-shih* degree was received). While these latter variables are not equal-interval measures, they can be made up in an ordered set of mutually exclusive categories. For example, any given individual in the sample cannot be from more than one stratum position.

When dealing with variables such as these, we can first present our data in tabular form. Each table will show the existence or non-existence of a relationship between the variables involved. The conventional measure of chi-square (X^2) will indicate the probability that the relationship could have occurred purely by chance. The measure we shall use to test the *degree* of relationship between the variables is Tau-$_b$ (T_b), introduced by Goodman and Kruskal (1954). Since we are interested in *comparing* the degree of association in several different tables with varying numbers of rows and columns, T_b is more satisfactory than some of the older measures. Like other measures, T_b varies between 1.0, when there is a perfect positive correlation, and -1.0, when there is perfect negative correlation. But since T_b shows a *lower* degree of association than the more popular measures, such as Pearson's C, I shall include at the bottom of each table in this study not only X^2, but, if the relationship is statistically significant, I shall also include both T_b and the square root of T_b. The latter measure, $\sqrt{T_b}$, gives results somewhat comparable to the more commonly used measures.

CHAPTER 6 BUREAUCRATIC VS. EXTRA-BUREAUCRATIC DETERMINANTS OF OFFICIAL ADVANCEMENT (1)

IN THIS CHAPTER, we begin the direct limited testing of our hypotheses, using a Chinese sample of 572 officials of the Ch'ing period. We shall be analyzing the interrelationships among a system of variables which we specified in Chapter II. As a system, these variables have the following characteristics. First, a change in one variable produces changes in the other variables. For example, depending upon which recruitment path is taken, rank reached, length of incumbency in high ranks, rate of promotion, and amount of seniority accumulated may all be influenced in determinate ways. Second, since these variables are interrelated, all are to some extent both "cause" and "effect." The age at which one received the *chin-shih* degree, for example, may be at once the "effect" of the stratum position of family of orientation, and the "cause" of later seniority accumulated. Third, some of these interrelationships are stronger than others: official advancement may be more dependent upon seniority accumulated than upon the stratum position of the family of orientation. Fourth, it is legitimate to treat some of these variables as "independent" with respect to others which are "dependent":

Independent variables

1. Stratum position of family of orientation
2. Recruitment path taken (also a dependent variable)
3. Bureaucratic seniority accumulated (also dependent)

Dependent variables

1. Official Recruitment
   a. Did or did not receive *chin-shih* degree
   b. Age at *chin-shih* degree
   c. Recruitment path taken ("regular" versus "irregular")
2. Official Advancement
   a. Highest rank reached during career
   b. Rate of promotion
   c. Length of incumbency in given high-rank posts
3. Seniority accumulated

As was shown in Chapter II, from a theoretical standpoint, our analysis is an attempt to test the influence of (*a*) bureaucratic factors—seniority and recruitment path taken, and (*b*) extra-bureaucratic factors—stratum position of family of orientation, upon (*c*) official recruitment and (*d*) official advancement. In the most general terms, our problem in this and the next chapter is to discover the precise determinants of intra-generational (career) elite mobility.

Does the burden of the evidence on Chinese stratification and mobility which we have reviewed thus far tend more toward the "bureaucratic hypothesis" or toward the "extra-bureaucratic" hypothesis? It is well to raise this question before we begin the analysis of our own elite sample: on the basis of what is already known and asserted in the field of Chinese studies, what results might we expect from our own study? Only if new research attempts to test the conclusions of previous research, to support, refine, or reject them, can we have intellectual continuity. Earlier in this study, we have taken pains to show that there is, by no means, consensus among scholars in the field of Chinese stratification and mobility. However, if the literature is carefully reviewed, greater support for the "extra-bureaucratic" hypothesis can be found than for the "bureaucratic" hypothesis. Many scholars have asserted that family background, nepotism, and other extra-bureaucratic factors were more significant determinants of official recruitment and advancement than were bureaucratic determinants, such as seniority. Fairbank states that there was little social mobility in China, for the "gentry" produced the scholar class and the scholar class produced officialdom (1948, p. 41). Lang (1946, p. 23) argued that "nepotism in old China reached proportions unparalleled anywhere else." Latourette comments, "The traditional ethics which stress devotion to one's family have often . . . made it right to use public office to restore the family fortunes and appoint relatives to public posts, even when to do so has jeopardized the well-being of the state" (1951, p. 667). Marion Levy has lent further credence to this viewpoint by arguing that "the bureaucracy failed to maintain universalistic standards and became highly particularistic. . . . In the long run the extremes to which the bureaucracy went to secure objectivity were not sufficient to maintain universalistic standards" (1949, pp. 222-23). Most recently, a study of Chinese military power at the end of the Ch'ing dynasty states that "the social structure was family centered with a resultant prevalence of nepotism" (Powell, 1955, p. 7).

Let us construct our specific hypotheses in accord with this generally held view that extra-bureaucratic factors were more significant than bureaucratic factors in shaping official recruitment and advancement. We shall test the following hypotheses in this and the next chapter:

1. The sons of Chinese official families are more likely to receive the *chin-shih* degree than Chinese from commoner families.

2. Among those who take the *chin-shih,* Manchus are likely to be significantly younger than Chinese from official families, and the latter, in turn, significantly younger than Chinese from commoner families.

3. Chinese from official families are more likely than Chinese from commoner families to take the preferred path of recruitment, the examination system.

4. Manchu officials are more likely than Chinese from official families to reach posts of a given high rank, and the latter more likely than Chinese from commoner families.

5. Manchu officials spend a significantly greater proportion of their total official careers in high-rank posts than do Chinese from official families, and the latter a significantly greater proportion than Chinese from commoner families.

6. The median incumbency of Manchu officials in given high-rank posts will be longer than that of Chinese from official families, and the latter will have longer incumbency than Chinese from commoner families.

7. "Regular"-path officials (examination system) are more likely than "irregular"-path officials to reach given high-rank posts. (This hypothesis does not assert the priority of extra-bureaucratic over bureaucratic influences. Rather, it follows the lead of some Chinese sources which argue that the examination path led to greater official advancement than other recruitment paths, the "irregular" path.)

8. Median incumbency of regular-path officials in given high-rank posts will be longer than that of irregular-path officials. (The basis of this hypothesis on the consequences of alternative recruitment paths is the same as that for Hypothesis 7.)

9. When the stratum position of family of orientation is held constant, the original relationship between recruitment path taken and later official advancement will be seen to be a spurious relationship, that is, it will be reduced or else it will disappear altogether.

10. When family stratum position is held constant, the original difference in incumbency in high-rank posts as between regular- and irregular-path officials will be reduced or will disappear altogether.

11. Manchus, Chinese from official families, and Chinese from commoner families will accumulate significantly different amounts of seniority: Manchus most, Chinese from official families next most, and Chinese from commoner families least.

12. Rank reached will vary independently of the amount of seniority accumulated; long seniority will not necessarily be found among those officials in high ranks nor little seniority among officials in low ranks.

13. Incumbency in given high-rank posts will vary independently of amount of seniority accumulated.

14. When family stratum position is held constant, whatever relationship may have existed between seniority and highest rank reached will be further reduced or will disappear altogether. That is, among Manchus, or among either group of Chinese officials, there will be no relationship between seniority and rank reached.

15. When seniority is held constant, the original differences in incumbency in given high-rank posts as between Chinese official sons and Chinese commoner sons will *not* be reduced.

16. "Regular"-path officials are likely to have a significantly higher rate of promotion than "irregular"-path officials. (The basis for this hypothesis is the same as that for Hypotheses 7 and 8.)

All these hypotheses, except numbers 7, 8 and 16, are based on the widely shared view that extra-bureaucratic factors had more impact upon official advancement in traditional China than did strictly bureaucratic factors. We may now proceed to see the extent to which our data support, refine, or refute this view.

Manchus and Chinese

On the basis of our historical analysis in Chapter III, a meaningful ordering of the variable "stratum position of the family of orientation" would seem to be as follows:

Highest stratum: All Manchus

Next highest stratum: Chinese official and local elite (degree-holding) families

Lowest stratum: Chinese commoner families

Although this ordering follows from our general discussion of Ch'ing stratification, it cannot be taken for granted in this particular sample; our first task is to examine the *internal consistency* of these three strata. Only after doing this should we attempt to use this ordering in our analysis. There are two problems here. First, is the highest stratum—the Manchus—internally consistent? Second, should Chinese Banner families be included with the Manchus because of their common Banner membership, or with Chinese official non-Banner families, because of their common ethnic status? Let us begin with the first of these questions.

Within the Manchu stratum in our sample, the social-legal-authority stratification is as follows: At the top are the sons of the various Emperors, Princes of the First Degree, e.g., Mien-k'ai, I-hsin, I-huan, I-tsung, Yin-hsiang, and other members of the Imperial family and nobility. Below them are the sons or later descendents of Manchus holding hereditary rank, high office, or tribal chieftainships. At the bottom of the Manchu stratum are men whose families were relatively obscure—for example, Te-hsing-a, Omutu, Hai-lan-ch'a, E-le-teng-pao, Tulisen, and A-k'o-tun; a total of sixteen Manchu officials in our sample appear to be from relatively obscure families. These sixteen Manchus held posts above the fourth rank (*ssu-p'in*) for 11 years on the average, as compared with 33.7 years for the 102 Manchus from higher stratum families, and they held first-rank posts (*i-p'in*) only 9.6 years on the average, in comparison to 21.3 years for the higher stratum Manchus, those from the Imperial family, nobility, and officialdom. The number of cases (16) is, of course, too small to allow much importance to be attached to this finding. Except for the fact that these lowest Manchus came from Banner families, their stratum position would be more similar to that of Chinese commoners than to that of the Manchu elite of the Imperial family and nobility. But because Banner membership gave one almost castelike privileges, we shall group together all these 118 Manchus. Their ethnic status and Banner membership operated more to give them a common position than the internal stratification among them operated to counteract these common factors.

We turn now to the second problem of internal consistency. We referred in Chapter III to the Banner military organization which the Manchus created. We pointed out that, during the Ch'ing period, Banner membership was hereditary and that Bannermen came to have great privileges and a castelike status. There were twenty-four Banner military divisions altogether: eight Manchu, eight Mongol, and eight Chinese. In our sample, 86 of the 118 Manchus were Bannermen (the remaining 32 were from the Imperial family, an even higher status than Banner membership *per se*). Among the Chinese from official families in our sample, 37 were from Banner as well as from official families, the remaining 247 from official but non-Banner families. Is it more valid to categorize these 37 Chinese with the 86 Manchus because of their common Banner status, or with the 247 Chinese from non-Banner official families, because of their common ethnic status? We shall see that this question of strata consistency has both methodological and substantive implications.

Official advancement in Table 13 is measured by the highest rank an official reached during his career. Table 13 shows that there are statistically significant differences between the advancement of Chinese Bannermen and that of Chinese from official non-Banner families ($\sqrt{T_b} = 0.2$). On

Table 13—Relation between Banner Membership and Official Advancement (by Highest Rank Attained During Career)

Highest Rank During Career	Manchu Bannermen Number	Manchu Bannermen Per Cent	Chinese Bannermen Number	Chinese Bannermen Per Cent	Non-Bannermen Official Families Number	Non-Bannermen Official Families Per Cent	Total Number
Rank 1	70	81	24	65	100	41	194
Rank 2-3	12	14	12	32	64	26	88
Rank 4-9	4	5	1	3	83	33	88
Total	86	100	37	100	247	100	370

$\chi^2 = 5.695$ $P < 0.10$ for columns 1 vs. 2.

$\chi^2 = 15.336$ $P < 0.001$ for columns 2 vs. 3.

$T_b = 0.05$ $\sqrt{T_b} = 0.23$ for columns 2 vs. 3.

the other hand, the differences in advancement between Chinese Bannermen and Manchu Bannermen are not statistically significant. The similarity in the advancement patterns of Manchu and Chinese Bannermen is seen most clearly in that 95 per cent of the former and 97 per cent of the latter reached posts in the highest three ranks; only 67 per cent of the Chinese from official non-Banner families reached posts in the three highest ranks. As far as *rank reached* is concerned, then, it appears that Chinese Bannermen are more validly categorized with Manchu Bannermen than with Chinese from official non-Banner families.

This impression is changed when the measure of more extreme official advancement—length of incumbency in high-rank posts—is used. In Table 14, official advancement is measured not merely by *highest rank reached,* but by the *median number of years* high-rank posts were held by officials.

Table 14—Relation between Banner Membership and Official Advancement (by Length of Incumbency)

Banner Membership	Median Years Incumbency	Number of Officials
Rank 1		
Manchu Bannermen	21.9	70
Chinese Bannermen	8.0	24
Non-Bannermen, official families	9.9	100
Rank 1-3		
Manchu Bannermen	31.6	82
Chinese Bannermen	25.2	36
Non-Bannermen, official families	23.2	164

Table 14 shows that although Manchu Bannermen were not significantly more likely than Chinese Bannermen to *reach* given high-rank posts, they tended to *hold* posts in these high ranks considerably longer. If a Chinese were a Bannerman, he could experience more advancement than Chinese from non-Banner official-elite families—*up to a point.* He tended to reach high-rank posts more often than his non-Banner Chinese counterparts, even though they were from official families. But, with respect to the duration of time he held these high-rank posts, his advancement was distinctly more like that of his fellow Chinese than like that of Manchu Bannermen. In fact, as Table 14 shows, he held first-rank posts, on the average, only 8 years, whereas Chinese from official but non-Banner families held these posts for 9.9 years. Also, only one-third of his time in posts in the highest three ranks was spent in first-rank posts, in contrast to two-thirds of the time Manchu Bannermen spent in the highest three ranks. This difference in advancement is greatest precisely at the highest rank in the bureaucracy: while the difference in incumbency between Manchu and Chinese Bannermen in rank 1-3 posts was 6.4 years (31.6–25.2 years), this gap increased to 13.9 years, on the average (21.9–8 years), in rank 1 posts, the highest posts in the imperial bureaucracy. Manchu Bannermen, therefore, had greater advancement than Chinese Bannermen. Further, the difference in advancement between Manchu and Chinese Bannermen was *greater* than the difference between Chinese Bannermen and Chinese from official non-Banner families. In this sense, we may conclude that it is more valid to categorize the 37 Chinese Bannermen in our sample with the 247 Chinese from official non-Banner families than to categorize them with the Manchus. We do not deny that, *up to a point*, Banner membership gave that minority of the Chinese population who were Bannermen *distinct privileges*. Our analysis has suggested that at many points of power and authority, except perhaps the most pivotal—indicated here by long incumbency in top-ranking posts—a Chinese Bannerman was better off than another Chinese from an official non-Banner family. The former was more likely to reach given high-rank posts than was the latter; Chinese Bannermen could intermarry with Manchus, whereas other Chinese could not. The Manchus, then, did not suppress all Chinese equally. But, in the last analysis, long incumbency in posts in the highest reaches of the bureaucracy went more to Manchu Bannermen than to Chinese Bannermen, in our sample.

A note of caution is necessary throughout the study as far as our Manchu sample is concerned. We cannot say how typical the advancement of these Manchus was of all Manchu officials. This is because many of the 118 Manchus in the sample were Imperial clansmen or members of highly placed Banner families. That Manchu Bannermen held high-rank posts considerably longer than any Chinese, be they Bannermen or otherwise, may be due to the unrepresentativeness of the Manchu Banner sample. One source of this possible bias may have been that the compilers of the ECCP included Manchus, to a greater extent than Chinese, only if the Manchus did reach topmost ranks. This point deserves further study, on the basis of more representative samples of Manchu and Chinese Bannermen. This research could tell us the extent to which the Manchus gave Chinese Bannermen equal access to ultimate authority in the Ch'ing dynasty.

We conclude our discussion of internal stratum consistency with the following marginal totals for our independent variable, stratum position of family of orientation. We shall, in our subsequent analysis, include the 37 Chinese from Banner families with the Chinese official-elite stratum, as in Table 15.

Table 15—Stratum Position of Family of Orientation of 572 Officials*

Family Position		*OFFICIALS*	
		Number	*Per Cent*
Manchus		118	20.6
Chinese Banner, official-elite		284	49.7
Chinese commoners		170	29.7
	Total	572	100.0

* To repeat, the "family of orientation" here consists of the generations of one's great-grandparents, grandparents, and parents. Thus, the 29.7 per cent of our sample from commoner families had no officials or local elite (degree-holders) in any of these three generations, while some of the 49.7 per cent from official families had only one official or degree-holder among these three generations.

Education and Degree-Attainment

There were impelling reasons, both positive and negative, for men who aspired to official careers to compete in the examination system. The expected "regular path" (*cheng-t'u*) of mobility was crowned by the attainment of the much coveted *chin-shih* degree, especially for would-be civil officials. Several high posts were slated only for high *chin-shih* graduates in their later careers. Also, *chin-shih* graduates often had such strong identification with each other that they formed cliques and factions while in office, facilitating each other's advancement as against other groups. There is anecdotal evidence that in the informal structure of the bureaucracy these cliques of examination-path officials directed prejudice and discrimination—in the form of jealousy, accusations, and punishments—not so much against those officials who rose from commoner family strata *per se*, as against those who rose through purchase or special examinations or through the ranks, rather than through the examination system. (See biographies of T'ien Wen-ching, Chu I-tsun, and Wang Ch'i-shu in ECCP, II, 720; I, 183; and II, 810, respectively.)

Hypothesis 1: Attainment of the *chin-shih* degree is a function of the stratum position of family of orientation; therefore, among Chinese, men from official families are more likely than men from commoner families to attain the degree. (Manchus were not encouraged to take the degree, especially the civil *chin-shih.*) Of our total sample, 309, or 54 per cent, took the *chin-shih* degree. Table 16 shows that ethnic factors were better predictors of getting the *chin-shih* than were stratum differences between Chinese from official and from commoner families. This seems to be due to the fact that Manchus had other means of official advancement and were therefore not so dependent upon the *chin-shih* as were Chinese. For this and other reasons, the *chin-shih* was largely a Chinese channel of advancement, as is seen in the correlation ($\sqrt{T_b}$) of 0.4 for Manchus vs. Chinese taking the *chin-shih.* Among the 454 Chinese in the sample, almost as high a percentage of men from commoner families took the *chin-shih* as men from official-elite families; the difference is not statistically significant. This indicates that education and the examination system were resorted to as much by commoners successfully mobile as by those from official families. In this sense, our data do not support Hypothesis 1, as far as Chinese officials are concerned. There does not seem to be a pattern of stratum *differentials* in the use of education as a means of mobility, although we shall see later that this finding must be qualified according to the degree of official advancement realized by the individuals in the sample. (For comparative data on education as a means of mobility in American society, see Kahl, 1953; Warner *et al.*, 1949, p. 61; Hyman, 1953; Barber, 1957, pp. 390-404.)

Table 16—Relation between Family Stratum Position and Chin-Shih Degree Attainment

	FAMILY POSITION						
	MANCHUS		CHINESE OFFICIAL-ELITE		CHINESE COMMONERS		Total
Degree Attained	Number	Per Cent	Number	Per Cent	Number	Per Cent	Number
Received *Chin-shih**	17	14	190	67	102	60	309
Did not receive *Chin-shih*	101	86	94	33	68	40	263
Total	118	100	284	100	170	100	572

$P < 0.01$ $T_b = 0.17$ $\sqrt{T_b} = 0.41$

* In our sample, the number of Manchus taking the *chin-shih* increased as the Ch'ing dynasty wore on. Of these seventeen Manchus, two were seventeenth-century *chin-shih*, five became *chin-shih* in the eighteenth century, and ten in the nineteenth century. Cf. Fang Chao-ying and Tu Lien-che, 1941.

We may also interpret these findings in the context of

the distribution of these two strata in the population as a whole. Here it is obvious that a heavily disproportionate number of Chinese from official families took the *chin-shih*. Indeed, so far is our sample distribution from being *representative* of the actual population distribution of commoners and official-elite strata that 190 men from official families took the degree, as compared with only 102 men from commoner families, i.e., 65 per cent of all *chin-shih* graduates in our sample were from official families. The 2 per cent of the population of China in the official and elite stratum produced 65 per cent of all the *chin-shih* graduates in our sample. In this sense, Hypothesis 1 is confirmed: official sons are more likely than commoner sons to attain the *chin-shih*. This finding is, of course, theoretically expected, and conforms to American and European findings which show the disproportionate recruitment of elites from near-elite family backgrounds.

Age at Chin-Shih *Degree*

It was desirable to try to get the *chin-shih* as early as possible in life, in order to launch one's official career sooner. The longer the career, as we shall see later, the more of the rewards of official status one could reap. Did the stratum position of one's family of orientation make for age differences in attaining the *chin-shih?* Hypothesis 2 states that: Age at *chin-shih* is inversely related to stratum position of family of orientation. Table 17 shows this relationship.

Family stratum position predicts some differences in age at *chin-shih*. But coming from an official-elite family gave one only a slight edge in launching one's career earlier, in comparison with coming from a commoner-family background; the difference is not statistically significant. The direction of the differences here is in accordance with theoretical expectations:

the small number of Manchus who did take the *chin-shih* did so the earliest in life; Chinese from official families were older than Manchus when they received the *chin-shih*, and Chinese commoners were the oldest before this hurdle was behind them. All the seventeen Manchus had the *chin-shih* before age thirty-five, in contrast to 80 per cent of the men from Chinese official families and 74 per cent of the men from commoner families. Of those for whom the *chin-shih* was a *fait accompli* by the age of twenty-six, there is a steady decrement of 13 per cent or 12 per cent as we move down from Manchus to Chinese official-family men and then to Chinese commoners' sons.

However, the amount of difference in age between men from official families and those from commoner families is rather slight, and, in this respect, theoretical expectations are not strongly supported. Only 12 per cent more men from official families than men from commoner families had the *chin-shih* behind them and their careers ahead by age twenty-six; only 6 per cent more by the age of thirty-five. We may conclude, tentatively, that while achievement of the *chin-shih per se* went disproportionately to Chinese from elite families, achievement in this channel *early in life* was not, to any appreciable extent, the monopoly of men from official

Table 17—Relation between Family Stratum Position and Age at the Chin-Shih Degree

	FAMILY POSITION						
Age at Chin-shih	*MANCHUS*		*CHINESE OFFICIALS**		*CHINESE COMMONERS*		*Total*
	Number	*Per Cent*	*Number*	*Per Cent*	*Number*	*Per Cent*	*Number*
Before 26	7	41	53	28	16	16	76
26-35	10	59	99	52	59	58	168
After 35	—	—	37	20	27	26	64
Total	17	100	189	100	102	100	308

$\chi^2 = 11.7348$ $P < 0.02$ for entire table
$\chi^2 = 6.053$ $P < 0.05$ for columns 2 vs. 3
$\chi^2 = 9.401$ $P < 0.01$ for columns 1 vs. 3

* One person's age is unknown, making the total here 189 instead of 190.

elite families. In this sense, our data do not support Hypothesis 2.

Do other social-stratification variables help explain the high mobility in the examination system of these 102 men from commoner families, and particularly the 16 men who received the *chin-shih* before age twenty-six? One factor is the presence or absence of *scholarly-intellectual traditions* in one's family—even though one's three previous generations had produced no degree-holders.

In our sample, 34 of the men from commoner families—20 per cent of the commoners—were from scholarly families. Among the fathers, grandfathers, and great-grandfathers of these men were teachers, tutors, heads of academies (*shu-yüan*), local students (*hsien hsüeh-sheng*), scholars, and literati. The other 80 per cent of the commoners are without indication of such intellectual family traditions. Table 18 shows the age difference between those two groups of commoners at the time of receiving the *chin-shih.*

Table 18—Relation between Intellectual Family Background and Age at Chin-Shih for Commoners

	INTELLECTUAL-FAMILY BACKGROUND				
	INTELLECTUAL FAMILIES		NO INDICATION OF INTELLECTUALS		
Age at Chin-shih	Number	Per Cent	Number	Per Cent	Total Number
Before 26	4	16	12	16	16
26-35	16	64	43	56	59
After 35	5	20	22	28	27
Total	25	100	77	100	102

$\chi^2 = 0.7752$ $P < 0.70$

The youngest *chin-shih* graduates from among these commoner families were *not* drawn mainly from intellectual families. The modal *chin-shih* age both for commoners from intellectual and from non-intellectual families was between twenty-six and thirty-five years old. Among commoners, intellectual versus non-intellectual family of orientation has no significant relationship with age at *chin-shih*. This can be seen in a more striking way in Table 19, which compares age at *chin-shih* among those from *either* official or from intellectual commoner families with the age of those from commoner families with no indication of scholarly-intellectual traditions. This shows the *combined* influence of official and intellectual family background upon age at *chin-shih*.

Table 19—Combined Influence of Official and Intellectual Family Background upon Age at Attainment of Chin-Shih

		CHINESE OFFICIALS' BACKGROUND				
		Official Families and Intellectual Commoner Families		Non-Intellectual Commoner Families		
Age at Chin-shih		Number	Per Cent	Number	Per Cent	Total Number
Before 26		57	27	12	16	69
26-35		115	54	43	56	158
After 35		42	19	22	28	64
	Total	214	100	77	100	291

$\chi^2 = 4.656$ $P < 0.10$

Table 19 shows that, although men from official and intellectual commoner families took the *chin-shih* degree at a slightly younger age than men from non-intellectual commoner families, this difference is not statistically significant. Furthermore, while 67 per cent of the men from official or intellectual families took the *chin-shih*, in contrast to 57 per cent of those from non-intellectual commoner families, this difference is also not statistically significant. The *combined* effect of official and intellectual commoner-family background, then, was neither a significantly younger age at receiving the *chin-shih* nor a significantly greater tendency to take the degree *per se*, in comparison with the effect of coming from a non-intellectual commoner family. That as many as 57 per cent of the commoners from non-scholarly families in our sample took the *chin-shih* suggests that it required more than the absence of intellectual family orientations to discourage men from competing in the highest level of the examination system. It is true, of course, that some of this group were from commoner families whose *wealth* permitted hiring tutors, etc., which would compensate for the lack of scholarship among the family members themselves. (We lack enough cases to test the influence of wealth upon *chin-shih* attainment.) Others of these *chin-shih* from non-intellectual commoner families clearly had neither learning nor wealth in their families. (Again, too few cases to analyze further.)

Thus, out of our total sample of 454 Chinese officials, 292 took the *chin-shih*, all but one of whose ages at the *chin-shih* level are known. Although the proportion of these *chin-shih* from official or intellectual commoner families is far greater than the proportion of these families in the population as a whole, among this sample *per se* the combined effect of official and intellectual commoner family background is *not* significantly related to taking the *chin-shih* or to age at taking the *chin-shih*. In this latter sense, it is necessary to reject our Hypothesis 2.

We shall now look at the attainment of *lower* degrees in the examination system, and compare men who took *any* of the "regular path" degrees with those who took the "irregular" path (*tsa-t'u*).

Regular versus Irregular Recruitment Paths

While taking the *chin-shih* was the most prestigeful way of embarking upon one's official career, one could still take the preferred, "regular" path (*cheng-t'u* or *k'o-t'u*) of recruitment by receiving one of the lower degrees in the competitive examination system—*chü-jen*, *kung-sheng*, or *yin-sheng*. (The *yin-sheng* was not competitive, but was awarded to the sons or grandsons of meritorious officials.) If an official had received no degree above the licentiate (*hsiu-ts'ai*, or *sheng-yüan*) except the *chien-sheng* by purchase, he was spoken of as having taken the "irregular path" (*tsa-t'u*) of recruitment. As we noted earlier, official appointment was not extended to those who held only the licentiate's degree (*hsiu-ts'ai*). Licentiates and men with no degrees could enter the bureaucracy only by means of the purchase system (*chüan-na chih-tu*), i.e., by purchasing the *chien-sheng* (*li chien-sheng*) or the *kung-sheng* (*li kung-sheng*) and the right to be appointed to office, or by rising from the lowest ranks (Hsu Ta-ling, 1950). As to the actual number of *yin-sheng*, appointed because of their father's merits, it was small in Ch'ing times, and it is small in our sample. Rising through the ranks without taking the higher degrees is technically classed as regular path, but in this study we shall take the liberty of defining officials who rose through the ranks, along with those who purchased degrees and rank, as *irregular path* officials. We shall reserve the term regular path for only those officials who took the *chin-shih*, *chü-jen*, *kung-sheng*, or *yin-sheng*.

Which strata in our sample resorted most to the regular path and which to the irregular path for their advancement? What were the consequences for advancement of having taken one or the other of these two paths? Table 20 takes up the first of these questions, in the light of Hypothesis 3: The recruitment path taken is a function of the stratum position of the family of orientation; therefore, Chinese from official families are more likely to take the preferred path (examinations) than are Chinese from commoner families.

In Table 16, we saw that 14 per cent of the Manchu sons, 67 per cent of the Chinese elite sons, and 60 per cent of the Chinese commoner sons took the highest degree, the *chin-shih*. Table 20 shows that each of these three strata produced a slightly higher percentage of sons who took one of the lower degrees: 10 per cent more Manchus, 13 per cent more Chinese elite sons, and 12 per cent more Chinese commoner sons were "examination path" men, though not holders of the most coveted degree.

The over-all results in Tables 16 and 20 are the same. In both tables, there is the high relation between ethnic status (Manchus vs. all Chinese) and path of recruitment (regular vs. irregular)—$\sqrt{T_b} = 0.4$ and $\sqrt{T_b} = 0.5$, respectively; the relationship between stratum position *among* Chinese (official vs. commoner families) and recruitment path continues to be statistically insignificant. Almost as high a percentage of commoners' sons who sought elite bureaucratic mobility resorted to the examination path as did men from official families. Thus, Hypothesis 3 is supported, though further specified. It holds for ethnic differences (Manchus vs. Chinese), but not for stratum differences among Chinese.

Thus far, we have treated regular and irregular recruitment paths as dependent upon family stratum position. We shall now regard recruitment path taken as an independent variable. We shall hypothesize that bureaucratic advancement varies according to both family stratum position and the recruitment path one takes. First, let us use the relation between family position and advancement as measured by

Table 20—Family Stratum Position of Officials Advancing by "Regular" and "Irregular" Mobility Paths

	FAMILY POSITION						
	MANCHUS		CHINESE OFFICIALS		CHINESE COMMONERS		Total
Mobility Path	Number	Per Cent	Number	Per Cent	Number	Per Cent	Number
"Regular" path (examinations)*	28	24	224	80	122	72	374
"Irregular" path†	90	76	60	20	48	28	198
Total	118	100	284	100	170	100	572

$P < 0.001$ for three columns, $T_b = 0.20$, $\sqrt{T_b} = 0.45$

$\chi^2 = 2.964$ $P < 0.10$ for columns 2 vs. 3

* Military and civil *chin-shih, chü-jen, kung-sheng, yin-sheng.*
† All other types of recruitment.

rank reached in the nine-rank bureaucracy. Hypothesis 4 states that highest rank reached is directly related to family stratum position. Therefore, we should expect Manchus to be more likely than Chinese from official families, and the latter to

Table 21—Relation between Family Stratum Position and Official Advancement

Highest Rank During Career	FAMILY POSITION: MANCHUS Number	Per Cent	CHINESE OFFICIALS Number	Per Cent	CHINESE COMMONERS Number	Per Cent	Total Number
Rank 1	99	84	124	44	74	43	297
Rank 2-3	15	13	75	26	47	28	137
Rank 4-9	4	3	85	30	49	29	138
Total	118	100	284	100	170	100	572

$P < 0.001$ $T_b = 0.07$ $\sqrt{T_b} = 0.26$ for entire table.
Manchus vs. all Chinese: $P < 0.001$ $\sqrt{T_b} = 0.26$

be more likely than Chinese from commoner families, to reach posts of a given rank.

In Table 21, as before, the break is more along ethnic lines than between Chinese from official and from commoner families. In fact, there is no significant relationship between official versus commoner background among the Chinese and their latter advancement, according to this table. There is a relation ($\sqrt{T_b} = 0.3$) between ethnic status and advancement, in that 84 per cent of the Manchus rose to first-rank posts, in contrast to only 44 per cent and 43 per cent of the two Chinese strata, respectively. All but 3 per cent of the Manchus reached posts in the highest three ranks, as compared with 30 per cent of the official-family Chinese and 29 per cent of the commoner-family Chinese. These ethnic differences agree with Zi's 1894 conclusion that, while intellectual achievement went to the Chinese (they monopolized the examination path), power and authority were monopolized by the Manchus. Thus, Hypotheses 3 and 4 are supported only for ethnic differences, not for stratum differences among Chinese officials. It should be remembered, however, that our Manchu sample is highly skewed in the direction of high stratum families, and may therefore exaggerate to some extent the differences in official advancement between Manchus and Chinese. In addition to this possibility, there is independent evidence that the mass of Manchu officials—those not from the Imperial clan, the nobility, or officialdom—had *less* official advancement than is shown in our sample. For example, in such central government organizations as the Censorate (*Tu Ch'a Yüan*) there were 115 Manchus and only 5 Chinese holding the low posts of clerks (*pi-t'ieh-shih*), ranks seven through nine (Hsiao, 1928, I, 465). Thus, in the bureaucracy as a whole, the official advancement of Manchus was not as great as is indicated here. The Manchus monopolized the power and authority during the Ch'ing period, but our sample exaggerates the influence of this monopoly upon the differences in official advancement between Manchus and Chinese.

We have another measure of official advancement, the *rate of promotion*, which gives a kind of career mobility profile. Hypothesis 5 states: The rate of promotion is directly related to the stratum position of family of orientation. Therefore, we should expect Manchu officials to spend a significantly greater proportion of their total careers in high-rank posts than do Chinese from official families, and the latter a significantly greater proportion than Chinese from commoner families.

In Table 22, rate of promotion was measured in this way: the total number of years all the individuals in our sample from each stratum held posts in given ranks was first computed. Of the 3,514 years during which the 118 Manchus (see Table 21) had official careers, *as a group*, 26 per cent of their career duration was spent in four- to nine-rank posts, 34 per cent of their time in third- and second-rank posts, and 40 per cent of their career duration was spent in first-rank posts. These data give a basis for comparing the rate of promotion of men from different strata family backgrounds.

Table 22—Relation between Family Stratum Position and Rate of Promotion*

RANK	CAREER YEARS SPENT, BY FAMILY POSITION									TOTAL NUMBER
	MANCHUS			CHINESE OFFICIALS			CHINESE COMMONERS			
	Career Years	Per Cent Total	Number	Career Years	Per Cent Total	Number	Career Years	Per Cent Total	Number	
Rank 1	1,406	40	99	1,374	18	124	621	16	74	297
Rank 2-3	1,186	34	15	2,051	27	75	1,056	27	47	137
Rank 4-9	922	26	4	4,229	55	85	2,282	57	49	138
Total	3,514	100	118	7,654	100	284	3,959	100	170	572

* Per cent of career years spent at various rank levels.

What can we conclude about the *rate of bureaucratic ascent* of each of these three strata—Manchus, Chinese official sons, and Chinese commoner sons—*as strata*? This table again confirms our generalization that the patterns of official advancement in the Ch'ing bureaucracy were shaped more by ethnic stratum differences between Manchu and Chinese than by stratum differences between Chinese official- and commoner-family sons. This generalization refers, of course, only to our own sample. There is virtually no difference in the mobility profile of those from official and those from commoner families: both strata's officials spent slightly over 50 per cent of their total career—as strata—in four- to nine-rank posts, about one-fourth of their career in third- and second-rank posts, and finally, 18 per cent and 16 per cent of their career duration, respectively, in first-rank posts. In this table, coming from an official family did not give one steeper ascent in the bureaucracy than coming from a commoner family. This failure to predict advancement within the bureaucracy on the basis of official- versus commoner-family background among Chinese is a serious fault in the hypothesis of extra-bureaucratic influence which we are testing.

One reason for the very similar advancement patterns between commoners and official-family men is the outside chance that the 89 of our commoners on whom there is no family background data in their biographies may be from official families. If some or all of these 89, out of the 170 men classed as commoners, were in fact from official or local elite families, this would account for the observed similarities between official-family sons and commoner sons. As we shall see later, it is highly unlikely that these 89 men were from official-elite families—we have examined many of the available sources, and in none of the biographies on these individuals is there any mention of office, etc., among immediate ancestors; these items are always listed if there *were* officials or degree-holders in one's family. But in order to strengthen our argument, we shall isolate these 89 "unknown background" cases from the other 81 commoners on whom we have *positive* data that they were from commoner families (see Table 23).

Table 23—Validity of the Official vs. Commoner Differentiation According to Highest Rank Attained

	ALL CHINESE					
	ALL COMMONERS		KNOWN TO BE FROM COMMONER FAMILIES		NO DATA ON FAMILY BACKGROUND	
Highest Rank During Career	Number	Per Cent	Number	Per Cent	Number	Per Cent
Rank 1	74	43	37	46	37	42
Rank 2-3	47	28	17	21	30	34
Rank 4-9	49	29	27	33	22	24
Total	170	100	81	100	89	100

$\chi^2 = 3.740$ $P < 0.20$ for column 2 vs. 3.

When the 89 officials on whom there is inadequate family background data are compared with the remaining 81 certain commoners, there is no significant difference in their official advancement. If the 43 per cent of all the commoners (170) who rose to first-rank posts truly had sons of official-elite families among them, making the mobility of the commoners appear to be higher than it was, column 2 should show a *drop in advancement*, for column 2 reflects the advancement of certain commoners. Column 2 does not show this drop. We feel this strengthens our argument that no officials or degree-holders are hidden among the 89 on whom we have no positive data on family position. We feel justified in lumping together the 81 certain commoners and the 89 probable commoners, in our future analysis. One possible source of error has been eliminated.

There is, however, another indication that all 170 of the commoners are validly categorized, and that they are all distinguishable from Chinese coming from official families. Our most sensitive measure of stratum differences in advancement—median years in high posts—shows a clear *difference* between Chinese from official families and those from commoner families. This supports Hypothesis 6: Length of incumbency in given ranks is directly related to family stratum position.

In Table 24 we observe a difference in advancement *both* along ethnic lines (Manchus vs. Chinese) and also between Chinese from official families and those from commoner families. The Manchus spent considerably less time in lower-rank posts and more time in higher-rank posts than either of the two Chinese strata. The rate of promotion of Manchus, at all stages, was greater than that of Chinese, regardless of their stratum background. Chinese from official families held higher-rank posts (both above rank four, in general, and in rank one) longer than Chinese from commoner families.

Note, however, that at the highest and most decisive point of bureaucratic advancement—length of time in first-rank posts—our hypothesis is not as strongly supported as

Table 24—Relation between Family Stratum Position and Length of Incumbency

Family Stratum Position	Median Years Incumbent	Number of Officials	
Rank 1			
Manchu	21.2	99	
Chinese Official	9.6	124	
Chinese Commoner	6.9	74	
			297
Rank 1-3			
Manchu	34.8	15	
Chinese Official	26.7	75	
Chinese Commoner	17.8	47	
			137
Rank 4-9			
Manchu	6.8	4	
Chinese Official	19.2	85	
Chinese Commoner	17.8	49	
			138

might be expected. Men from official families held these posts only 2.7 years longer (9.6 vs. 6.9 years) than men from commoner families. Although these differences are in the anticipated direction—Manchus have the longest incumbency, Chinese official sons next longest, commoners' sons shortest—the difference is slight enough to reflect again the inadequacy of the hypothesis of "extra-bureaucratic influence." If some men from relatively low-evaluated families, legally commoners, could hold the highest posts in the Empire only 2.7 years less time than men from official families, we are left with one of two conclusions: either there was considerable upward mobility and "circulation of elites," or else there were *other* independent variables at work, which we have not yet measured. In the first of these alternatives, the 6.9 years during which the commoners were occupying first-rank posts were *that many years* during which *that many men* from official-elite families were *deprived* of the authority, privileges, etc., of incumbency in those posts. We shall return to this line of analysis later; at the present, we turn to the second possible explanation for the high mobility of Chinese commoners' sons.

Earlier, we saw that the Manchus typically took the "irregular" or non-degree path of mobility, while Chinese of both strata typically took the "regular path." What was the relation between these recruitment paths taken and one's subsequent advancement? Is the path one chose for bureaucratic recruitment the factor which explains later advancement differences, where family stratum position fails to explain any but slight differences among Chinese? Table 25 shows the relationship between recruitment path and highest rank reached in the bureaucracy, in the light of Hypothesis 7: Rank reached is a function of recruitment path taken. Therefore, we should expect "regular path" officials to be more likely than "irregular path" officials to reach given high-rank posts.

Table 25—Relation between Rank Attained and Recruitment Path Taken

	HIGHEST RANK ATTAINED						
Recruitment Path Taken	Rank 1		Rank 2-3		Rank 4-9		Total
	Number	Per Cent	Number	Per Cent	Number	Per Cent	Number
"Regular" path	160	43	100	27	114	30	374
"Irregular" path	137	69	37	19	24	12	198
Total number	297		137		138		572

$P < 0.001$ $T_b = 0.04$ $\sqrt{T_b} = 0.20$

In Table 26 we shall test Hypothesis 8: Incumbency in high-rank posts is a function of recruitment path taken. Therefore, the median incumbency of regular-path officials will be longer than that for irregular-path officials. There are correlations here between recruitment path taken and *both* bureaucratic rank reached ($\sqrt{T_b} = 0.2$) and length of time one held posts in high ranks. But the relationship goes in the opposite direction from that posited by Hypotheses 7 and 8, and also appears to contradict the view of several

Table 26—Relation between Length of Incumbency and Recruitment Path Taken

Recruitment Path	INCUMBENCY Rank 1 Median Yrs. Incumbent	Rank 1 Number of Incumbents	Rank 1-3 Median Yrs. Incumbent	Rank 1-3 Number of Incumbents
"Regular" path	8.7	160	20.1	260
"Irregular" path	10.8	137	31.6	174

Chinese scholars. Chang Chung-li (1955, p. 10), for example, states that higher-ranking officials came almost exclusively from the examination system or regular path. Or, in a biography of Liu Lun (1711-73), one of the officials in our sample, it is stated, "Liu Lun was the only Chinese Grand Secretary (*ko-ch'en*) during the Ch'ing dynasty who did not take the examination path (*k'o-mu-t'u*) (*Kuo-ch'ao ch'i-hsien lei-cheng*, 26/35a). Actually, Liu Lun was a stipendary licentiate (*ling-sheng*) and also passed the special *po-hsüeh hung-tz'u* examination. But he had not taken the orthodox degrees of *chü-jen* and *chin-shih*.

The discrepancy between this view and our finding that men from the irregular path rose to high-rank posts more often and held them longer than men from the regular path has this explanation: our sample includes Manchus, whereas this generalization refers only to Chinese officials. We have consistently seen that, in our sample, the Manchus had a much greater advancement than both Chinese official sons and commoner sons. But, as we shall see later, even among Chinese in our sample, irregular-path men had greater advancement than regular-path men. Hence, in our sample, the only sense in which the traditional view of greater advancement for regular-path officials is valid is when it is limited to *Chinese* officials, and limited to *civil* rather than military posts. The irregular-path men in our sample had more advancement than regular-path men because of these two closely linked facts: although the number of Manchus and Chinese in top posts was about equal, the percentage of all

Manchus who held top posts was higher than the percentage of all Chinese; Manchus, typically, did not take the examinations, but rose through the military. Therefore, our findings show that non-examination-path and military officials had greater official advancement than examination-path men. Were our sample limited to officials in high *civil* posts, we should probably see that most of these officials were products of the examination system. Also, in favor of the view that the regular path led to more advancement in office, it must be pointed out that even with the many Manchus and military officials in our sample, regular-path men had *steeper ascent* than irregular-path men. In Table 26, regular-path officials spent almost *half* of the time they were in the highest three ranks specifically in first rank posts (8.7 years out of 20.1 years), in comparison to only about one-third of the time for irregular-path officials (10.8 years out of 31.6 years).

From our point of view, rising to high military posts is advancement just as much as is rising to high civil posts. While, in the lower ranks, civil posts were generally admitted to have higher prestige than military posts, in the higher ranks the prestige of civil and military office was more equalized. High provincial officials, for example, held concurrent military and civil posts. Omutu, one of the officials in the sample, while a Sub-chancellor (*hsüeh-shih*) in the Chung Ho Tien and in the Nei Ko—both civil posts— was also involved in military campaigns. There was also the tradition of the Confucian scholar-general, which again made the line between military and civil officials more tenuous.

For us, the significant datum is not the prejudice sometimes operative against military officials, but the fact that officials not rising through the examination system or in civil posts attained high advancement in the Ch'ing period.

Summary. We have seen that family stratum position and recruitment path taken are both positively correlated with official advancement. Family position correlates with ethnic differences in advancement ($\sqrt{T_b} = 0.3$), i.e., differences between Manchus and all Chinese, but *among* Chinese officials there is no correlation between family background and official advancement. Recruitment path taken correlates with later advancement ($\sqrt{T_b} = 0.2$), and, in our sample, irregular-path officials had more advancement than regular-path officials.

We have also seen that there is a positive correlation of 0.5 between the two "test factors," or independent variables—family position and recruitment path taken. But this relationship holds only for ethnic differences, not for stratum differences among Chinese. That is, most Manchus took the irregular path while most Chinese took the regular path, but almost the same percentage of Chinese commoner sons as of Chinese official sons resorted to the regular path.

We are now ready for a higher level of statistical analysis—partial correlation. What is the relation between path taken and subsequent advancement when family position is held constant? Does path taken have an independent role in explaining later advancement, or is this relation actually a function of family background differences?

One way of answering this is to compare ascription factors with achievement factors. In American stratification research it has proved fruitful to ask: If manual workers' sons graduate from college, are they subsequently more mobile than business men's sons who do *not* go to college? This tests the relative influence of status ascription versus personal achievement. Did the status which the business fathers ascribed to their sons give the sons greater career mobility, even without a college education, than the achievement represented by a college education helped the sons of manual workers, for whom the status ascribed by their fathers was of little benefit?

The analogous question in our Chinese elite sample is, did Chinese commoners' sons, by taking the *preferred* path (examination), have greater advancement during their careers than the sons of Manchus and of Chinese official families who did not take the preferred path? The hypothesis of "extra-bureaucratic influence" we are testing would suggest that they did not, and this is in part what Table 27 shows:

Table 27—Role of the Examination System in Official Advancement

	Highest Rank Attained During Career						
	Rank 1		*Rank 2-3*		*Rank 4-9*		*Total*
Recruitment Path	*Number*	*Per Cent*	*Number*	*Per Cent*	*Number*	*Per Cent*	*Number*
Manchus: Irregular	79	88	10	11	1	1	90
Chinese Officials: Irregular	32	54	16	27	11	19	59
Chinese Commoners: Regular	49	40	36	30	37	30	122

$P < 0.01$ $T_b = 0.12$ $\sqrt{T_b} = 0.34$ for entire table.
χ^2 3.837 $P < 0.20$ for rows 2 vs. 3

	Length of Incumbency			
	Rank 1		*Rank 1-3*	
	Median Yrs.	*Number*	*Median Yrs.*	*Number*
Manchus: Irregular	21.3	79	33.1	89
Chinese Officials: Irregular	9.9	32	30.5	48
Chinese Commoners: Regular	6.2	49	10.9	122

Chinese from commoner families who took the preferred path of recruitment did not have significantly greater advancement than Chinese from official families who took the less prestigeful "irregular" path. In fact, these regular path commoners' sons appear to have had even slightly less advancement than the irregular path officials' sons, although this difference is not statistically significant. As to incumbency in high-rank posts, however, Chinese from official families clearly outdistanced Chinese from commoner families, despite differences in the recruitment paths. Table 27 also shows that these regular-path Chinese from commoner families had much less advancement than Manchus who took the irregular path. This holds for rank reached, and especially for length of time in high ranks. The original over-all correlation between family position and advancement is not reduced, but remains 0.3. In this sense, the examination system had definite limitations as a mobility channel for commoners. This would indicate that the correlation between path taken and later advancement was actually a function of stratum differences in family background, especially for Manchus.

A second way of seeing this is that Manchus were encouraged to take the irregular path. Therefore, we can compare Manchus who deviated from this norm and who took the degree path, with Chinese from commoner families who *conformed* highly in that they took the degree path. Was it a consequence of Manchus' getting literary degrees that they would have less advancement?

As shown in Table 28, our generalization still stands: even mobile-deviant Manchus had greater advancement than mobile-conformist Chinese from commoner families. This difference is statistically significant, with a correlation of $\sqrt{T_b} = 0.2$.

Table 28—Advancement of Manchu and of Chinese Commoner Regular Path Officials

Family Position, Regular Path	*Rank 1*		*Rank 2-3*		*Rank 4-9*		*Total*
	Number	*Per Cent*	*Number*	*Per Cent*	*Number*	*Per Cent*	*Number*
Mobile deviant Manchu	20	71	5	18	3	11	28
Mobile conformist Chinese commoner	49	40	36	30	37	30	122
Total number	69		41		40		150

$\chi^2 = 9.300$ $P < 0.01$ $T_b = 0.04$ $\sqrt{T_b} = 0.19$

Thus far, family stratum position has been seen to be a more important factor than path taken, in explaining later advancement. To clinch this argument, let us now observe the complete relationship between recruitment path taken and later advancement, when family background is held constant (see Table 29). This will fully test Hypothesis 9, which states that rank reached is *more* a function of family position than of recruitment path taken.

Table 29—Relation between Recruitment Path Taken and Highest Rank Attained When Family Position Is Held Constant (1)

	HIGHEST RANK DURING CAREER						
Recruitment Path by Family Position	*Rank 1* Number	Per Cent	*Rank 2-3* Number	Per Cent	*Rank 4-9* Number	Per Cent	*Total* Number
Manchu							
"Regular"	20	71	5	18	3	11	28
"Irregular"	79	88	10	11	1	1	90
Chinese Official							
"Regular"	92	41	59	27	74	32	225
"Irregular"	32	54	16	27	11	19	59
Chinese Commoner							
"Regular"	49	40	36	30	37	30	122
"Irregular"	25	52	11	23	12	25	48
Total number	297		137		138		572

$P < 0.05$ for Manchus; $P < 0.10$ for Chinese officials' sons;
$P < 0.50$ for commoners' sons.

Correlations between recruitment path taken and later advancement are here consistently reduced by holding family background constant. The original correlation between path taken and advancement was 0.2; in Table 29 this relationship between path taken and advancement is no longer statistically significant *for any of the three strata.* Among Manchus, among Chinese from official families, and among Chinese from commoner families, the original correlation of 0.2 is now wiped out. The point is that the original relation is *consistently* eliminated when family position is held constant.

Originally, we saw that 43 per cent of regular-path officials in the sample as a whole, as against 69 per cent of irregular-path officials, had risen to first-rank posts. Now, within each of the three family background strata, the difference in percentage of men from regular and from irregular path reaching a given level post is much less.

One's family stratum position precedes in time the recruitment path one chose to take. Further, variations in family position in our sample are a *cause* of variations in both path taken and later official advancement; the partial correlation between path taken and later mobility is *lower* than when family position is not held constant. Therefore, we may conclude that the original relation between path taken and later advancement is at least partly attributable to the fact that path taken and later official advancement have a *common source of variation*: family stratum position.

We saw that, within the bureaucracy, regular-path officials sometimes discriminated against irregular-path officials. In this sense, the recruitment *path* one had taken could significantly affect one's career. But our data show quite clearly that ethnic differences between Manchus and Chinese were more fundamental than path taken in accounting for general patterns of advancement. Hypothesis 9 is thus confirmed.

Does this conclusion hold for our most sensitive measure of bureaucratic advancement—the number of years in high-rank posts? Hypothesis 10, in line with the general hypothesis of "extra-bureaucratic influence," states: Length of incumbency in high posts is more a function of family position than of recruitment path taken. Therefore, we should expect that when family stratum position is held constant, the original differences in incumbency in high posts as between regular- and irregular-path officials will be reduced or will disappear altogether.

Within each of the strata in Table 30, irregular-path officials continue to hold posts longer than regular-path officials. This generalization holds both before and after family position is held constant. But it holds with considerable variation from stratum to stratum. In some respects the original differences between path taken and years in high-rank posts have been *increased* (e.g., among Manchus); in other respects they have been *decreased* (as among Chinese from official families), as a result of holding family position constant.

Table 30—Relation between Recruitment Path Taken and Later Advancement When Family Position Is Held Constant (2)

Rank by Family Position	PATH OF RECRUITMENT Regular	Irregular
Rank 1		
Manchus	12.0 yrs.	21.3 yrs.
Chinese Officials	9.6	9.9
Chinese Commoners	6.2	8.5
Rank 1-3		
Manchus	32.8	33.1
Chinese Officials	21.9	30.5
Chinese Commoners	10.9	18.8

For Manchus, according to Table 30, recruitment path taken was unimportant as far as years spent in posts above the fourth rank were concerned. But in first-rank posts, Manchus who had taken the irregular path (as they had been encouraged to do) had much longer incumbency than those who had taken the degree path. In the last analysis, this difference must be attributed not to path taken, *per se*, but to the fact that about 77 per cent of these 79 miscellaneous-path Manchus in first-rank posts were *also* the sons or descendents of members of the imperial family, nobility, tribal chieftains, and high ranking officials. Their long incumbency was due not so much to the path they had taken as to the pre-eminent position of their families.

As for Chinese, both those from official and from commoner families were better off taking the irregular path, in the interests of high mobility. The one exception to this is that, in first-rank posts, it made little difference for official-family sons whether they took the regular or irregular path: both paths are associated in this sample with about the same length of time in first-rank posts. Thus, Hypothesis 10 is not supported for the Chinese officials in our sample.

Path taken, then, was not entirely inconsequential, not only because regular-path officials discriminated against irregular-path officials, but also because, *in all respects*, taking the irregular path would at least give one *as high bureaucratic advancement* as would taking the regular path; and in some instances, taking the irregular path increased one's advancement. For example: Chinese from official families as a whole in our sample served, on the average, 26.7 years in posts in the highest three ranks, but those officials' sons who took the irregular path served 30.5 years in these posts. Or, commoner-family sons, as a group, served an average of 6.9 years in first-rank posts, while irregular-path commoners served 8.5 years in these first-rank posts.

We know that there are differences in our sample between irregular- and regular-path Manchus: the former, more than the latter, were from extremely high royal and noble families. But *within* the stratum of Chinese from official families, the only factor in our analysis known to differentiate them is the factor of path taken. We cannot say, as we could for the Manchus, that officials' sons who took the irregular path came from more highly elite families than did officials' sons who took the regular path. All we know in the case of Chinese officials' sons is that they had taken different bureaucratic paths; we cannot say whether there were any other systematic factors differentiating irregular-path elite sons from regular-path elite sons. What has been said for Chinese sons of officials is equally true for Chinese commoners' sons: path *does* seem to make a difference in advancement.

Thus, until future research uncovers new variables which determine advancement, we must accept the conclusion that, at least among the Chinese in our sample, *both* the stratum position of one's family and the path one took were determinants of one's advancement.

We are still left with the problem of deviant case analysis: that Chinese from commoner families in our sample could, by taking the irregular path, achieve almost as much advancement as Chinese from official families who took the degree path is a datum to be explained. Irregular-path Chinese officials of commoner background held first-rank posts 8.5 years, only about one year less than official-family sons' incumbency in the first-rank posts. What was there about the irregular path followed by 48 commoners in our sample that made their mobility patterns deviate from theoretical expectation? If we analyze these 48 cases intensively, the major fact that emerges is that, by having a career in the *military bureaucracy*, irregular-path commoners in the sample could achieve extreme upward mobility. The numerous military campaigns of the Ch'ing period provided opportunities for rapid promotion in the military hierarchy, as rewards for victory and so forth. This is particularly well seen if we divide these 48 men into three groups: the 25 who reached first-rank posts, the 11 who reached second- or third-rank posts, but not first-rank posts, and the 12 who never rose above the fourth rank.

Of the 25 who rose from Chinese commoner families through the irregular path to first-rank posts, *all but one* man served principally or wholly in the military bureaucracy, rising in office during the Ming-Ch'ing struggle for supremacy, or during the "pacification" of various uprisings (Miao, Mohammedans, Chahar Mongols, Pai Lien Chiao, Taiping, Nien Fei, etc.), or during the campaigns in such regions as Burma, Taiwan, Annam, the Ili Valley, and Turkestan. Of the 11 who rose to third- or second-rank posts, 7 were mainly military officials; the other 4, civil officials (Chang Yin-huan, Jung Hung, Liu Jui-fen, and Ting Jih-ch'ang), were all connected with mid- and late-nineteenth-century roles as diplomats to Western nations, Westernizers in China, and in the general field of foreign affairs. These roles were distinctly progressive, even deviant (Teng and Fairbank, 1954, p. 97).

Of the 12 officials who never rose above fourth-rank posts, only one was a military official. This group typically had only short official careers, which were greatly overshadowed by their scholarly and intellectual activities. Of the 11 civil officials in this group, one, Wu Chien-chang, was also associated with foreign relations with the West.

Thus, many non-degree-path officials of commoner background who were the most upward mobile did what Ts'ui Shu's Ming dynasty ancestor had done: they "raised the family by military achievement" (*i chün-kung ch'i chia*) [*Pei-chuan-chi,* 39/5a]). Fei Hsiao-t'ung has noted, for the twentieth century (Republican period, 1912-49), that a military career was a better way to get ahead than through the slow climb of agricultural accumulation over the generations (Fei, 1945, p. 277). Others have also pointed out the possibilities of upward mobility through the military, even during the traditional period (Wittfogel, 1957, pp. 339-40; Powell, 1955, p. 7). In our sample, several Chinese from obscure commoner families rose by going over to the Manchu side (*lai kuei*) as military officials during the Ming-Ch'ing struggle for supremacy (see, e.g., biography of Ning Wan-wo). Another period of upward mobility for commoners in our sample was the Taiping Rebellion in the mid-nineteenth century. Of the 32 officials in our sample from commoner-non-degree-path backgrounds who served in the military bureaucracy, 29 *of them* were associated with either the Manchu-Ming conflict or the Taiping Rebellion. Of those not in the military, high mobility was realized by some non-degree-path commoner sons in the nineteenth century in connection with "China's response to the West." New roles as technological and ideological reformers provided a mobility channel for non-degree-path commoners at that time.

We have seen that a military career provided greater advancement than a civil career for all three strata in our sample, but since Manchus and Chinese from official-elite families were from high stratum backgrounds to begin with, it was chiefly Chinese commoners for whom the military path was a channel of greatest mobility. By taking the military path, the commoner could circumvent the expensive and time-consuming process of preparing for and taking the several examinations. In our sample, there are commoners who, by the age of thirty, had barely taken the *chin-shih* and started their career, while some others—military non-degree-path men—were, by thirty, already Colonels, with a dozen years' seniority and campaigns behind them. The biography of Liu Ming-ch'uan, 1836-96, an official in our sample, well illustrates this point:

> His ancestors had for generations been farmers. Resourceful, ambitious, and discontented with his father's occupation, he became the head of a band of freebooters. . . . When the Taipings threatened [his native place] . . . he organized a powerful volunteer corps which became famous. . . . [He was a major by the age of 26]. . . . In cooperation with the commanders of other volunteer corps, he finally took Changchow . . . and captured a powerful insurgent commander. . . . For restoring peace in Kiangsu, this rustic of only twenty-nine *sui* was made an official of the first rank and commander-in-chief of Chihli (1864). [ECCP, I, 526.]

We have also seen that the son of an official family could have longer incumbency in high posts even *without* taking the examination path than a commoner's son who had taken the examinations. This shows the limits of the examination system in facilitating the advancement of commoners' sons.

To sum up our findings thus far. Hypotheses 1 through

10 (with the exception of Hypotheses 7 and 8) were based upon the general hypothesis that extra-bureaucratic factors, to a greater extent than bureaucratic factors, determined official recruitment and advancement in the Ch'ing period. To what extent is this general hypothesis supported by our findings? First, it is *fully supported* only in Hypotheses 6 and 9: we found that incumbency in high-rank posts *does* vary directly with family stratum position, and that the relationship between recruitment path taken and rank reached is a spurious relationship, actually dependent upon family stratum position. Second, it is *partially supported* by Hypotheses 3, 4, 5, 7, 8, and 10: in most of these hypotheses, differences in official recruitment and advancement were correlated with *ethniic differences* between Manchus and Chinese, but were not correlated with *stratum differences* between Chinese from official and Chinese from commoner families. Third, the case for the priority of extra-bureaucratic influences is weakened by the fact that Hypotheses 1 and 2 are *not supported*: Chinese from official families in our sample are not more likely than Chinese from commoner families to receive the *chin-shih* or to receive it at a significantly younger age.

There are, to repeat an earlier point, at least two *base-lines* against which all the findings in this study can be interpreted. One base-line is the proportion of each stratum in the population of Chinese society as a whole. From this point of view, even Hypotheses 1 and 2 support the notion of extra-bureaucratic influences on advancement, for the proportion of Chinese officials' sons receiving degrees in the examination system or holding posts at a given level is *always far greater* than their proportion in the society as a whole. The other base-line, and the one we emphasize in this study, considers only officialdom, not the population of China as a whole. From this latter base-line, the criterion is: *among* officials, do those from different strata backgrounds have significant differences in their advancement? The hypothesis of extra-bureaucratic influences, then, is always supported in the sense that there are larger proportions of official-family men, and smaller proportions of commoner-family men, in the bureaucracy than their respective proportions in the society as a whole. But the hypothesis of extra-bureaucratic influence is *less well supported* in the sense that, *of the commoners* in the bureaucracy, as many take a given recruitment path or advance in the bureaucracy as do the sons of official families.

Perhaps the best simple summary thus far, then, is that the hypothesis of extra-bureaucratic influences on advancement is not fully supported, but only partially supported by our findings.

CHAPTER 7 BUREAUCRATIC VS. EXTRA-BUREAUCRATIC DETERMINANTS OF OFFICIAL ADVANCEMENT (2)

IN THIS CHAPTER we shall conclude the testing of our hypotheses concerning Chinese elite mobility. We shall first examine the influence of another aspect of family stratum position—the "strength" of official tradition in one's family—upon official advancement. This will take us briefly from the intra-generational aspects to the inter-generational aspects of elite mobility. The culminating point of our analysis will be a comparison of the influence of family stratum position and bureaucratic seniority upon official advancement. After this confrontation of the problem of bureaucratic versus extra-bureaucratic determinants of official advancement, we shall conclude our analysis with discussions of economic stratification in our Chinese elite sample and of the processes of mobility in China.

Strength of Official Family Tradition

Since the "family of orientation" of the officials in our sample consists not only of their parents, but also of their grandparents' and great-grandparents' generations, there are important variations among the 284 officials from official-elite families with respect to *how many* officials and degree-holders there had been in their three previous generations. In some cases, there was only one official or degree-holder; in other cases, several.

An attempt to measure this variable of the *strength* of official tradition in one's family was made by Kracke in 1947. Whereas Kracke's Sung data were limited to paternal ancestors, our data bear on maternal line also. Thus, even if the only official ancestor a man had was his maternal grandfather, he is still classified in our study as coming from an official family. Kracke distinguished four degrees of strength in official family tradition:

Paternal ancestors who were officials.—1. "Prevalent"—father, grandfather, and great-grandfather, or father and grandfather, or father and great-grandfather. 2. "Strong"—grandfather and great-grandfather, or father only. 3. "Minor"—grandfather or great-grandfather. 4. "None"—neither father, grandfather, nor great-grandfather.

Table 31 presents the results obtained by applying these

Table 31—Official Tradition in Family of 454 Non-Manchu Officials

Strength of Official Tradition		NON-MANCHU OFFICIALS	
		Number	Per Cent
1. Prevalent		63	14
2. Strong		125	28
3. Minor		64	14
4. None		202	44
	Total	454	100

definitions to our sample, exclusive of Manchus. Using these marginal totals, we may hypothesize: the "strength" of official tradition in one's family is a special case of the variable, stratum position of the family of orientation. Therefore, we would expect officials from "prevalent" official families to have greater advancement than officials from "strong" official families; we would expect officials from the latter type of official family to have greater advancement than officials from families with a "minor" official tradition, etc. Table 32 tests this new version of the hypothesis of "extra-bureaucratic influence": official advancement varies directly with Kracke's variable, the "strength" of official tradition in one's family.

Table 32—Relation between Strength of Official Family Tradition and Advancement (by Highest Rank Attained)

	STRENGTH OF OFFICIAL TRADITION								
	Prevalent		*Strong*		*Minor*		*None*		*Total*
Highest Rank During Career	*Number*	*Per Cent*	*Number*	*Per Cent*	*Number*	*Per Cent*	*Number*	*Per Cent*	*Number*
Rank 1	28	44	60	48	23	36	87	43	198
Rank 2-3	21	33	31	25	17	27	54	27	123
Rank 4-9	14	23	34	27	24	37	61	30	133
Total	63	100	125	100	64	100	202	100	454

$\chi^2 = 5.264$ $P < 0.70$

Table 32 does not support the Kracke-derived hypothesis. It shows that there was not a significant relationship between the "strength" of official tradition in one's family and one's own bureaucratic advancement. Officials with no official-family tradition reached first-rank posts more often than did men with "minor" official-family traditions. Men with no official tradition reached first-rank posts almost as often as men from families with "strong" and even "prevalent" official traditions. All differences here are insignificant; there is no predicted trend, but rather, an irregular function.

When we observe the relation between this variable of strength of official tradition and *length* of time one held posts in a given rank, a correlation more consistent with the hypothesis of extra-bureaucratic influence emerges, as indicated in Table 33.

Table 33—Relation between Strength of Official Family Tradition and Advancement (by Length of Incumbency)

Strength of Official Tradition	Median Years Incumbent	Number of Officials	
Rank 1			
Prevalent	19.0	28	
Strong	10.4	60	
Minor	8.5	23	
None	6.9	87	
			198
Rank 1-3			
Prevalent	35.5	49	
Strong	25.2	91	
Minor	21.7	40	
None	18.8	141	
			321

Here, the more officials among one's immediate forebears, the longer was one likely to hold high office. Officials from families with no official tradition held posts above the fourth rank about one-half as long as officials from families with "prevalent" official traditions, and held first-rank posts about one-third as long as officials from "prevalent" official families. This again conforms to our hypothesis—the ratio between extremes of official-family tradition ("prevalent" vs. "none") is greater in the highest rank posts than in first- to third-rank posts in general. That is, the gap in incumbency in office between sons of "prevalent" official-tradition families and sons of no-official-tradition families *increased* as they moved from third- and second-rank posts into first-rank posts.

We are seeing a recurrent pattern. Whether we measure

social-legal-authority stratification in terms of "stratum position of family of orientation" or in terms of the "strength of official family tradition," it does not correlate well with bureaucratic *rank reached.* In our sample, commoners, men with no official-family tradition, reached high posts *about as often* as sons of official families, even sons of families with "prevalent" official traditions. But men from official families with stronger official tradition held high-rank posts *longer* than men from lower, commoner families. With reference to officials in large bureaucracies, Schumpeter (1955, p. 123) has noted that there is a "discrepancy between those qualities that enable a man to *reach* a leading position and those that enable him to hold it." The latter qualities, Schumpeter affirms, involve articulateness, the ability "to woo support, to negotiate with and handle men with consummate skill," and mastery of the art of "advancement." Were these the qualities that enabled the sons of official families to hold high posts longer than commoners' sons? If so, was this due to the experience of being reared in an official family, where one early came into contact with these psychological qualities and role models? These are questions we can raise, but not answer, at this time.

Despite this recurrent pattern of official-family sons holding high posts longer than commoners' sons, there is still considerable circulation of elites observable in our data. Men from official families of long standing may have had the greatest advancement in the bureaucracy, but (*a*) men from commoner families in our sample were not far behind them in their advancement, and (*b*) the majority of officials in our sample did not come from official families of long standing. Let us clarify both these points.

In Table 33 we saw that officials with no official-family tradition held first-rank posts only 1.6 years less (6.9 years *vs.* 8.5 years) than those with "minor" official tradition, and only 3.5 years less (6.9 years *vs.* 10.4 years) than those with "strong" official traditions in their immediate ancestry. Similarly, officials from completely non-official families held posts above the fourth rank only 2.9 years less (18.8 years *vs.* 21.7 years) than those from families with minor official traditions.

One element of status ascription seems to have prevailed in the Ch'ing bureaucracy: the officials with the greatest advancement—those holding high-rank posts the longest—were typically either Manchu or from Chinese official-elite families of long standing. But a second crucial element of status ascription was absent: there is, in our sample, an inverse relation between the number of generations official position had been maintained in a family and the number of officials in our sample belonging to these families. This can be seen in Tables 34 and 35, which present our findings on *inter-generational* elite mobility in China. Table 34 presents

Table 34—Number of Successive Generations in Office

	Number	Per Cent
One generation—the respondent himself	230	51
Two generations—not successive	22	5
Two generations—successive*	144	32
Three successive generations	38	8
Four or more successive generations	20	4
Total	454	100

* These 144 include 122 cases where only the respondent and his father were officials, and 22 cases where the two successive generations were not the respondent and his father, but the grandfather and great-grandfather or the father and grandfather.

an analysis of our data in terms of the number of successive generations in office; Table 35, in terms of the total number of generations in office.

In both these tables, the advancement patterns of our sample officials and their immediate ancestors are in accordance with the theory of the circulation of elites. Only 4 per cent of the sample produced four or more generations of officials. Over 80 per cent of the sample, on the other hand, had fewer than three generations in office. There is some evidence that this was also true apart from our sample. For example, during the entire Ch'ing period, only six families are said to have had four consecutive generations admitted to the Hanlin Academy (ECCP, I, 491). These findings on inter-generational mobility again call into question the general hypothesis of the priority of extra-bureaucratic influences on mobility. This general hypothesis suggests much *less* inter-generational mobility than we have, in fact, observed.

We are still confronted, therefore, with the possibility of considerable upward mobility in our sample, with a degree of vertical mobility which is quite unaccounted for by a theory of status-ascription on the basis of family stratum position and other extra-bureaucratic influences.

Was the amount of inter-generational elite mobility relatively constant throughout the Ch'ing period, or did it vary with the "dynastic cycle" or with some other processes of disequilibrium or change? To give a tentative answer to this question on the basis of our sample, we have divided the Chinese sample into ten generation-specific subsamples. Each subsample covers a thirty-year period. Thus, all respondents the mid-point of whose official government career fell between the years 1590 and 1619 were classified in the first Chinese generation-specific subsample; all whose career mid-point fell between 1620 and 1649 were classified in the second subsample, etc. Table 36 presents the findings.

According to Table 36, the period of greatest elite mobility was 1620-49, when 46 per cent of the sample officials rose from below-elite families. Other periods of relatively

Table 35—Total Number of Generations in Office

	Number	Per Cent
One generation—the respondent himself	230	51
Any two generations	144	32
Any three generations	60	13
Four or more generations	20	4
Total	454	100

high upward mobility were; 1590-1619 (35 per cent); 1800-1829 (31 per cent); and 1830-59 (30 per cent). The periods of lowest mobility—from 1680 to 1770—were the years of the middle of the Ch'ing dynasty, a period generally regarded as one of prosperity, relative peace, and social order. There is a rough relationship between the periods of greatest social disequilibrium, conflict, and dynastic decline—those periods at the beginning and at the end of the Ch'ing dynasty—and the time of the greatest upward mobility into officialdom. The most upward mobility occurred during the chaotic period of the Ming-Ch'ing struggle for supremacy, a time of transition from one dynastic rule to another. Further indication that this pattern held is provided from the ECCP (I, 191): "from 1621 to 1644 the presidents of the Six Ministries changed 116 times. . . . In fifty-four instances the occupants were dismissed from office, and in twenty of these they suffered death or confiscation of property. In the corresponding

Table 36—Amount of Chinese Elite Mobility, by 30-Year Periods, 1590-1900 (Relation between Status of Father and of Official-Son)

Period During Which Mid-point of Official Career Occurred	Fathers Also Elite		Fathers Below Elite*		Total Number
	Number	Per Cent	Number	Per Cent	
1590-1619	18	65	10	35	28
1620-49	43	54	37	46	80
1650-79	58	71	24	29	82
1680-1709	58	84	11	16	69
1710-39	33	79	9	21	42
1740-69	41	82	9	18	50
1770-99	37	74	13	26	50
1800-29	34	69	15	31	49
1830-59	39	70	17	30	56
1860-1900*†	48	73	18	27	66
Total number	409		163		572

* This includes other individuals of the same generation as one's father, e.g., uncle or step-father, in the cases where they, rather than the biological father, reared the respondent, gave him his early status, etc.

† The tenth subsample runs from 1860 to 1900, 40 years, because there were only seven officials the mid-point of whose career fell after 1890. All of these seven officials had career mid-points between 1890 and 1900.

twenty-four years of the preceding century there had been only seven cases of dismissal and five of punishments inflicted on presidents of the Six Ministries." This does not necessarily mean that commoners' sons took these posts, but at least there was instability in incumbency in periods of dynastic disorder. After the Ch'ing dynasty had achieved supremacy, and during its "golden age" in the eighteenth century, fewer men entered the elite from "below elite" families. This correlation between the amount of upward mobility and the phase of the "dynastic cycle" can be seen most clearly if we recombine our 572 respondents and then classify them according to a trichotomous periodization, one that is con-

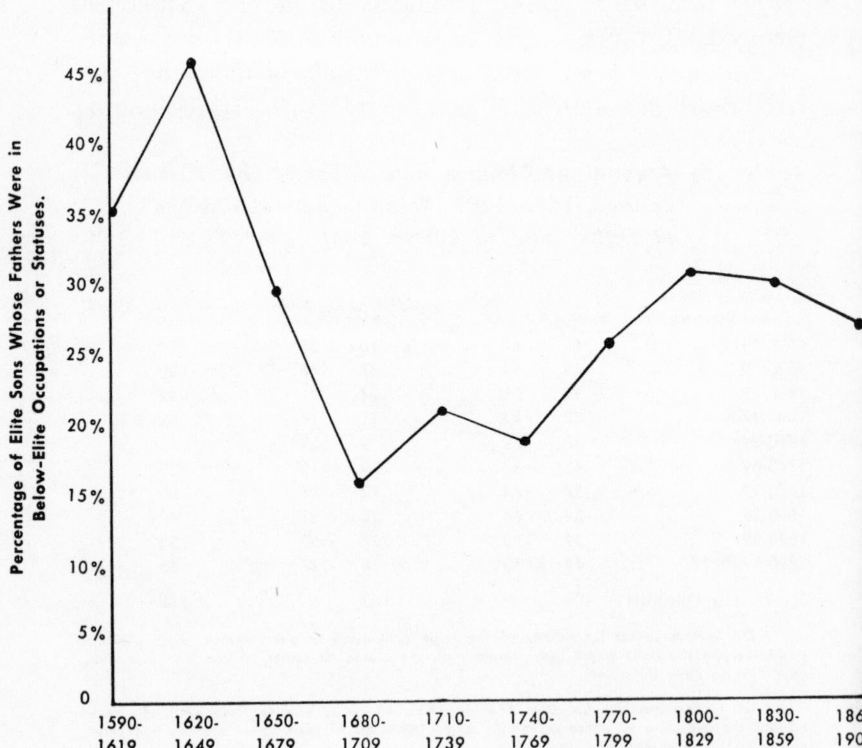

gruent with major turning points during these three centuries. Such a classification is presented in Table 37.

Table 37—Relation between the Dynastic Cycle and the Amount of Mobility, 1590-1900 (According to Relation between Status of Father and Official-Son)

Period During Which Mid-point of Official Career Occurred*	Fathers Also Elite Number	Per Cent	Fathers Below Elite Number	Per Cent	Total Number
1590-1683: Late Ming-early Ch'ing; Ming Dynastic decline; Ming-Ch'ing struggle	131	64	73	36	204
1684-1780: "Golden Age" of Ch'ing supremacy; Relative peace and order	136	81	32	19	168
1781-1900: Ch'ing dynastic decline; peasant rebellions; Western encroachments	141	71	58	29	199
Total number	408		163		571
$P < 0.01$	$T_b = 0.02$		$\sqrt{T_b} = 0.15$		

* 1683 was chosen as the first cutting point because it was the date of the fall of the last effective opposition to the Ch'ing during their conquest of China. In 1683, Shih Lang, with a large Manchu fleet, forced the surrender of the descendents of Cheng Ch'eng-kung, the Pescadores, and Formosa. The year 1780 was chosen as the second cutting point because it was the approximate time in the latter Ch'ien Lung reign when the administration began to deteriorate; Ho-shen and his clique rose to tremendous power and became extremely corrupt. As the ECCP puts it, "The Ch'ing dynasty, which reached its peak during the Ch'ien Lung period, slowly but steadily declined thereafter—the disintegration unquestionably beginning during the reign when Ho-shen was in power. . . . There can be no doubt that the corruption and nepotism which marked the beginning of his ascendancy had a permanently debilitating effect upon the government" (ECCP, I, 290).

We may conclude, from Table 37, that upward elite mobility was greatest at the beginning of the Ch'ing period; that it declined during the more stable period of the middle of the dynasty; and that it increased again during the last third of the dynasty, but not so much as to reach the level of mobility in the early decades of the dynasty. There is a statistically significant relationship between the "dynastic cycle" and the amount of elite mobility, as measured here, with a correlation ($\sqrt{T_b}$) of 0.2. The hypothesis suggested here is that status was ascribed from fathers' to sons' generation more fully during periods of dynastic stability than during periods of instability and conflict. Periods of turmoil and crisis enhanced the opportunities for upward mobility into the elite.

Seniority

It is possible that variations in bureaucratic advancement in our sample are the result, not of stratum position of family of orientation in any of the several forms in which we have measured it, or of recruitment path taken, but of bureaucratic *seniority,* i.e., length of career. We must consider briefly the relation of seniority to other determinants of official advancement. Let us think of a *continuum,* along which the various determinants of advancement may be located. We shall label the two extremes on this continuum "complete particularism" and "complete universalism," respectively. At the former extreme, advancement would be determined primarily by "who one was," for example, the son of a certain official with whom one had a private "understanding," etc. The influence of family background and the phenomenon of nepotism would operate at the "particularistic" extreme of the continuum. At the opposite end of the continuum, one's advancement would be determined not by "who one was," but by *what one did,* that is, one's performance, merit, and the like. In this case, one's promotion would depend on outstanding service rather than on family background, "pull," etc.

Seniority belongs in the middle of this continuum. It is not fully universalistic because, to a certain extent at least, officials can rise because of *long* service, even if their service is not outstanding. Seniority is not fully particularistic either, because a commoner's son has as much chance for advancement as an official's son, providing that he has equivalent seniority. Parsons (1951, p. 185) regards seniority as a contravention of the principle of advancement purely on the basis of competitive achievement. This is perhaps going too far; at the most, seniority is only a *partial* contravention of universalistic-achievement criteria. Also, in the Chinese bureaucracy, as in most other bureaucracies, the accumulation of seniority presupposes at least a *minimum* standard of performance. In China, the operation of seniority did not mean automatic promotion. Rather, as a rule, only a first-class recommendation from the Board of Civil Office, plus seniority, made one eligible for promotion in the Ch'ing bureaucracy. Hence, in our subsequent analysis, we shall treat seniority as a *relatively* universalistic or quasi-universalistic determinant of advancement.

First, we must show the relationship between family stratum position and seniority, or length of career. Hypothesis 11 states that total seniority accumulated is a function of family stratum position; that Manchus, Chinese from official families, and Chinese from commoner families will have significant differences in seniority. Table 38 tests this hypothesis.

Table 38 shows that Manchus were able to accumulate

Table 38—Relation between Family Stratum Position and Seniority Accumulated

SENIORITY	FAMILY POSITION						
LENGTH OF CAREER (Years)	MANCHUS		CHINESE OFFICIALS		CHINESE COMMONERS		Total Number
	Number	Per Cent	Number	Per Cent	Number	Per Cent	
2-15*	22	19	61	21	54	32	137
16-29	34	29	101	36	60	35	195
30-43	43	36	84	30	44	26	171
Over 43	19	16	38	13	12	7	69
Total	118	100	284	100	170	100	572

$\chi^2 = 15.787$ $P < 0.02$ for entire table.
$\chi^2 = 8.808$ $P < 0.05$ for column 2 vs. 3.
$\chi^2 = 45.187$ $P < 0.001$ for column 1 vs. 3.

* An official had to serve at least two years to be included in our sample.

only slightly more seniority than Chinese from official families. Similarly, Chinese from official families were able to accumulate somewhat more seniority during their careers than Chinese from commoner families. Of the Manchus, 52 per cent served thirty years or more, as compared with 43 per cent of the Chinese from official families and 33 per cent of the Chinese from commoner families. The variations are in the *direction* expected by our hypothesis, but none of the differences are statistically significant, except that between Manchus and Chinese from commoner families.

If there is very little relationship between *family background* and seniority, there is a relation between seniority and rank reached during one's career. Hypothesis 12, which states that rank reached varied *independently* of seniority, is thus *not* supported. This is shown in Table 39.

Table 39—Relation between Seniority and Advancement in Office (Highest Rank Attained and Number of Officials by Total Years in Office)

	TOTAL YEARS IN OFFICE								
	2-15		16-29		30-43		Over 43		
Highest Rank During Career	Number	Per Cent	Number	Per Cent	Number	Per Cent	Number	Per Cent	Total
Rank 1	33	24	81	42	122	71	61	88	297
Rank 2-3	24	18	62	32	43	25	8	12	137
Rank 4-9	80	58	52	26	6	4			138
Total	137	100	195	100	171	100	69	100	572

$P < 0.001$ $T_b = 0.15$ $\sqrt{T_b} = 0.39$

This relationship between seniority and bureaucratic advancement ($\sqrt{T_b}=0.4$) is also found when length of time in high-rank posts is measured, thus also rejecting Hypothesis 13, which stated that incumbency in high-rank posts varied independently of seniority accumulated. (See Table 40.)

Were there a high relationship between family position and seniority, we might expect that the relation between seniority and advancement was spurious, i.e., that *both* the seniority and the advancement of officials were due to family stratum position. But we have seen that there was no significant relationship between family background and seniority. Therefore, it appears that seniority is not spuriously related to advancement, but that it is a determinant of advancement. In any case, the issue can be settled by testing this relation between seniority and advancement, when the preceding factor, family position, is held constant. It will be recalled that Hypothesis 14 stated that when family position is held constant, the relationship between seniority and rank reached would be further reduced or would disappear altogether.

Table 41 shows that the original correlation between seniority and official advancement ($\sqrt{T_b} = 0.4$) is *not* reduced by holding family stratum position constant, except for the Manchu group. Seniority remains correlated with advancement among the Chinese, both those from official families ($\sqrt{T_b} = 0.4$) and those from commoner families ($\sqrt{T_b} = 0.4$). The relation between seniority and advancement disappears among the Manchus. This suggests that the relation

Table 40—Relation between Seniority and Advancement in Office (Median Length of Incumbency and Number of Officials by Total Years in Office)

Total Years in Office	Median Years Incumbency	Number of Officials	
Rank 1			
2-15	5.3	33	
16-29	5.9	81	
30-43	10.6	122	
Over 44	28.2	61	
			297
Rank 1-3			
2-15	5.4	57	
16-29	10.4	143	
30-43	23.4	165	
Over 44	39.0	69	
			434

between seniority and advancement tends to be spurious for the Manchus, but not spurious for the Chinese from official and from commoner families.

What this means is that, among Manchus, *both* seniority and advancement were a result of the high stratum position of their families. Advancement among the Chinese in our sample, on the other hand, was a result of the seniority they accumulated, more than of their family stratum background. In our sample, a Manchu tended to have great advancement in his official career *whether or not he accumulated considerable seniority;* among Chinese officials, however, those with the greatest advancement tended to be those with the most seniority, *whether they were from official or from commoner families.* Thus, Hypothesis 14 holds

Table 41—Relation between Seniority and Advancement, When Family Position Is Held Constant

Total Years in Office	HIGHEST RANK DURING CAREER Rank 1 Number	Rank 1 Per Cent	Rank 2-3 Number	Rank 2-3 Per Cent	Rank 4-9 Number	Rank 4-9 Per Cent	Total Number	Total Per Cent
Manchus:								
2-15	15	68	5	23	2	9	22	100
16-29	28	82	6	18	—	—	34	100
30-43	38	88	3	7	2	5	43	100
44 & over	18	95	1	5	—	—	19	100
Chinese Official-Elite:								
2-15	9	15	7	11	45	74	61	100
16-29	30	30	34	33	37	37	101	100
30-43	53	63	28	33	3	4	84	100
44 & over	32	84	6	16	—	—	38	100
Chinese Commoners:								
2-15	9	17	12	22	33	61	54	100
16-29	23	38	22	37	15	25	60	100
30-43	31	70	12	27	1	3	44	100
44 & over	11	92	1	8	—	—	12	100
Totals	297		137		138		572	

Manchus: $\chi^2 = 6.490$ $P < 0.50$

Chinese Officials' Sons: $P < 0.001$ $T_b = 0.17$ $\sqrt{T_b} = 0.4$

Chinese Commoners' Sons: $P < 0.001$ $T_b = 0.19$ $\sqrt{T_b} = 0.4$

only for the Manchu officials in our sample. That it does not hold for stratum differences among Chinese officials is further evidence *against* the general hypothesis of extra-bureaucratic influence.

Among the officials in our sample, it appears that one set of generalizations applies throughout to Manchus, another set to Chinese. For Manchus, being a Manchu was more important than accumulating seniority, as far as rank reached in the bureaucratic hierarchy was concerned. (As we have repeatedly said, this generalization is subject to revision on the basis of studies of more representative samples of Manchu officials.) Among Chinese officials in this study, family background did not reduce the original correlation between advancement and seniority.

This same relationship can be seen in our most sensitive measure of advancement, the median number of years high-rank posts were held. Hypothesis 15 stated that when seniority is held constant, the original differences in incumbency between Chinese from official and from commoner families will *not* be reduced. It will be recalled that in Table 24 Chinese from official families held posts in the three highest ranks 8.9 years longer than commoners' sons. This considerable difference is now reduced when we hold seniority constant, as in Table 42.

Among officials with the shortest careers (less than 16 years), Chinese from official families held posts in the three

Table 42—Relation between Family Position and Advancement When Seniority Is Held Constant

	TOTAL YEARS IN OFFICE			
Years in Rank 1-3 by Family Background	*2-15*	*16-29*	*39-43*	*44 & over*
Chinese Official				
Median Yrs.	8.5	9.7	19.8	32.7
Chinese Commoner				
Median Yrs.	3.9	8.9	18.1	36
Difference	4.6	0.8	1.7	−3.3

highest ranks 4.6 years longer, on the average, than Chinese from commoner families, instead of 9 years, as in Table 24. For officials with more seniority—16-29 years and 30-43 years —this difference in average incumbency is further reduced, to only 0.75 years and 1.7 years, respectively. Finally, of those officials with more than 43 years' seniority, Chinese from commoner families *actually reversed* the tables and held high-rank posts 3 *years longer*, on the average (36 years vs. 32.7 years), than Chinese from official families.

There are two striking things about this finding. First, it does not support Hypothesis 15, but, rather, shows seniority to be a more important determinant of advancement than family background. Second, one can clearly observe *the slow but cumulative process by which Chinese from commoner families began their careers* under a considerable handicap in comparison to Chinese from elite families, but thenceforth steadily "caught up" with and even outdistanced Chinese officials from official families. Seniority is seen to work significantly in favor of Chinese from less-privileged (commoner) families. The more seniority they accumulated, the more likely were the Chinese from commoner families to catch up with and even outdistance Chinese from official families, with respect to incumbency in high-rank posts.

To relate this finding to an earlier assertion: Chinese from commoner families, by taking the miscellaneous path, getting an early start in their (military) careers, and by accumulating seniority over those who had started later because of having to take the arduous examinations, could achieve as much advancement as official-family sons.

Note, however, that getting into the bureaucracy in the first place was heavily determined by official family background, among the Chinese. But, once in, rising through the ranks was not so much determined by family background as by such factors as path taken and seniority.

The objection may be raised that, while these data on seniority may argue against nepotism, they do not necessarily eliminate the possibility of *other forms of favoritism.* That is, due to seniority, men with official family connections did not have a strong advancement edge over commoners' sons. But favoritism may have operated along non-kinship lines, and in this form it may have been beyond the control of the seniority principle. We know that high officials could recommend (*pao-chü*) lower officials as having great talent, and could request the Emperor to give these subordinates more responsibilities and to promote them. Was this practice abused in such a way that promotions were determined more by favoritism than by merit or seniority? There is reason to believe that favoritism did not operate strongly, at least not through recommendation, during the Ch'ing period. Recommendation on the basis of pure favoritism was held in check by the fact that, if the person recommended subsequently violated bureaucratic rules, the punishment would befall the official who had recommended him. Hsieh comments, "the responsibility of the protector for the offense of the protégé made this act too much of a burden. This power [of recommendation], therefore, was seldom exercised" (1925, p. 104).

Thus far, we have uncovered at least two career sources of the upward mobility of Chinese from commoner families: promotions for military success at times like the Manchu-Ming struggle or the Taiping rebellion, and promotions because of seniority accumulated. Both these sources of mobility were based upon one's *performance* in office—the seniority principle did not mean automatic promotions. Rather, every three years, every official's record would be examined by the Board of Civil Service, and only the one-third or one-fourth of the officials with the best record would be promoted, the rest either being transferred to another office of the same rank, demoted, or otherwise punished. Nevertheless, it appears that the *types of performance* involved in (*a*) a military victory and (*b*) the more routine tasks of civil office were often quite distinct, especially when we compare military office in times of crisis and civil office in times of stability and peace. It appears that performance in military posts was of a more decisive, dramatic nature than performance in civil posts. We have already seen that irregular-path officials had greater advancement than regular-path officials. Given the *less routinized* nature of performance in military posts than in civil posts, let us test Hypothesis 16, which states that "regular" path officials were likely to have a significantly higher rate of promotion than "irregular" path officials.

Of our 170 Chinese from commoner families, there is no sharp difference in total length of career between the 122 who took the regular path (examination system) and the 48 who took the irregular path. The median length of career for the regular-path commoners was 21.5 years; for irregular-path commoners, 24.4 years. If the seniority principle—with its normally slow, regularized promotion—operated *equally* in both these groups of commoners, it would follow that both groups would have the same rate of promotion, that is, spend the same percentage of their total career in given rank posts. Table 43 makes the assumption that if one spent 50 per cent or less of his total career in the 3 highest ranks, his rate of promotion was determined mainly by standardized

Table 43—Rate of Promotion among "Regular" and "Irregular" Path Chinese Commoners' Sons

Per Cent of Total Career in Rank 1-3 Posts	Recruitment Path: Regular Path Number	Regular Path Per Cent	Irregular Path Number	Irregular Path Per Cent	Total Number
Over 50 per cent of career	33	27	24	50	57
50 per cent or less	89	73	24	50	113
Total	122	100	48	100	170

$P < 0.01$ $T_b = 0.05$ $\sqrt{T_b} = 0.22$

seniority; if one spent more than 50 per cent of his total career in the three highest ranks, his rate of promotion was determined by factors other than standardized seniority.

There is a relationship here between path taken and rate of bureaucratic advancement ($\sqrt{T_b} = 0.2$). Non-examination-path officials, mostly military officials, were promoted significantly faster than examination-path officials, mostly in civil posts. There is evidence here that non-examination-path Chinese from commoner families, to a greater extent than examination-path commoners' sons, did not have to depend on the slow-operating seniority principle for their promotions. Much anecdotal evidence indicates that although, among civil officials, rapid promotions occurred, these were exceptions rather than the rule. In our sample, the following cases are illustrative: Ch'en Ta-shou, *chin-shih* of 1733, was given, in 1737, the "*unusual promotion*" from rank seven to rank five, and in 1738 was promoted to rank two (ECCP, I, 99); Lü Kung, optimus *chin-shih* of 1647, was a first-rank official within seven years by *not* "*having to adhere to the rule of seniority*" (ECCP, I, 550); Yao Ch'i-sheng "*rose rapidly*" (ECCP, II, 899) and Kuo Hsiu was "*rapidly promoted*" to a first-rank post nineteen years after taking his *chin-shih* (ECCP, I, 436). These cases indicate that the *usual* promotion did conform to the one-half-rank-at-a-time law of the Board of Civil Office. Put slightly differently, among officials from commoner families, those who took the non-examination or military path could often benefit from *two* sources of promotion: accumulated seniority and extraordinary promotion based on military success. Regular-path commoners, to a greater extent, were dependent solely upon seniority for their official advancement.

A few other concluding remarks are in order. First, seeking advancement in military posts was probably a greater gamble, for the decisive nature of the performance in military office worked in both directions: It gave some commoners very great advancement; it undoubtedly gave others heavy punishment and downward official mobility for failure. Failure could be quite as decisive as success.

Second, a hypothesis that invites further study is that the prejudice and discrimination directed by examination-path officials against non-examination-path officials were closely related to the *greater bureaucratic advancement* realized by non-examination-path military officials. The function of this widespread scorn for military officials may have been to discourage new candidates for office from taking the military path and eschewing the examination system.

Of all the problems that demand further research, perhaps none is so crucial as that of economic stratification. Let us consider this briefly.

Economic Stratification

We have seen that the general hypothesis of the priority of extra-bureaucratic influences, such as family position, over bureaucratic influences, such as recruitment path taken and seniority accumulated, in determining differences in official advancement, is by no means as well supported by our findings as was expected. In this chapter, hypotheses 11 through 16, all based on the notion of extra-bureaucratic influences, have all failed to be supported by our data. In Chapter VI, we found some support for the hypothesis of "extra-bureaucratic influence," in the sense that Chinese from official families held high posts *longer*, on the average, than did Chinese from commoner families. But in this chapter, even this difference was called into question by the fact that if Chinese from commoner families accumulated the same amount of seniority as Chinese from official families, they tended to have equal advancement. To say the least, then, the predictive power of the hypothesis of "extra-bureaucratic influence" leaves something to be desired.

There is a sizable number of highly mobile officials from commoner families, privileged neither socially nor legally, in our elite sample. The question arises: were they from *economically* privileged families? This question is especially important from the viewpoint of the theory of extra-bureaucratic influences upon advancement. This theory asserts that the stratum position of the family of orientation is ascribed to its individual members, thereby influencing their "life chances" for mobility. We have tried to test the *social and legal* aspects of family stratum position, as they influenced official advancement; another aspect of family stratum position, which we have not yet studied, is economic position. If men from poorer families could attain high office through such *career* sources as the seniority principle and more rapid promotion because of military success, it follows that the theory that family stratum position tends to determine advancement is *less well borne out* than if the commoners' sons with the greatest advancement were, in fact, from *wealthy* commoner families. If the commoners' sons with the greatest advancement were shown to be from wealthier families, it would not be necessary to invoke special *ad hoc* conditions outside the theory, such as the seniority principle and military success. We could assert that a combination of sociolegal and economic factors *within the theory* explains elite mobility.

In principle this would be a valuable analytic step; in fact, the data on the economic stratum position of the families of our sample are so meager that no determinate conclusions are possible. Chang Chung-li found no indication of economic status in 446, or 36 per cent, of his cases (Chang, 1955, p. 227, Table 41), and we find no adequate economic data in the majority of our cases.

Among the 170 officials from Chinese commoner families, we have positive indication of economic position in only 56 cases (24 from poor families; 15 from wealthy families; 17 from poor but scholarly-intellectual families, though not degree-holders). The remaining 114 cases have either no indication or inadequate indication of economic position, although 17 of these officials were from scholarly-intellectual families. In all respects, the number of cases with positive data is too small to allow any conclusive analysis. There are many speculative suggestions for inferences about economic position, but none of these leads has yet proved conclusive enough.

Thus, we shall rest our case with this assertion: There is no positive evidence that the officials in our sample from commoner families typically came from either wealthy or from poor families. This question must be left open. (See Chapter III for a general discussion of economic stratification in the Ch'ing period.)

Processes of Social Mobility

The operation of bureaucratic processes in equalizing the advantages of officials from higher- and lower-strata family backgrounds presupposes that lower-strata individuals have been recruited for a bureaucratic career in the first place. Seniority promotions and promotions for extraordinary performance could be a source of mobility only for those whose initial bureaucratic appointment was a *fait accompli*. We must, therefore, attempt to identify those *pre-career* processes of elite mobility which, in combination with *career* factors, produced the observed amount of mobility in Chinese society.

The first of these pre-career processes of mobility concerns the relationship between the upward mobile individual and his kin group. Barber has shown that the "processes of social mobility in societies where the extended family is predominant differ typically from those in societies where the nuclear family is the . . . predominant type" (1957, pp. 361-66). This suggests that kinship arrangements associated with both high and low degrees of "familism" or kinship solidarity could contribute, as functional alternatives, to processes and amounts of elite mobility. In what ways, then, did the traditional Chinese lineage ("common descent group," "clan") contribute to elite mobility? The relatively high degree of kinship solidarity made it possible and legitimate to *pool* the resources of the extended family in order to assist one or more lineage members in their mobility. Mobility was defined as mobility for a *large* and *extensive* kin group. P'an and Fei (1947) have noted that offspring could be helped by even distant relatives (*ch'in-shu*), including father's patrilineal (*tsung-ch'in*), mother's patrilineal (*wai-ch'in*), and the wife's patrilineal relatives (*ch'i-ch'in*). The lineage, or "common descent group" (*tsu*) was characterized by a feeling of mutual responsibility. To share one's wealth with one's kinsmen, immediate and remote, was highly sanctioned. Since wealth *per se* was not highly valued in the Confucian system, if a wealthy man wanted to have his biography in the local history, one way of achieving this, aside from distinction as an official, writer, or scholar, was to be known for looking after the welfare of near and remote kinsmen (Ho Ping-ti, 1954, pp. 167-68).

Pooling operated as follows. A lineage might include both wealthy and poor branches (*fang*). But the poorer branches could receive financial help from the wealthier branches. There were several institutionalized mechanisms for this, so far was it from being left to chance. Nor did the institutionalization of pooling conflict with the private property which each branch used for its own livelihood. Pooling in no way required the *general* acceptance of socialistic values. Rather, a well-organized lineage had a certain amount of common property set aside from the private property of its individual branch families.[1] The income from this lineage-held property—fields (*i-t'ien*) and estates (*i-chuang*)—was used for ritual, *educational*, and relief purposes, in the common interests of the lineage.[2] Indeed, providing funds for the education of impecunious younger members of the lineage was one of the primary uses of this common income. Much evidence attests to this.[3] This common lineage property (*tsu-ch'an*), which was set aside for education, was referred to as "study fields" (*tu-shu t'ien, hsüeh-t'ien*) and "free school fields" (*i-shu t'ien, i-t'ien*). Income from this property was used not only to support lineage schools but also to pay for the travel and other expenses of those going to compete in the examinations (Sung, 1956, pp. 26-27; Niida, 1952, pp. 11, 67, 158). This common lineage property was the symbol of the unity of the lineage. If a lineage could pool enough resources to get one member into office, he in turn would increase the lineage's common property and thus put the lineage in an even better position. Sacrificial land (*chi-t'ien*), though mainly set aside for ancestor worship, was also used to support those who were poor but ready to take the examinations (Sung, p. 18). Even the government encouraged and helped lineages to set up common lineage property. During Ch'ing times and earlier, tax exemptions were sometimes given to a lineage so that it would have more surplus for its common property. From the point of view of the government, it was said that lineage pooling helped the public morale, prevented crime, etc. (Sung, p. 77). The government rewarded individuals cited by local officials for helping their kinsmen (Sung, p. 78). There were many cases where common lineage property was set up or increased by many small donations from relatives, each of whom had very little surplus, instead of by large contributions from only one or two wealthy members (Sung, pp. 102, 138). One form of literature—Records of Common Lineage Property, Records of Lineage Schools (*I-chuang chi, I-t'ien chi, I-hsüeh chuang chi*)—dealt exclusively with the development of a given lineage's arrangements for pooling its resources for education, examination competition, and the like.[4]

An important problem in connection with pooling as a mobility process in China is how widely distributed this process was. What proportion of Chinese elite mobility was the result of lineage pooling? We cannot answer these questions of magnitude in a satisfactory way. Students disagree; the view I have presented is similar to that of Chang Chung-li, Ho Ping-ti, and some other Chinese scholars. It is typified in Chang's argument (1953, p. 490, *et passim*) that, given the great concentration of income in the elite stratum, the *plowing back* of at least some of this income into the lineages to which the elite individuals belonged, and thereby to the *poorer branches* of their lineages, was an adaptive mechanism for the society as a whole. It served as a device for income redistribution. The philosophical basis for lineage pooling of resources can be traced from the ancient classic, the *Chou Li, The Ritual of the Chou*, down through Fan Chung-yen (989-1052), Ku Yen-wu (1613-82) and others.[5]

This view is challenged as somewhat idealistic by Maurice Freedman. Freedman's view is that "the gentry were not likely to allow kinship rules to interfere with their exercise of power" (1958, p. 67). In theory, all lineage members had equal claims on the property owned corporately by the lineage, but in practice, "access to power and benefits was unequally ascribed. An elite in the lineage wielded much of the power and controlled the distribution of economic and ritual privileges. . . ." (p. 69). This is an empirical question, and only further research can determine the actual extent to which the sons of the poorer branches of a lineage were aided in their mobility-striving by contributions from wealthier branches of the lineage.

Our discussion, up to this point, has assumed that the lineage had some wealth to pool in the first place. However, in numerous cases, it is unlikely that the lineage could raise enough common income for the education of even *one* of its members. As Hu has admitted:

> While, without a doubt, many a poor man's son benefited from . . . the educational assistance derived from the common funds of his group . . . it is the boy from families slightly above the subsistence level up through the upper class who profited most from the system since he could be spared by his family to spend years in studying and thus qualify for the civil examinations. [1948, p. 88.]

The implication here is that, at the subsistence level, even when a youth had the requisite intelligence and motivation, his *labor* could not be forfeited by the family.

Thus, much of the discussion of pooling in the literature simply begs the question. Lineage pooling is not likely to account for the upward mobility of relatively poor commoners. The question remains: how did the commoners' sons in our sample who, *after their official career was under way*, were aided in their mobility by seniority and extraordinary promotion—how did these men become eligible to launch an elite career in the first place?

Non-kin sources of educational subsidies. China provided formal subsidies for education during the Ch'ing period, although again we are unable to determine the magnitude of these subsidies. We know that there were free schools (*she-hsüeh*, *i-hsüeh*, and *i-shu*), although we have no data on the extent to which individuals in our Chinese sample were helped in their pre-career mobility by these institutions. These free schools were established by public funds (*kung-k'uan*) or private capital (*ssu-tzu*) and taught the sons of poor families. They resembled private study halls (*ssu-shu*). Wang (1954, p.

158) asserts that in Ch'ing times these free schools became relatively widespread. Tutors were hired for these schools from among scholars of good repute. Poor students were given stipends (*hsin-shui-kao-huo*).

The case of Wu Hsun is revealing. Wu was a Shantung beggar who died in 1896. Poor and orphaned as a youth, he turned to begging by day and weaving by night. He gradually accumulated money, did not marry or spend lavishly. He loved to help the poor and, since he hated his own illiteracy, he bought land and established free schools (*i-hsüeh*) in four different places, all the while remaining a beggar himself. He is said to have been so sincere that, whenever a teacher or a student became lazy, he got on his knees and begged him to work hard.

There is evidence that some officials from commoner families in our Ch'ing sample established free schools. Shen Chin-ssu, the son of a poor farmer, established a free village school for illiterate children in 1709, while he was serving as magistrate (ECCP, II, 639). Ch'en Hung-mou, 1696-1771, from a commoner family, established more than 650 free schools in Yunnan. In these schools Miao and other border aborigines could become literate, and some even rose to take degrees (ECCP, I, 86-87).

From the historian Hsiao I-shan I am grateful for this suggestion: if some families could afford a tutor, poor children might also be allowed to sit in on the instruction. This would constitute a free school for some pupils.

Solidarity in China was based on geography as well as on kinship. Accordingly, *provincial inns* (*hui-kuan*) in the capital and elsewhere, where men from the same province could congregate and live while away from home, also provided a kind of educational subsidy which influenced mobility processes. These inns gave men of a given province food and lodging, even though at the time they were unable to pay for it, e. g., while they were studying for the metropolitan examinations. In return, when success was theirs, donations for the support of these inns were made so that other fellow provincials might also be helped in their mobility. In general, we may say that subsidizing impecunious students, even though they were not kin, was a highly sanctioned and highly rewarding type of investment in Chinese society. Yang (1957, p. 304) relates a traditional story in which examination candidates were likened to real estate investments by those who had assisted them in their pre-career mobility.

The "Deferred Gratification" Pattern. If the family one is born into has a low stratum position, successful mobility-striving may involve the postponement of gratification of certain desires until the upward mobility has been realized. In American society, for example, while middle-class youth may enter middle-class occupations without sacrificing extracurricular activities in high school, for lower-class youth to enter middle-class occupations it is often necessary that they work after school in high school, etc. The mobility process followed by these lower-class youth who postpone their gratifications is termed the "deferred gratification" pattern (Schneider and Lysgaard, 1953). There is indication that this process operated in Chinese elite mobility. For example, when Li Wen-t'ien, an official in our sample, was fourteen, his father died. This was an economic calamity, and the family fortunes declined. The family depended on the "ten fingers" of the mother from morning till night. Li, to lessen his mother's toil, wanted to abandon study and to take gainful employment. His tutor said, "You have talent and will early be able to reach high office. As to poverty, it is the common lot of scholars." It is clear here that the tutor admonished Li not only to continue to defer his and his mother's gratifications, but also to temporarily take as his reference group scholars, who were poor, rather than officials or others who were wealthy. In this way, one's reference group may help one to adjust to the deferred gratification pattern (cf. Merton, 1957, pp. 225-80).

Throughout our discussion of the processes of mobility in China, the inadequacy of our empirical knowledge has been painfully evident. However, subject to revision in the light of future research, we have argued that the following processes of social mobility operated in Ch'ing China and have accounted for our somewhat unexpected finding that the hypothesis of "extra-bureaucratic influence" is not strongly supported by our data.

1. Pre-career-recruitment mobility processes
   a. Pooling within the kinship system
   b. Free schools
   c. Provincial inns
   d. The "deferred-gratification" pattern
2. Post-recruitment career mobility processes
   a. The leveling of original family background differences by the bureaucratic seniority principle
   b. Bureaucratic promotion independent of the seniority principle, in cases of extraordinary performance

Conclusion

Earlier research on Ch'ing stratification and mobility, although not in complete agreement as to conclusions, tended in general toward the view that differences in official recruitment and advancement were more a result of extra-bureaucratic factors than of formal bureaucratic rules. Thirteen of the sixteen hypotheses we have tested were based on the assumption that this hypothesis of "extra-bureaucratic influence" was valid. The major conclusion we have reached is that, as far as our sample of 572 officials is concerned, this general hypothesis is *not* valid. The majority of our hypotheses which asserted the priority of extra-bureaucratic over bureaucratic influences have not been supported by the data.

Perhaps our most important finding is that, among Chinese officials, seniority tended to *equalize* the chances of advancement for men from official and from commoner families—once they were *in* the bureaucracy. Furthermore, if the seniority rule enhanced the opportunities of some commoners' sons, it also did not retard the advancement of other, more exceptional commoners. The latter commoners' sons did not have to adhere to the seniority principle, but instead had rapid ascent as a result of military successes and the like.

Although officials sought to use their position to advance the interests of their families, the resulting nepotism was thus constrained by the bureaucratic rules of seniority, recommendation, avoidance of kin while serving in office, and mutual responsibility for misdemeanors. This is not to say that an official's commitment to his family ceased to impinge upon his official role. Rather, it took other forms, such as the "squeeze." If an official could not influence his relatives' advancement in obvious ways, he could at least manipulate the perquisites of his position for the needs of his family, for investments in land and pawnshops, and so forth. Many memorials to the throne attest to the frequency of financial corruption among officials, and it was apparently the rare official who did not amass a fortune during his career. Favoring relatives in posts in the capital was usually a dangerous activity; but amassing wealth through posts in the provinces for the use of relatives back home was much more typical, and less easily discoverable.

One other implication of our findings must be noted. Max Weber argued that in societies like China, where officials have the highest social position, they would come mainly from socially and economically privileged strata. He asserted that there would be a "guild-like closure of officialdom typically found in patrimonial and . . . praebendal officialdoms of the past" (Weber, 1946, p. 200; . . .). Our data confirm this: the officials in our sample were recruited disproportionately from the socio-economically privileged strata of Ch'ing China. Weber also expected American elites to exhibit more vertical mobility than Chinese bureaucratic elites. He contrasted the closure of praebendal bureaucracies with the situation in democratic societies where, he felt, the development of a closed status group of officials is prevented, in the interest of a universal accessibility of office (1946, p. 226).

For Weber, the traditional Chinese bureaucracy was an example of the "patrimonial-praebendal" type of administration. The administrative staff was supported by "benefices," that is, allowances in kind or in money from the stores of the emperor, and the appropriation of taxes by this staff. Such a bureaucracy was based on "praebends"; thus the term "patrimonial-praebendal." Weber's astute observations of historical bureaucracies of this type led him to generalize: "In patrimonial administrations, it is common for slaves or freedmen to rise even to the highest positions" (1947, p. 343). He went on to state that in this type of bureaucracy, "it is possible to maintain a *system of promotion on a basis of seniority or of particular objectively determined achievements*" (p. 351, italics mine). There is, then, a marked congruence between our major findings and Weber's theoretical and historical analysis. While the officials *recruited* to the bureaucracy in the first place came mainly from the privileged strata, the officials with the greatest *advancement* in the bureaucracy were as likely to be from commoner families as from official families, as a result of such bureaucratic criteria of promotion as seniority and objectively determined achievements.

CHAPTER 8 SUMMARY, CONCLUSIONS, AND FUTURE RESEARCH

Summary and Implications of Findings

THE FOLLOWING FINDINGS of this study should be of interest to sociologists and to students of Chinese society and mobility during the Ch'ing period.

(1) As to terminology, we have proposed substituting "local elite" for "gentry" because the latter term carries several connotations which, though they apply to England's traditional landed squires, do not apply to *shen-shih*, or degree-holders, or to the local leadership group in the Ch'ing period. "Local elite" can be distinguished from "elite of the realm," i.e., officialdom, the imperial family, and nobility. The term "local elite" is preferable to "gentry" because it is more neutral, and can be defined by the particular social, economic, intellectual, and other characteristics of the leadership group in a given society.

(2) Because a large number of the Manchus in our sample

were sons or other descendents of the imperial family, nobility, tribal chieftains, and higher, hereditary officials, they rose higher in the bureaucracy and held high-rank posts longer than both Chinese from official-elite families and Chinese from commoner families in our sample.

(3) Of those officials who received degrees in the examination system, the proportion from Chines official-family backgrounds was far greater than the proportion of official families in the total population of China. That the examination system had definite limitations as a mobility channel for commoners is also shown by the fact that Chinese from official families held high-rank posts longer *without* taking the "regular path" (*cheng-t'u*), i.e., the examinations, than Chinese commoners' sons, even though they did take the "regular path."

(4) In our sample, Chinese from official families did not tend to receive the *chin-shih* degree much earlier in life than Chinese from commoner families. This suggests either that these commoner's sons were more talented than the sons of officials or that their families had other advantages on which we have no data, and that these advantages allowed the commoners' sons to begin to prepare for the examinations at an early age.

(5) Using Kracke's measure of the "strength" of official-family tradition, we found, for our sample, that the more officials there had been among one's father, grandfather, and great-grandfather, the longer one held posts in the highest ranks of the bureaucracy.

(6) Whether we measure mobility in relation to a threefold division of family background—Manchu, Chinese official-elite, and Chinese commoner—or in relation to Kracke's "strength" variable—prevalent, strong, minor, and none—we find in our sample that commoners' sons were about as successful as officials' sons in *reaching* high-rank posts, once they were in office, but not as successful in *holding* these high-rank

posts for a long time, unless they had the same amount of seniority as the sons of official families (see 9 below).

(7) The mobility patterns over a four-generation period of the officials in our sample and of their fathers, grandfathers and great-grandfathers are in accordance with the theory of the circulation of elites. In 51 per cent of the cases only one generation of the family was in office; in 32 per cent of the cases, two of the four generations of a family were officials; in 13 per cent of the cases, three generations were officials; and in only 4 per cent of the cases were all four generations in a family officials. Elite families rose and fell.

(8) Upward mobility into officialdom was most common during the early Ch'ing, somewhat less in late Ch'ing, and least frequent during the middle period of the Ch'ing. The prevalence of upward mobility varied with the phases of the "dynastic cycle."

(9) Finally, what is perhaps the most significant finding of this study: although Chinese from official families held posts in the high ranks *longer* than Chinese from commoner families, this difference in incumbency was not as great as would be expected, on the basis of family background differences. In this sense, we may say that commoners' sons had considerable upward mobility. What explains this? The main hurdle for a commoner's son was to get into the bureaucracy in the first place, for, as we have stated, the tiny fraction of the population who were degree-holders and officials were greatly overrepresented numerically in the bureaucracy, while the mass of the population was greatly underrepresented. (This finding is similar to Chang Chung-li's point that it was more difficult to move from commoner to "lower gentry" than to move from lower to "upper gentry.") The key to the upward mobility of our commoners appears to be that once an individual had succeeded in entering the bureaucracy, norms began to operate that tended to *equalize* the mobility chances of men from official and from commoner families. That is, although the

vast majority of commoners' sons never got official appointment, those commoners' sons who did enter office were able to achieve almost as great advancement as the sons of official families. Commoners who did not take the examinations (*K'o-t'u*) avoided the time-consuming preparation for these competitions. In this way, they began their official career at a younger age and thus built up more seniority than the sons of official families who took the "examination path" and who did not begin their official career until later in life. We have shown that officials with the same amount of seniority—the same number of years in the bureaucracy—tended to rise to posts in the same rank, and to occupy those posts for about the same length of time *regardless* of whether they came from official or from commoner families.

We feel that this finding argues against the often-asserted notion that nepotism was rampant in the Chinese bureaucracy. Whatever the extent of family favoritism in Chinese business or other spheres, we feel that advancement in the Ch'ing bureaucracy was influenced by the seniority principle, which offset the operation of family favoritism.

A second mechanism by which non-examination-path commoners' sons in our sample attained high office was by having a career in the *military* bureaucracy, especially if their careers coincided with the great Manchu-Ming struggle or with the Taiping rebellion. We have seen that if a military official scored a victory in these crucial campaigns, he tended to be rapidly promoted, whether or not he was the son of an official family. For our purposes, the main criterion of upward mobility was movement into posts in higher ranks of the bureaucracy; whether their posts were civil or military was a less important consideration.

It is hoped that, in the future, students of Chinese social mobility will regard such questions as the amount of mobility, the rates of mobility for commoners' sons as opposed to officials' sons, the operation of nepotism as opposed to seniority and impartial bureaucratic rules, and the rapidity of promotions for non-degree-holding military officials, as research problems which are not settled issues (as they have been treated at times) but, instead, as very much open.

Conclusion

Families in China, as elsewhere, jealousy guard the rights and privileges attached to their stratum position against encroachment and diminution. Unless adaptive structures develop, elite positions tend to be monopolized from generation to generation by a small, privileged minority of the population. One important adaptive structure which developed in China was the bureaucratization of the governmental administration. Insofar as an individual's mobility chances became determined by the rules of this bureaucracy, the ascriptive tendencies of the family were undercut. The Chinese bureaucracy, like any bureaucracy, had as its functional prerequisites the maintenance of certain standards of administrative performance and the handling of new problems. These pre-requisites could not have been met had nepotism been allowed to override the bureaucratic rules of seniority and merit. This is clearly the major implication of our findings. On the other hand, the bureaucracy was part of a more inclusive system, the society, where universalistic and other bureaucratic rules were much less operative. The bureaucratized segment was not able to prevent the conferring of advantages on a kinship basis, *before* adult occupational recruitment took place, as well as at other points in the system. The result was that, as in other societies, the elite were recruited disproportionately from the 2 per cent of the population in the elite stratum, rather than from the 98 per cent of the population in the below-elite, or commoner, stratum.

Future Research

It is well to examine some of the possible methodological weaknesses of the present study. The major fault with our sample of 572 officials drawn from the *Eminent Chinese of the Ch'ing Period* is that this source was not meant to provide a statistical sample from which generalizations could be made to a larger, determinate population. The ECCP represents the informed judgment of specialists as to what individuals had "left marks on Chinese society and had obviously *made* history." In this sense the officials in our sample are highly unrepresentative of the large mass of Ch'ing officials whose common attitude was "never mind seeking merit, but seek to avoid committing transgression (*pu ch'iu yu kung, tan ch'iu wu kuo.*")

Since our conclusions stem from an achievement-based sample, it will be necessary in future research to test these conclusions with more truly random, representative samples, drawn from all Ch'ing officialdom—high and low, outstanding and mediocre. The best source for this future research is the Official Directories titled *T'ung-kuan lu*, for various years and provinces. These contain information on family background, education, and method of entering the bureaucracy, and on subsequent careers for officials serving in a given province in a given year. The writer has already undertaken the analysis of several of these directories, drawn from the late eighteenth and nineteenth centuries. If the results of this further study support the present findings, we shall have a much firmer basis for asserting that bureaucratic factors such as seniority were more important than extra-bureaucratic factors such as family background, in determining official advancement under the Empire. On the other hand, future research may show that extra-bureaucratic determinants were *more* significant than the formal, impersonal bureaucratic rules specified in the several editions of the *Ta-Ch'ing hui-tien* and elsewhere. In that event, we shall have a clearer knowledge of the limitations of sources like *Eminent Chinese of the Ch'ing Period* for the study of social mobility and bureaucratic advancement. Knowing this is especially relevant in view of the ongoing or anticipated compilations of similar large-scale biographical dictionaries for the post-1912 and Ming periods.

A second major task for future research is the comparative analysis of social mobility. The results of a number of mobility studies made in a variety of countries and periods can be compared by the use of a method developed by Goldhamer and by Rogoff (1953). This method helps to distinguish between the occupational mobility which is due to (*a*) differences in the occupational structure of societies and (*b*) that which occurs independently of these inter-societal differences in occupational structure. Societies differ in their degree of industrialization and, correlatively, in their demand for elite skills. This means that the elite occupations—governmental decision-making, the professions, etc.—may constitute different proportions of the total working force in different societies or at different periods in time. The Rogoff method enables us to hold constant the occupational structure—e.g., the proportion of the working force at the elite level—and to see if there remain differences in the amount of mobility within this constant occupational demand structure. If differences do persist, they can be attributed to differences between the societies in individuals' freedom to move up and down occupationally within the limits set by the demand factor.

The significance of a given amount of elite mobility, then, differs according to whether it is the product of an increased proportion of elite jobs in the society or whether it represents opportunities for upward mobility independent of an increase in the number of elite openings. A society may become more "open" in two ways—either through a "demand" factor or through what can be called "social distance" factors. The latter category is residual, for it includes all factors *other than* changes in the occupational opportunity structure which influence the amount of mobility. This residual category of "social distance" factors could include increased access to educational facilities, reduction in discriminatory practices in hiring, and so forth (Rogoff, p. 14).

In sum, ". . . we wish to isolate an expression for social distance mobility alone, in which variation in the demand factor is ruled out for all the expressions that we compare. Or stated otherwise, we wish to compare amounts of mobility between various positions for a fixed unit of demand. This can be accomplished very simply by *defining social distance mobility as total mobility divided by the demand factor*" (Rogoff, p. 31).

One illustration of the way Rogoff's formula (Rogoff, pp. 31-32) could be adapted to comparative analysis is as follows. Let us suppose our data showed that the occupations we classified as "elite" constituted 2 per cent and 4 per cent of the working force of Ch'ing China and twentieth-century America, respectively. The elite demand would be twice as great in America as in Chinese society. Suppose, further, that various elite mobility studies showed that 60 per cent of the American elite had fathers in below-elite occupations. The comparable figure for China, let us say, is 30 per cent. Thus, while the amount of mobility at the elite level was twice as great in American as in Chinese society (60 per cent *vs.* 30 per cent), since the elite demand is also twice as great in American society (4 per cent *vs.* 2 per cent), it would follow that the two societies had an *equal amount* of "social distance" mobility. It will be difficult to get valid and reliable data on these variables for China and some other societies, and the problem of the definition and operationalization of the concept of "the elite" in a comparative framework is far from solved. Nevertheless, the contributions this kind of research could make to our knowledge make it well worth the effort. To cite again the case of Chinese-American societal comparisons, if research showed that virtually all the American elite mobility which has occurred can be accounted for by the increased size of the elite, important implications could be derived. One of these might be that there are *functional alternatives* to the presumably American mobility processes of "going it alone," weakening kin ties, and the like. In the case of China, such alternative processes as clan pooling of resources, provincial inns, etc., would take on greater significance as processes making for what Rogoff calls "social distance" mobility.

Through such research on the sources of "openness" in societies—occupational demand factors versus processes making for "openness" within a relatively constant occupational structure—a more adequate theory of comparative stratification and mobility could be developed.

APPENDIX I 572 OFFICIALS IN *EMINENT CHINESE OF THE CH'ING PERIOD*, CLASSIFIED BY MANCHU, CHINESE OFFICIAL, OR CHINESE COMMONER FAMILY BACKGROUND

1. Manchus:

A-k'o-tun
A-kuei
Asitan
Bahai
Bolo
Ch'ang-ning
Chao Hui
Chi-er-hang-a
Chih-jui
Ch'i-shan
Ch'i-ying
Ch'ung-hou
Ch'ung-shih
Ebilun
Eidu
E-le-teng-pao
Enggeder
Fiongdon
Fiyanggu
Fu-ch'ang-an
Fu-ch'ing
Fu-heng
Fu-k-'ang-an
Fu-lung-an
Funinggan
Furdan
Fu-te
Gali
Giyesu
Gubadai
Hai-lan-ch'a
Hesu
Ho Lin
Ho-shen
Hurhan
I-ching
I-hsin
I-huan
I-hui

I-liang
I-li-pu
Ingguldai
I-shan
I-tsung
Jalangga
Jangtai
Jidu
Jirgalang
Jung-lu
Kangguri
Kuan-wen
K'uei-hsu
Kuei-liang
Labu
Langtan
Lekedehun
Le-pao
Lin-ch'ing
Lungkodo
Maci
Mandahai
Manggultai
Maska
Mien-k'ai
Minggadari
Mingju
Ming-jui
Ming-liang
Mishan
Mu-chang-a
Na-yen-ch'eng
Nikan, died 1652
Nikan, died 1660
Oboi
O-er-t'ai
Omutu
Pao-t'ing
Pengcun
Sabsu
Sahaliyen
Sarhuda
Seng-ko-lun-ch'in
Sheng-yü
Shu-ho-te
Singde
Songgotu
Sunu
Su-shun
T'a-ch'i-pu
Te-hsing-a
Te-leng-t'ai
Te-pei
T'ieh-pao
Tsai-chu'üan
Tuan-fang
Tuhai
Tulisen
T'ung Kuo-ch'i
T'ung Kuo-kang
T'ung Kuo-wei
T'ung T'u-lai
T'ung Yang-chen
Ubai
Wasan
Wen-ch'ing
Wen-hsiang
Yangguri
Yeksu
Yen-hsin
Yin-chi-shan
Yin-hsiang
Ying-ho
Yolo
Yoto
Yü-ch'ien
Yung-ch'eng
Yung-hsüan

2. Chinese Official and Elite Families:[1]

Bandi
Cha Li
Cha Shen-hsing
Ch'a Ssu-t'ing
Chang Chao
Chang Chih-tung
Chang Chih-wan
Chang Ch'üan
Chang Hsüeh-ch'eng
Chang Huang-yen
Chang Kuang-ssu
Ch'ang Ling
Chang P'ei-lun
Chang Po-hsing
Chang T'ing-shu
Chang T'ing-yü
Chang Wei-p'ing
Chang Wen-t'ao
Chang Ying
Chang Yü-shu
Chao Chih-hsin
Chao Huai-yü
Chao Liang-tung
Chao Shen-ch'iao
Ch'en Kuo-jui
Ch'en P'eng-nien
Ch'en Shih-kuan

[1] Including six Mongols.

Ch'en Shou-ch'i
Ch'en T'ing-ching
Ch'en Tzu-chuang
Ch'en Tzu-lung
Ch'en Wei-sung
Cheng Chen
Cheng Ch'eng-kung
Cheng Chih-lung
Cheng Ching
Cheng Hung-k'uei
Ch'eng Chin-fang
Ch'eng En-tse
Ch'eng K'o-kung
Chi Chen-i
Chi Tseng-yün
Chi Yün
Ch'i Chün-tsao
Ch'i Piao-chia
Ch'i Yün-shih
Chiang Ch'en-ying
Chiang Liang-ch'i
Chiang T'ing-hsi
Chiao Hung
Ch'ien Ch'en-ch'ün
Ch'ien Ch'i
Ch'ien I-chi
Ch'ien Ta-hsin
Ch'ien T'ai-chi
Ch'ien T'ang
Ch'ien Tien
Ch'ien Tsai
Ch'ien Wei-ch'eng
Chin Chien
Chin Fu
Ch'in Hui-t'ien
Ch'iu Feng-chia
Ch'iu Yüeh-hsiu
Ch'ou Chao-ao
Chu Chien
Chu Kuei
Chu Kuei-chen
Chu I-tsun
Ch'ü Shih-ssu
Chu Yün
Chuang Ts'un-yü
Ch'ung-ch'i
Fa Jo-chen
Fa-shih-shan
Fan Ch'eng-mo
Fan Ching-wen
Fan Wen-ch'eng
Fang I-chih
Fang Kuan-ch'eng
Fang Pao
Feng Ch'üan
Fu Wei-lin
Hao Shuo
Hao Yü
Ho Ch'ang-ling
Ho Ch'iu-t'ao
Ho Ch'o
Ho Shao-chi
Ho T'eng-chiao
Hou T'ung-tseng
Hsiao Yung-tsao
Hsieh Chi-shih
Hsieh Sheng
Hsü Chi-yü
Hsü Ch'ien-hsüeh
Hsü Ching-ch'eng
Hsü Ch'iu
Hsü Kuang-ch'i
Hsü Kuang-chin
Hsü Sung
Hsü Tzu
Hsü Yüan-wen
Hsüeh Fu-ch'eng
Hu Hsü
Hu Lin-i
Huang Ching-jen
Huang Fang-shih
Huang Fang-t'ai
Huang P'eng-nien
Huang Shao-chi
Huang Shu-lin
Huang T'i-fang
Huang T'ing-kuei
Huang tsun-hsien
Huang Tsung-hsi
Huang Yü-chi
Hui Shih-ch'i
Hung Chün
Hung Liang-chi
Juan Ta-ch'eng
Juan Yüan
Kao Chin
Kao Pin
Keng Chi-mao
Keng Ching-chung
Ku K'uei-kuang
Kung Tzu-chen
K'ung Kuang-sen
K'ung Shang-jen
Kuo Shang-hsien
Lang T'ing-chi
Lang T'ing-tso
Li Chao-lo
Li Ch'eng-liang
Li Ch'ing
Li Hsing-yüan
Li Hung-chang
Li Hung-tsao
Li Shih-yao
Li Shu-ch'ang
Li Shuai-t'ai
Li T'ang-chieh
Li T'iao-yüan
Li T'ien-ching
Li T'ien-fu
Li T'ing-i
Li Tsung-wan
Li Tz'u-ming
Li Wei

Li Yüan-tu
Liang Chang-chü
Liang Kuo-chih
Liang Shih-cheng
Liang T'ung-shu
Lin Chi
Lin Tse-hsü
Liu Feng-lu
Liu Hsi-hai
Liu K'un-i
Liu Lun
Liu Pao-nan
Liu T'ai-kung
Liu T'ing
Liu Tsung-chou
Liu T'ung-hsün
Liu Yung
Lu Chien-tseng
Lu Hsi-hsiung
Lu Lung-chi
Lu Wen-ch'ao
Lu Fei-ch'ih
Ma Hsin-i
Ma Hsiung-chen
Ma Kuo-han
Ma Wen-lung
Mei Ku-ch'eng
Meng Ch'iao-fang
Mi Wan-chung
Ni Yüan-lu
Nien Keng-yao
Niu Yün-chen
P'an Lei
P'an Shih-en
P'an Tsu-yin
P'eng P'eng
P'eng Sun-yü
P'eng Ting-ch'iu
P'eng Yü-lin
P'eng Yün-chang
Pien Yung-yü
Po Huang
Shang Chih-hsiao
Shang Chih-hsin
Shang K'o-hsi
Shao Chin-han
Shen T'ing-fang
Shih I-chih
Shih K'o-fa
Shih Lang
Shih Shih-lun
Shih Shih-p'iao
Sun Chia-kan
Sun Hsing-yen
Sun Shen-hsing
Sun Ssu-k'o
Sun Yen-ling
Sun Yü-t'ing
Sung Lao
Sung Wan
Sung Ying-hsing
Sung-yün
Tai Ming-shih
T'an Y'ing
T'ang Chiung
T'ang Hsien-tsu
T'ang Pin
T'ao Chu
Teng T'ing-chen
T'ien Wen
T'ien Wen-ching
Ting Pao-chen
Ts'ai Hsin
Ts'ai Yü-jung
Ts'ao Chen-yung
Ts'ao Yin
Ts'en Yü-ying
Tseng Chi-tse
Tseng Kuo-ch'üan
Tseng Kuo-fan
Tso Tsung-t'ang
Ts'ui Shu
Tu Li-te
Tu Shou-t'ien
Tung Kao
Tung Pang-ta
Wan Ching
Wan Yen
Wang An-kuo
Wang Chien
Wang Ch'ung-chien
Wang Hsi
Wang Hsiang-ch'ien
Wang Hsiang-chin
Wang Hsü-ling
Wang Hua-chen
Wang Hui-tsu
Wang Hung-hsü
Wang I-jung
Wang Ming-sheng
Wang Nien-sun
Wang Shan
Wang Shih-chen
Wang Shih-min
Wang Yin-chih
Wang Yüan-ch'i
Wei Hsiang-shu
Wei I-chieh
Wei Yüan
Weng Hsin-ts'un
Weng Shu-yüan
Weng T'ung-ho
Wo-jen
Wu Ju-lun
Wu K'o-tu
Wu San-kuei
Wu Ta-ch'eng
Wu Wei-yeh
Yang Chieh
Yang I-tseng
Yang Kuang-hsien
Yang T'ing-yün
Yang Wen-ts'ung

Yao Nai
Yeh Fang-ai
Yeh Ming-ch'en
Yeh Ying-liu
Yin Chia-ch'üan
Yü Ch'eng-lung (b. 1617)
Yü Ch'eng-lung (b. 1638)
Yü Min-chung
Yu T'ung
Yü Yüeh
Yüan Ch'ang
Yüan Shih-k'ai
Yüeh Chung-ch'i
Yün Ching

3. Chinese Commoner Families:[2]

Ch'ai Ta-chi
Chang Ch'i
Chang Hui-yen
Chang Ming-chen
Chang P'eng-ko
Chang Ts'un-jen
Chang Yin-huan
Chang Yung
Chao Chih-ch'ien
Chao I
Chao Shih-lin
Ch'en Chao-lun
Ch'en Ch'i-yü
Ch'en Hung-mou
Ch'en Meng-lei
Ch'en Ming-hsia
Ch'en Ta-shou
Ch'en Wen-shu
Cheng Hsieh
Ch'eng Hsüeh-ch'i
Ch'i Shao-nan
Chiang Chung-yüan
Chiang Hsiang
Chiang Shih-ch-üan
Chiang Yüeh-kuang
Ch'ien Ch'ien-i
Ch'ien Feng
Chin Chih-chün
Chin Pao
Chin Sheng-huan
Ch'in Liang-yü
Chou Liang-kung
Chou Yung-nien
Chu Chih-hsi
Chu Kuo-chen
Chu Li
Chu Shih
Fang Tsung-ch'eng
Feng Kuei-fen
Feng P'u
Feng Teng-fu
Feng Tzu-ts'ai
Fu I
Fu I-chien
Ha Yuan-sheng
Han T'an
Hang Shih-chün
Hao I-hsing
Ho Kuo-tsung
Hsiang Jung
Hsiao Ch'i-chiang
Hsiung T'ing-pi
Hsiung Tz'u-li
Huang Chi
Huang Tao-chou
Huang Te-kung
Huang Wu
Hung Ch'eng-ch'ou
I Pi
Jung Hung
Kao Chieh
Kao Shih-ch'i
Keng Chung-ming
Ku Ying-t'ai
Kung Ting-tzu
Kung Yu-te
Kuo Hsiu
Kuo Sung-tao
Lan Ting-yüan
Li Ch'ang-keng
Li Ch'eng-tung
Li Chih-tsao
Li Fu
Li Hsü-pin
Li Ju-chen
Li Kuang-ti
Li Shan-lan
Li Tu-no
Li Wen-t'ien
Li Yung-fang
Liang T'ing-nan
Ling T'ing-k'an
Liu Ch'ang-yu
Liu Jui-fen
Liu Liang-tso
Liu Ming-ch'uan
Liu Tse-ch'ing

[2] Including some Mohammedans.

Lo Ping-chang
Lo Shih-lin
Lo Tse-nan
Lu Hsin-yüan
Lü Kung
Ma Shih-ying
Ma Su
Ma Te-kung
Man Kuei
Mao Ch'i-ling
Meng Ch'ao-jan
Ning Wan-wo
Pao Ch'ao
Pi Kung-ch'en
Pi Yüan
Shao I-ch'en
Shen Ch'in-han
Shen Chin-ssu
Shen Pao-chen
Shen Te-ch'ien
Shih Jun-chang
Shih Yün-yü
Sun Ch'eng-tse
Sun Ch'eng-tsung
Sun Chia-nai
Sun Shih-i
Sun Yüan-hua
Sung Ch'ing
Sung Ch'üan
Tai Chen
Tai Hsi
Tai Tun-yüan
T'ang Chin-chao
T'ien Hsiung
Ting Jih-ch'ang
Ting K'uei-ch'u
Ting Yen
Ts'ao Jung
Tseng Ching
Tso Liang-yü
Tso Mou-ti
Tsu Ta-shou
Tu Chen
Tuan Yu-ts'ai
Tung Ch'i-ch'ang
Tung Hsün
Wang Ch'ang
Wang Cheng
Wang Chi
Wang Ch'i-shu
Wang Chih-ts'ai
Wang Ch'ing-yün
Wang Fu-ch'en
Wang Tsai-chin
Wang Wan
Wang Wen-chih
Wang Yung-chi
Wen T'ing-shih
Wen Fang-kang
Wu Cheng-chih
Wu Ch'i
Wu Chien-chang
Wu Hsi-ch'i
Wu Jen-ch'en
Wu Jung-kuang
Yang Fang
Yang Hao
Yang Lien
Yang Su-yün
Yang Yü-ch'un
Yao Ch'i-sheng
Yao Wen-t'ien
Yen Ch'ang-ming
Yen K'o-chün
Yü Chi
Yü Chih-ting
Yüan Chia-san
Yüan Chung-huan
Yüan Chi-hsien
Yüan Mei
Yüan Ying-t'ai

APPENDIX II SUPPLEMENT TO FAMILY BACKGROUND DATA FOR THE CHINESE SAMPLE

THE FOLLOWING respondents in the Chinese sample were classified differently from the indication in the *Eminent Chinese of the Ch'ing Period (1644-1912)* regarding family background. First, the ECCP had no mention at all of the following officials' social origins; Chinese sources showed their families to have been in the government bureaucracy. Though most of these men's families had produced only low-ranking officials, there are some notable cases of omissions in the ECCP of high-ranking official-family background. Also, it must be kept in mind that, by any standards, the position of even low officials in Chinese society was highly significant in relation to the mass of the population.

Name and Family Background Data:

1. Chang Chao: Father was a Department Director (*lang-chung*), 5A rank, in the Board of Punishments in Peking (*Lou hsien chih*, 26/1a).

2. Chang Ch'üan: Father was a *chin-shih* and official (*ta-ssu-ma*) (*Ch'in-shui hsien-chih*, 8/12a).

3. Chang Po-hsing: Father was an Assistant Department Magistrate (*chou-ssu-ma*), 6B rank. His great-grandfather and grandfather were licentiates and local students (*ling-shan-sheng* and *i-yang-sheng*) (*Pei Chuan Chi*, 17/1a).

4. Chang Ying: Paternal uncle held 2B rank post (*Ch'ing-tai cheng-hsien lei-pien*.)[1]

5. Chao Liang-tung: Father was a Lieutenant-Colonel, 3B rank (*Pei Chuan Chi*, 14/19a).

6. Ch'en Tzu-lung: Father was a *chin-shih* and official (*Sung-chiang fu-chih*, 55/15b).

7. Chi Yün: Father was a *chü-jen* and official. Wang Lan-yin, "Chi Hsiao-lan hsien-sheng nien-p'u" in *Shih-Ta Yüeh-k'an*, I, No. 6 (1933).

8. Ch'i Yün-shih: Family was influential in Shansi (*Kuo-ch'ao ch'i-hsien lei-cheng*,[2] 132/3a). Ch'i's father was a *sheng-yüan* and held an 8A rank post of District Director of Studies (*chiao-yü*) (CTCHLP).

9. Ch'ien Wei-ch'eng: Grandfather held a 7B rank post (CTCHLP).

10. Fu Wei-lin: Father was a *chin-shih* who rose to a very high post of 1B rank (CTCHLP).

11. Gubadai: Father held hereditary title of *Ch'ing-ch'e-tu-wei*, 6B rank hereditary noble, and grandfather was a Captain (*tso-ling*) of the 4A rank (KCCHLC, 51/36a).

12. Ho Teng-chiao: Father was a senior licentiate and 8A rank official, Department Director of Studies (*Li-p'ing fu-chih*).

13. Hsü Sung: Father was an official in Peking (*Hsü Pei Chuan Chi*, 78/1a).

14. Hsü Yüan-wen: Great-grandfather was a *chin-shih* and 3B rank official, *T'ai-p'u-ch'ing-ying-p'ing*, and his grandfather and father were senior licentiates (CTCHLP and KCCHLC, 8/16a).

15. Huang Shu-lin: Grandfather was a 6B rank official; father, a District Director of Studies, 8B rank (KCCHLC, 64/4b).

16. Hung Liang-ch'i: Great-grandfather was a Prefect, 4B rank. Grandfather was a 6B rank official. Father was a *chien-sheng* in the Kuo Tzu Chien (KCCHLC, 132/21a).

17. Li T'ien-fu: Father held the hereditary post in First Class Transport Station, 4A rank, and was also a licentiate (*Pei Chuan Chi*, 13/1a).

18. Liu Lun: Great-great-grandfather and great-grandfather were

[1] Hereafter cited as CTCHLP.

[2] Hereafter cited as KCCHLC.

officials. Grandfather was a *chü-jen*. Father was a student (KCCHLC, 26/29a).

19. Ma Hsin-i: Great-grandfather and father were District officials. Some of his immediate ancestors were degree-holders and local students (*Ma Tuan-min-kung nien-p'u*).

20. Mao Wen-lung: Maternal uncle was a 6B rank official in the Board of Punishments in Peking. This uncle introduced him to a Brigade-General, and he secured the commissioned rank of *ch'ien-tsung* (Lieutenant), 6B rank (*Hang-chou fu-chih*, 1922, 128/23b).

21. Meng Ch'iao-fang: Father was a Brigade-General and the family had for nine generations held the rank of *yung-p'ing-wei* (KCCHLC, 149/14b and *Ch'ing Shih Kao*, 243/7a).

22. P'an Lei: Great-grandfather rose to 5B rank after taking a *chin-shih* (KCCHLC, 118/16a).

23. P'an Shih-en: Great-grandfather, grandfather, and father were all low officials (*Hsü Pei Chuan Chi*, 3/10b).

24. P'eng P'eng: Great-grandfather was a Senior Secretary in one of the Six Boards. Grandfather was a magistrate, 7B rank (KCCHLC, 157/23b).

25. Tai Ming-shih: Grandfather was an official in Kiangsi (*Pei Chuan Chi Pu*, 8/6b).

26. T'ang Hsien-tsu: Ancestors within four generations were senior licentiates and officials (*Pei Chuan Chi*, 82/5a).

27. Tu Li-te: An ancestor in the early 15th century had a 5A hereditary rank (*Pei Chuan Chi*, 7/16a).

28. Wang Ch'ung-chien: Foster father was an official (*Wang Wen-ching-kung tzu-chuan nien-p'u*).

29. Wang Hua-chen: Father was an official (*Chu-cheng hsien-chih*, 32/1b).

30. Wang Shu-yüan: Great-grandfather was a licentiate. Grandfather was a *chin-shih* and Hu-Kuang Governor, 2B rank. Father was a *chien-sheng* in the Kuo Tzu Chien (KCCHLC, 59/1a and CTCHLP).

31. Wu K'o-tu: Grandfather was a senior licentiate by imperial favor (*en-kung-sheng*) and District Director of Studies (*chiao-yü*), 8A rank (*Hsü Pei Chuan Chi*, 54/25b).

32. Yü Ch'eng-lung (1638-1700): An ancestor and father were officials (KCCHLC, 158/1a).

Second, the ECCP had some reference to the families of the following men, but the Chinese sources indicated that their stratum position was higher than the ECCP revealed. For example, where the ECCP stated only that the ancestors were "scholars and teachers," the Chinese sources showed that there had also been degree-holders or even officials.

Name and Family Background Data:

1. Ch'en P'eng-nien: From sixth generation ancestor to his grandfather were all licentiates; grandfather a *chü-jen* (KCCHLC, 164/11b).

2. Cheng Chen: His uncle, who was his tutor, was an official (*Ch'ing-tai Kweichow Ming-hsien hsiang-chuan*, 52-69).

3. Ch'eng Chin-fang: Father, though from a salt merchant family, was a *chih-yen-ts'e*, acting as an agent for officials in the registry and administration of salt consumption (KCCHLC, 130/32a; cf. *Yen-cheng tzu-tien* [Salt Administration Dictionary] for definition of *Yen-ts'e*; cf. also Yang Lien-sheng's review of Wittfogel and Feng, in *Harvard Journal of Asiatic Studies*, XIII [1950], 219).

4. Chi Ch'en-i: Father was an official in the Board of Civil Service (*T'ai-hsing hsien-chih*, 20/21b).

5. Liang Shih-cheng: Father was an expectant District Director of Studies (*Hsien shun-tao*), 8B rank (KCCHLC, 23/1a).

6. Shen T'ing-fang: Maternal grandfather was a *chin-shih* and had a 3A sinecure post in Peking (KCCHLC, 177/31a).

7. T'ao Chu: Father was a senior licentiate (*Jen-ming ta tzu-tien*).

8. Wang An-kuo: Grandfather and father were senior licentiates (CTCHLP; KCCHLC, 76/32a; *Pei Chuan Chi*, 29/11a).

9. Wang Yüan-ch'i: Grandfather was a 4B rank official (KCCHLC, 56/9a).

10. Wei Hsiang-shu: Father was an Archivist (*chu-pu*) of 7A rank (KCCHLC, 44/1a).

11. Wu Ju-lun: Grandfather was a district student. Father was a senior licentiate (*Hui-shih t'ung-nien chih-lu*, 1865; *Hsü Pei Chuan Chi*, 81/15a).

12. Wu Ta-cheng: Great-grandfather, grandfather, and father were students at the Kuo Tzu Chien and Hanlin bachelors. Great-grandfather was also a Law Secretary (*Pu Cheng Ssu li-wen*), 6B rank,

in the Provincial Governor's Office (*Hui-shih t'ung-nien chih-lu*, 1868).

It was also necessary to check the ECCP against the Chinese sources for bureaucratic career data. In many instances, the career *began* at an earlier date than listed in the ECCP. For example, the ECCP lists, as Li Ch'ing's first office, that of censor in Peking, 1638-40. The KCCHLC (474/47) states that Li was in office as early as 1631. His career was therefore longer. Similarly, the ECCP implies that Hu Hsü held his first office in 1714; KCCHLC (71/28a) shows that he was a local educational official (*chiao-yü*) in An-yang before this. These additional data add to the reliability and validity of our measurement of length of career.

APPENDIX III THE FORMAL HIERARCHY OF THE CH'ING BUREAUCRACY

WHAT WAS the nature of the formal hierarchy of the civil and military bureaucracy of the Ch'ing dynasty, within which our sample individuals experienced their elite mobility? This problem is all the more vital because the *rank* or grade of the bureaucratic offices reached and held by our sample individuals is one of our major methods of *measuring* our dependent variable, elite mobility. In order that these ranks and the corresponding offices and organizations in the bureaucracy may be somewhat more explicit, the following outline is presented.

What follows is an outline of the most important organizations and offices of the nine-rank (*chiu-p'in*) hierarchy of the Chinese governmental bureaucracy during the Ch'ing period.[1]

In the Ch'ing period, bureaucratic offices (*chih*) were classified in the following ways: first, as to location of appointment—inside the capital and outside the capital; second, as to whether the post was

[1] Sinologists will recognize our attempt as a modest version of what des Rotours did for the T'ang period. Robert des Rotours, *Traite des fonctionnaires et traite de l'armée, traduits de la nouvelle histoire des T'ang*, 2 vols. (Leyden: E. J. Brill, 1947), chaps. 46-50.

military or civil; third, as to ethnic factors—some posts were open only to Manchus or Mongols, others were for a specified number of Chinese and Manchus, etc. Finally, offices were classified as to rank. Each of the nine ranks—*chih-p'in*, substantive ranks (as opposed to *lu-chih*, honorary ranks)—had two levels (*cheng* and *tsung*), and below these eighteen levels was one more level, the "unclassed" (*wei-ju-liu*), making nineteen levels in all. Our outline concentrates upon the top fourteen levels, because almost all the officials in our sample held posts in these levels, rather than in the lowest five levels.

Our outline is a collation of several Chinese sources on the official system. This collation was made necessary by the fact that the official hierarchy changed somewhat over the three-century period from 1600 to 1900. Thus, the best English-language source, Brunnert and Hagelstrom's *Present Day Political Organization of China*, published in 1912, best represents the formal structure at the very end of the Ch'ing dynasty, when many bureaucratic reforms appeared; it must be supplemented by other, Chinese sources for a reliable view of the structure at earlier periods. For this, we compared the *Huang-ch'ao T'ung-tien* and the *Huang-ch'ao wen-hsien t'ung k'ao*, covering the period from early Ch'ing to 1785, with the 1848 edition of the *Ta-Ch'ing chin-shen ch'üan-shu*, the *Ta-Ch'ing Chung-shu pei-lan*, and the *Huang-ch'ao hsü wen-hsien t'ung-k'ao*, all covering the period of the last half of the Ch'ing dynasty. Other sources on formal bureaucratic structure are the *Ta Ch'ing Hui Tien*, the *Ch'ing Shih Kao*, and the *Ch'in-ting chih-kuan piao*.[2]

Our outline attempts only to give a general view of the kind of organizations, their manifest functions, and the offices within these organization, organized in terms of the nine-rank hierarchy. If every change in rank for a given office during this 300-year period were included in this outline, it would be unnecessarily complicated. Again, our interest is in the general structure rather than in the *history* of that structure. This much may be said: the deviations from our outline which could be found at different periods between 1600-1900 do not in any instance constitute a marked alteration from the structure presented here. Our outline is organized as follows:

1. Organizations
2. Notes on the Manifest Functions of Certain Organizations
3. Offices

[2] For these sources, see Bibliography.

Organizations

Officials in the nine-rank hierarchy were appointed to offices (*chih*) in one or more of the following organizations:

I. CIVIL ORGANIZATIONS IN THE CAPITAL

A. Most Powerful Organizations:

1. Grand Secretariat	内閣
After 1730: Grand Council	軍機處
2. Six Boards	六部
a. Civil Service	吏部
b. Revenue	户部
c. Rites	禮部
d. War	兵部
e. Punishments	刑部
f. Works	工部
3. Censorate	都察院
4. Supreme Court of Judicature and Revision	大理院
5. Court of Colonial Affairs	理藩院

B. Less Powerful Organizations:

1. Hanlin Academy	翰林院

2. Imperial Academy of Learning 國子監

3. Imperial Board of Astronomy 欽天監

4. Transmission Office 通政司

C. Imperial Clansmen Organizations 帝室

1. Imperial Clan Court 宗人府

2. Imperial Household 內務府

3. Supervisorate of Imperial Instruction 詹事府

4. The Four Courts 四寺

a. SACRIFICIAL WORSHIP 太常寺

b. BANQUETING 光祿寺

c. IMPERIAL STUD 太僕寺

d. STATE CEREMONIAL 鴻臚寺

5. Imperial Medical Department 太醫院

II. CIVIL ORGANIZATIONS OUTSIDE THE CAPITAL (Provincial Administration)

A. Offices of Viceroys and Governors 總督衙門 巡撫衙門

B. Offices of the Lieutenant-Governors 布政司

C. Offices of the Provincial Judges or Judicial Commissioners — 按察司

D. Offices of the Directors of Studies — 提督學政

E. Salt Gabelle Administration — 鹽政

F. Conservation of the Yellow River and the Grand Canal — 河道

G. Tax Grain Transport — 漕運

H. Customs — 関税

I. Prefectural and *Chou* Administrations — 府，州

J. District Administrations — 縣

K. Administration of Dependencies and Tribute States — 藩屬

L. Tribal Administration (of Miao, Lolo, Shan, etc.) — 土司

M. Administration of Taoist and Buddhist Religions — 道錄司，僧錄司

III. MILITARY ORGANIZATIONS

A. Imperial Bodyguard — 領侍衛府

B. Eight Banners: Manchus, Mongols, Chinese — 八旗：滿洲，蒙古，漢軍

1. Metropolitan Banners — 京旗

a. HOUSEHOLD BANNERS — 内旗

b. PEKING AND ENVIRONS' BANNERS 外旗

2. Banner Garrisons 駐防

C. Chinese Army 綠營

D. Imperial Equipage Department 鑾輿衛

E. Gendarmerie 步軍統領

Notes on the Manifest Functions of Certain Ch'ing Bureaucratic Organizations.[3]

I. *Grand Secretariat and Grand Council.* The Grand Secretariat, a purely Chinese institution deriving from Ming and earlier times, was the supreme organ of the Central Government until about 1730. It was the focal point of bureaucratic communications–memorials, reports, and imperial decrees–between the Emperor and the highest provincial officials. Grand Secretaries in the Grand Secretariat and in other Halls and Pavillions gradually lost their political influence during Ch'ing times. After 1730, the Grand Council, a Manchu innovation, usurped the supreme power of the Grand Secretariat. Ministers in the Grand Council had daily audiences with the Emperor, and formed a kind of Privy Council, though ultimately only the Emperor could issue edicts, decrees, and orders.

II. *The Six Boards.* The Six Boards' manifest functions are indicated in their several titles, e.g., supervision of the selection, promotion, demotion, etc., of officials (Board of Civil Service); taxes, population, treasury, coinage (Board of Revenue), and so forth.

III. *Censorate.* The Censorate functioned as the "eyes and ears" of the Emperor, censoring officials for any neglect or incompetency in their public or private lives, and supervising public morals in general.

---

[3] It is important to distinguish between the *manifest* and the *latent* functions of these organizations, even though we cannot here discuss the latent functions. See R. K. Merton, "Manifest and Latent Functions," in *Social Theory and Social Structure.*

There was a special organization for the scrutiny of Metropolitan officials. The Censorate, the Board of Punishments, and the Supreme Court of Judicature and Revision together were the "Three High Courts of Judicature."[4]

IV. *Supreme Court of Judicature and Revision.* The highest legal-judicial organ, it administered criminal law and tried criminal cases.

V. *Court of Colonial Affairs.* It was in charge of colonization and other relationships with Mongolia, Kokonor, and Mohammedan Princedoms in West China, Russia, etc. In 1861, the *Tsungli Yamen* took over its functions. No Chinese was ever appointed to this Court.

VI. *Hanlin Academy.* The Hanlin Academy was the highest academic and research organ, and the most prestigeful establishment of learning in the Empire. It also drew up government documents and histories, and supervised the studies of the highest-ranking *chin-shih* graduates.

VII. *Imperial Academy of Learning.* This was the highest educational organ, though, in Ch'ing times, it was more involved in supervising the Examination (*k'ao-shih*) system than in actual teaching.

VIII. *Imperial Board of Astronomy.* This Board compiled the calendar and made astronomical and meteorological observations, often of political consequence.

IX. *Transmission Office.* It received, recorded, and transmitted all memorials received from the provinces for the Grand Council. It was also a depot for all petitions addressed directly to the Emperor.[5]

X. *Imperial Court and Clansmen.* The Emperor, the royal family, and nobility, descendents of the acknowledged founder of the Ch'ing dynasty, Hsien-tzu, Nurhaci. This group did not have official rank in the nine-rank system *per se,* but were *above* it, with a hierarchy of their own. Individuals among this imperial group at times held substantive rank in the nine-rank hierarchy, when they held a substantive post.

XI. *Imperial Clan Court.* The Imperial Clan Court was directly below the imperial family and clansmen and exercised judicial and disciplinary authority over them. The great factional rivalry within

---

[4] Cf. Li Hsiung-fei, *Les Censeurs sous la dynastie Mandchoue, 1616-1911, en Chine,* (Paris: Presses Modernes, 1936).

[5] See J. K. Fairbank and S. Y. Teng, "On the Transmission of Ch'ing Documents," *Harvard Journal of Asiatic Studies,* V (May, 1939), 12-46, and Fairbank and Teng, "On the Types and Uses of Ch'ing Documents," *Harvard Journal of Asiatic Studies,* V (January, 1940), 1-71.

the imperial kindred made this Court necessary. The highest posts in the Court were *above* the nine-rank bureaucratic hierarchy.

XII. *Imperial Household.* It was more private than governmental. It served the needs of the Imperial Court, e.g., privy purse, food, clothing, entertainment, schools, etc.

XIII. *Supervisorate of Imperial Instruction.* It directed the studies of the Heir Apparent. But in eight of the ten Ch'ing reigns between 1644 and 1912 the Heir Apparent whom the Emperor had chosen was not known until the time of the death of the Emperor. Nor did the Manchu throne automatically descend to the eldest son. Therefore, except for the two instances, this organization offered mostly sinecure posts.[6]

XIV. *The Four Courts.* Their manifest functions are indicated in their several titles: The Banqueting Court supervised food supplies for banquets for vassal envoys, new graduates, old men, etc. The Court of Sacrificial Worship was in charge of sacrifices performed by the Emperor himself or by his deputies, and supervised the temples and Imperial Mausolea. The Court of State Ceremonial informed guests at banquets about proper etiquette.

XV. *Viceroys.* The several Viceroys had supreme control over the civil and military affairs of two or three provinces, and could forward memorials directly to the Emperor.

XVI. *Provincial Governors.* The Provincial Governor had complete control over the military and civil affairs of his province.

XVII. *Salt Gabelle Administration.* It was in charge of the provincial salt monopolies at Tientsin, Tsinanfu, Yangchow, Hangchow, and Canton, and the revenue derived therefrom.

XVIII. *Conservation of the Yellow River and the Grand Canal.* This office superintended the embankment of the Yellow River and maintained the sluices along the Imperial Canal.

XIX. *Tax Grain Transport.* This office supervised the system by which rice, as tax grain, was conveyed from the southern provinces to Peking. A special military organization was attached to both this and to the office for the conservation of the Yellow River and the Grand Canal.

XX. *Military Bureaucracy.* In the Ch'ing period, there were two kinds of military organizations: the Eight Banners and the Chinese Army. In the beginning, the Manchu forces were organized into eight Banners; later, Mongol armies and *Han* Chinese, who had willingly surrendered to the Ch'ing in the Northeast, were also set up with the

[6] Hsieh Pao-chao, *The Government of China,* pp. 41-43, 379.

Eight-Banner system. After the mid-Ch'ing period, the Eight Banners and the Chinese Army all became degenerate and were not usable during national emergencies. To protect their own provinces, local leaders trained their own guards. The *Hsiang-chün* (Hunan Army) and *Huai-chün* (Anhwei Army) were both developed from local guards.

OFFICES

I. CIVIL ADMINISTRATION

A. Central Administration—
Civil Offices in the Capital:

Rank 1A

Grand Preceptor of the Emperor	太師
Grand Tutor of the Emperor	太傅
Grand Guardian of the Emperor	太保
Grand Secretaries in the Halls and Pavillions within the Forbidden City	大學士

Rank 1B

Junior Preceptor of the Emperor	少師
Junior Tutor of the Emperor	少傅
Junior Guardian of the Emperor	少保

Grand Preceptor of the Heir Apparent	太子太師
Grand Tutor of the Heir Apparent	太子太傅
Grand Guardian of the Heir Apparent	太子太保
Presidents of the Boards and Courts	各部院尚書
Senior Presidents of the Censorate	都察院左都御史
Junior Presidents of the Censorate	都察院右都御史
Rank 2A	
Junior Preceptor of the Heir Apparent	太子少師
Junior Tutor of the Heir Apparent	太子少傅
Junior Guardian of the Heir Apparent	太子少保
Vice Presidents of Boards and Courts	部院左右侍郎
Ministers in the Imperial Household	內務府總管
Rank 2B	
Chancellors of the Grand Secretariat	內閣學士
Chancellors of the Hanlin Academy	翰林院掌院學士

Rank 3A

Senior Vice President of the Censorate	都察院左副都御史
Junior Vice President of the Censorate	都察院右副都御史
Vice Director of the Imperial Clan Court	宗人府府丞
Commissioner in the Transmission Office	通政司通政使
Director of the Court of Judicature and Revision	大理寺卿
Chief Supervisor of Instruction in the Imperial Supervisorate of Instruction	詹事府詹事
Directors of the Court of Sacrificial Worship	太常寺卿
Prefects of Shun-t'ien, the Metropolitan Prefecture, and of Feng-t'ien (Mukden)	順天府尹 奉天府尹
Director of the Imperial Armory	武備院卿
Director of the Palace Stud	上駟院卿
Director of the Bureau of Imperial Gardens and Hunting Parks	奉宸苑卿

Rank 3B

Director of the Banqueting Court	光祿寺卿

Director of the Court of the Imperial Stud	太僕寺卿

Rank 4A

Deputy Commissioners in the Transmission Office	通政司副使
Sub-Director of the Court of Judicature and Revision	大理寺少卿
Supervisors of Instruction in the Supervisorate of Imperial Instruction	詹事府少詹事
Sub-Directors of the Court of Sacrificial Worship	太常寺少卿
Sub-Directors of the Residence for Envoys of the Four Tributary States (Korea, Siam, Tonkin, and Burma)	會同四譯館少卿
Sub-Directors of the Court of the Imperial Stud	太僕寺少卿
Director of the Court of State Ceremonial	鴻臚寺少卿
Vice Prefects of Shun-t'ien and Feng-t'ien	順天府丞 奉天府丞

Rank 4B

Readers in the Grand Secretariat	內閣侍讀學士
Readers in the Hanlin Academy	翰林院侍讀學士

Expositors in the Hanlin Academy
翰林院侍講學士

Libationers in the Imperial Academy of Learning
國子監祭酒

Rank 5A

Senior and Junior Deputy Supervisors of Instruction in the Imperial Supervisorate of Instruction
左右春坊庶子

Secretaries in the Transmission Office
通政司參議

Sub-Directors of the Imperial Banqueting Court
光祿寺少卿

Senior Metropolitan Censors of the Six Sections of the Office for the Scrutiny of Metropolitan Officials
六科掌印給事中

Administrators in the Imperial Clan Court
宗人府理事官

Junior Metropolitan Censors
給事中

Department Directors in the Boards and Courts
各部院郎中

Sub-Prefects in Shun-t'ien and Feng-t'ien
順天府治中
奉天府治中

Assistant-Managers in the Imperial Household
内務府管領

Directors of the Imperial Board of Astronomy
欽天監監正

Commissioner of the Imperial Medical Department	太醫院院使
Rank 5B	
Sub-Readers in the Hanlin Academy	翰林院侍讀
Sub-Expositors in the Hanlin Academy	翰林院侍講
Librarians in the Supervisorate of Imperial Instruction	司經局洗馬
Sub-Directors of the Court of State Ceremonial	鴻臚寺少卿
Sub-Readers in the Grand Secretariat	內閣侍讀
Assistant - Administrators of the Imperial Clan Court	宗人府副理事官
Assistant Department Directors of the Boards and Courts	各部院員外郎
Rank 6A	
Assistant Readers in the Grand Secretariat	內閣侍讀
Secretaries in the Supervisorate of Imperial Instruction	左右春坊中允
Tutors in the Imperial Academy	國子監司業
Secretaries in the Boards and Courts	各部院主事

Secretaries in the Imperial Clan Court	宗人府主事
Registrars in the Registry Office of the Imperial Clan Court	經歷
Registrars in the Registry of the Censorate	都察院經歷
Officials in the Chancery of the Censorate	都事
Secretaries in the Court of Colonial Affairs	理藩院主事
Junior and Senior Secretaries in the Court of Judicature and Revision	大理寺左右寺丞
Vice Directors of the Imperial Board of Astronomy	欽天監監副
Astronomers	五官正
Police Magistrate of Peking	兵馬司指揮
Magistrate of Peking	直隸州州同

Rank 6B

Assistant Secretaries in the Supervisorate of Imperial Instruction	左右春坊贊善
First-Class Hanlin Compiler	翰林院修撰
Directors of the Banqueting Court	光祿寺署正

Manchu Astronomers	滿五官正
First-Class Assistant Department Magistrate of Chihli	直隸州州同

Rank 7A

Second-Class Compilers in the Hanlin Academy	翰林院編修
Archivists in the Transmission Office	通政司知事
Secretaries in the Transmission Office	通政司經歷
Assistant-Secretaries of the Court of Judicature and Revision	大理寺評事
Archivists in the Grand Secretariat	內閣典籍
Learned Doctors of the Court of Sacrificial Worship	太常寺博士
Overseers	典簿
Proctors in the Imperial Academy of Learning	國子監監丞
Inspectors in the Boards and Courts	各部院司庫
Inspectors in the Imperial Household	內務部司庫
Clerks in the Boards and Courts	各部院七品筆帖式

Director of Studies of the Metropolitan Prefecture	京府教授
Sub-Director of Studies of the Metropolitan Prefecture	京府訓導
District Councillors of the Metropolitan District	京縣縣丞
Seventh-Rank Korean Assistant Interpreters	七品朝鮮通事
Imperial Physicians in the Imperial Medical Department	太醫院御醫
Sub-Archivists	典籍
Calligraphers	書寫

Rank 7B

Correctors in the Hanlin Academy	翰林院檢討
Secretaries of the Imperial Patent Office	中書科中書
Secretaries of the Grand Secretariat	内閣中書
Archivists in the Supervisorate of Imperial Instruction	詹事府主簿
Archivists in the Banqueting Court	光祿寺典簿
Assistant Directors of the Department of Music	署丞

Learned Doctors of the Imperial Academy of Learning	國子監博士
Assistant Teachers	助教
Secretaries in the Imperial Guard	鑾儀衛經歷
Supervisors of the Observatory in the Imperial Board of Astronomy	欽天監灵台郎
Second-Class Assistant Department Magistrate for Chihli	直隸州州判
Secretaries of Shun-t'ien and Feng-t'ien Prefecture	順天府經歷 奉天府經歷

(For Rank 8A posts, see below, Provincial Administration and Military Offices.)

Rank 8B

Sub-Archivists in the Imperial Academy of Learning	國子監典簿

B. Provincial Administration – Civil Offices in the Provinces:

Rank 2A

Governor-General of the Provinces	各省總督
Directors-General of Conservancy on the Yellow River and the Grand Canal	河道總督
Directors-General of Grain Transport	漕運總督

Rank 2B	
Provincial Governors	各省巡撫
Lieutenant Governors	布政使司布政使
Rank 3A	
Judicial Commissioner	按察使司按察使
Rank 3B	
Salt Controller	塩運司運使
Rank 4A	
Circuit Intendants	各省守巡道
Grain Intendants	糧道
Rank 4B	
Assistant Salt Controller	塩運司運使
Prefects	各府知府
Rank 5A	
First-Class Sub-Prefects	各府同知
Magistrates of Independent *Chou*	各直隸州知州
Inspector of the Salt Distribution	塩運監掣同知
Rank 5B	
Circuit Censors	各道監察御史

Deputy Assistant Salt Controller 塩運司運副

Salt Inspector 塩運司提舉

Chou Magistrates 各州知州

Rank 6A

Second-Class Sub-Prefects 各府通判

Rank 6B

Secretaries in the Lieutenant Governors' Offices 布政司經歷

Law Secretaries 理問

Salt Officers 塩運使

Sub-Assistant Salt Controller 塩運司通判

First-Class Assistant *Chou* Magistrates 州同

Superiors and Preachers of the Buddhist Priesthood 僧錄司闡教

Superiors and Hierophants of the Taoist Priesthood 道錄司演法

Rank 7A

Registrars of Studies 四氏學教授

Assistant Police Magistrates 兵馬司副指揮

Secretaries in the Office of the Judicial Commissioner 按察司經歷

District Magistrates	各縣知縣
Registrars of Studies in Prefectural First-Class Grain Transport Stations	各府衛學教授

Rank 7B

Assistant Secretaries in the Office of the Lieutenant Governor	布政司都事
Second-Class Assistant *Chou* Magistrates	州判
Secretaries in the Office of the Salt Controller	塩運司經歷
Secretaries in the Grain Transport Stations	各衛經歷

Rank 8A

District Director of Studies	各縣教諭
Archivists in the Office of the Judicial Commissioner	按察司知事
Salt Receiver	塩課司大使
Salt Examiner	批驗大使
Prefectural Secretaries	各府經歷
Chou Director of Studies	學正
Assistant District Magistrate	縣丞

Rank 8B	
Chou Sub-Director of Studies	訓導
Archivists in the Salt Controller's Office	塩運司知事
Rank 9A	
Jail Wardens	照磨
District Registrars	各縣主簿
Prefectural Archivists	各府知事
Rank 9B	
Jail Wardens	司獄
Salt Watchers	塩巡檢
Prefectural Receiver of Duties and Taxes	稅課司大使
Examiner of Taxes	宣課司大使
Deputy Police-Master and Jail Warden	吏目
Sub-District Magistrates	巡檢
"Unclassed" Rank	
Salt and Tea Examiners	塩茶大使
Customs Examiner	關大使
River Police Inspector	河泊所官

Granary Keepers	倉大使
Jail Wardens	典吏

II. MILITARY OFFICES

Rank 1A

Chamberlain of the Imperial Bodyguard	三旗領侍衛内大臣
Field Marshall	大將軍

Rank 1B

Senior Assistant Chamberlain of the Imperial Bodyguard	掌統領侍衛親軍内大臣
Lieutenant-General in the Banners	八旗都統
Manchu General-in-Chief (or "Tartar General")	外省駐防將軍
Provincial Commander-in-Chief of the Chinese Army (*Lu-ying*)	提督
General	正都統

Rank 2A

Commandants of the Left and Right Wings of the Vanguard Division	左右翼前鋒統領
Captain-General of the Guards Division of the Eight Banners	八旗護軍統領

General Commandants of the Divisions of the Gendarmerie	提督九門
Adjutant of the Five Battalions of Police of the Gendarmerie	巡捕五營步軍統領
Deputy Lieutenant-General	軍副都統
Commissioners of the Imperial Equipage Department	鑾輿使
Deputy Lieutenant-Generals of the Outer Banners	外省駐防副都統
Brigade General	總兵
Rank 2B	
Junior Assistant Chamberlains of the Imperial Bodyguard	散秩大臣
Major General	協都統
Colonel	副將
Rank 3A	
First-Level Senior Bodyguards in the Imperial Bodyguard	一等侍衛
Chief Marshals of the Imperial Equipage Department	冠軍使
Brigadiers of Artillery and Musketry Division of the Banners	火器營翼長

Brigadiers of Scouts	健銳營翼長
Deputy Provosts of the Gendarmerie	步軍翼尉
Captain-General of the Guards Division of Bondservants	包衣護軍統領
Commandants of the Summer Palace Guards Division of the Banners	圓明園八旗護軍營總統
Commandants of the Artillery and Musketry Division	虎槍營統
Colonel of the Vanguard Division	前鋒參領
Colonel	正參領
Colonel of the Guards Division of the Banners	護軍參領
Manchurian Colonel	驍騎參領
Chief Controller (of the Imperial Hunting Preserves, Heilungkiang Boats, etc.)	總管
Commandant of a Minor Manchu Provincial Garrison	城守尉
Commandant of a Prince's Palace	王府長史
Lieutenant Colonel	參將

Rank 3B

Bondservant Commandant of the Summer Palace	圓明園包衣營總
Colonels (in Bondservants and Guards Divisions, in Kirin, Heilungkiang, and Chahar)	參領
Brigade Commanders in Banner Garrisons outside the capital	駐防協領
Major	游擊
Lieutenant Colonel	參將

Rank 4A

Second-Level Bodyguards in the Imperial Bodyguard	二等侍衛
Assistant Chief Marshals in the Imperial Equipage Department	雲麾使
Bodyguards in the Vanguard Division	前鋒侍衛
Lieutenant Colonels (in the Guards Division, in Artillery and Musketry, and in other Divisions of the Banners)	副護軍參領
Captain	佐領
Police Majors in the Guard Stations of Peking	步軍協尉

Controllers (of Alarms and Signal Guns, etc.) 信礮總管

Brigadier of the Hunting Preserves 圍場翼長

Commandant of Second-Class of Minor Manchu Provincial Garrisons 防守尉

Major-domos in the Palaces of the Princes of the Blood of the Third Degree (Beile) 司儀長

First Captain 都司

Captain 協參領

Rank 4B

Captains of the City Gate Guards 城門領

Lieutenant Colonels (Bond-servants in the Guards Divisions, in the Artillery and Musketry Division, etc.) 包衣護軍參領

Captain 佐領

Assistant Major-domo in Princes' Palaces 王貝勒府四品典儀

Second-Level Guards in Princes' Palaces 王府二等護衛

Rank 5A

Third-Level Senior Bodyguards 三等侍衛

Assistant Section Chiefs in the Imperial Equipage Department	治儀正
Police Captain	步軍副尉
Police Lieutenant	步軍校
Assistant Controller of Alarms and Signal Guns	監守信礮官
Captains by Non-Hereditary Selection	分管佐領
Captains (Keepers of the Seal, etc.)	掌印防禦
First Lieutenants	正軍校
Rank 5B	
Fourth-Level Senior Bodyguards	四等侍衛
Deputy Imperial Guardsmen of the Vanguard Division	委署前鋒參領
Second Captain	守備
Deputy Imperial Guardsmen of the Other Divisions	委署護軍參領
Fifth-Level Assistant Majordomos in the Princes' Palaces	五品典儀
Third-Level Guards in the Princes' Palaces	三等護衛
Gate Guards Lieutenants	守禦所千總

Rank 6A

Bodyguards 藍翎侍衛

Lieutenants in the Emperor's Personal Bodyguard 親軍校

Lieutenants (in Vanguard, Guards, Artillery and Musketry Divisions, etc.) 校

Gate and Camp Lieutenants 門營千總

Second Lieutenants 副軍校

Rank 6B

Deputy Police Lieutenants 委署步軍校

Sixth-Level Assistant Major-domos in the Princes' Palaces 六品典儀

Rank 7A

City Gate Clerks 城門吏

Sub-Lieutenant 協軍校

Sub-Lieutenant 把總

Seventh-Rank *Chien-sheng* by the *Yin* Privilege 七品蔭監生

Rank 7B

Police Captains of Mukden 盛京游牧副尉

Assistant Major-domos in the Establishments of Beitzu and Nobles 貝子公副典儀

Rank 8A	
Ensigns	司務長
Eighth-Rank *Chien-sheng* by the *Yin* Privilege	八品廕監生
Rank 8B (Petty officers)	
First-Class Sargeant	上士
Sub-Lieutenant	委署驍騎校
Assistant Major-domos of the Establishments of Nobles	公府典儀
Rank 9A	
Sargeant of the Second Class	中士
Rank 9B	
Sargeant of the Third Class	下士
"Unclassed Offices"	
Corporal	催領
First and Second Class Privates	馬甲，敖爾布
Supernumeraries	養育兵
Bannermen at Large	閑散

NOTES

CHAPTER I

1. "The Foxes' Revenge," a story of the T'ang dynasty, in *The Courtesan's Jewel Box: Chinese Stories of the Xth-XVIIth Centuries* (Peking: Foreign Language Press, 1957), p. 96.

2. See, for example, what is perhaps the most famous of these satirical novels, the *Ju-lin wai-shih*, by Wu Ching-tzu, written in the eighteenth century and translated into English as *The Scholars* (Peking, Foreign Language Press, 1957).

3. For accounts of the Taiping Rebellion, in relation to the present context, see Vincent C. Y. Shih, "The Ideology of the T'aip'ing T'ien-Kuo," *Sinologica*, III (January, 1951), 1-15; also "Interpretations of the Taiping Tien Kuo by Noncommunist Chinese Writers," *Far Eastern Quarterly*, X (May, 1951); Franz Michael, *Documentary History of the Taiping Rebellion* (forthcoming, University of Washington Press, Seattle); Eugene P. Boardman, "Christian Influence upon the Ideology of the Taiping Rebellion," *Far Eastern Quarterly*, X (1950-51), pp. 115-24; T. T. Meadows, *The Chinese and Their Rebellions* (Stanford, Academic Reprints, 1954).

CHAPTER II

1. In the simplest preliterate folk societies, stratification may be at a minimum. Cf. such societies as the aborigines of Australia, the Bushmen, the Eskimos, and the Semitic mounted nomads.

2. For the formulation of this theory of stratification, we are indebted most directly and fully to Bernard Barber, *Social Stratification: A Comparative Analysis of Structure and Process* (New York: Harcourt, Brace & Co., 1957), especially chaps. 1-3 and 10.

CHAPTER III

5. See Sir George Staunton, *Ta Tsing Leu Lee*, being a translation of *The Fundamental Laws and Supplementary Statutes of the Great Penal Code of China* (*Ta Ch'ing Lü Li*) (London: Bart., F. R. S., 1810), p. 5 Also, R. I. (anonymous), "The Chinese Government and Constitution," *Chinese Repository* (1836), pp. 11-17. For much of this Elite of the Realm stratification, I am also indebted to Brunnert and Hagelstrom, *Present Day Political Organization of China*, a translation of the work of A. Bettchenko and E. E. Moran, based upon the *Ta Ch'ing Hui Tien* (Shanghai: Kelley and Walsh, 1912).

6. *Ch'ing-ch'ao T'ung-Tien* (Wan-yu wen-k'u ed.; Shanghai, 1937, 40), 2235-6.

7. *Ta Ch'ing Hui Tien Shih Li* (Li Pu, 1818 ed.), 305/1b, 4a.

8. *Ta Ch'ing Hui Tien Shih Li* (Hu Pu, 1828 ed.), 134/25a-27a; see also the *Ch'ing Shih Lu* (1937 ed.); *Shih-Tsung Shih Lu*, 56/23b-28b; *Jen-Tsung Shih Lu*, 223/25a-b.

1. Mencius, *Meng-Tzu*, T'eng-wen-Kung (Shanghai: Commercial Press, 1929), 5/11a.

2. For a classic "utilitarian" analysis of "the problem of order," see Thomas Hobbes, *Leviathan*, Part I. For a modern commentary on this problem, see Talcott Parsons, *The Structure of Social Action* (Glencoe, Ill.: The Free Press, 1949), chap. 3.

3. For data on the British landed gentry from 1837 to 1952, see *Burke's Genealogical and Heraldic History of the Landed Gentry* (17th ed.; London: Burke's Peerage, Ltd., 1952).

4. See P. Selznick, *TVA and the Grass Roots: A Study of Formal Organization* (Berkeley: University of California Press, 1949), for a discussion of the concept of cooptation.

9. Liang Ch'i-ch'ao, *Chung-Kuo wen-hua shih, She-hui Tzu-chih p'ien*, "chieh-chi" (Class), (Taipei: Chung-hua shu chü, 1956), pp. 45-50; M. Sano, *Shincho Shakai Shi* (History of Ch'ing Society) "Social Class" (Tokyo: Bunkyodo, 1947), sec. 3, pp. 64-71.

10. For general analyses relevant to economic stratification in the Ch'ing period, see Mao Tse-tung, "Chung-kuo she-hui ko chieh-chi-ti fen-hsi," in *Mao Tse-tung Hsüan-chi* (Peking: Jen-min ch'u-pan she, 1951), I, 3-11, and Mao Tse-tung, "Tsen-yang fen-hsi nung-ts'un chieh-chi," *op. cit.*, pp. 123-26; English translation: Mao Tse-tung, *Selected Works* (London: Lawrence and Wishhart, Ltd., 1954). Chia Chih-fang, *Chin-Tai Chung-Kuo ching-chi she-hui* (Shanghai: T'ang-ti Ch'u-pan she, 1949); M. Sano, *op. cit.*, Part II, *Shakai Kaikyu*. Yü T'ing-ts'an, "Fu-min" (Wealthy People), in *Ching-shih Wen-pien*, chap. 36. Saeki Tomi, "Shindai niokeru eng yu shihon nitsuite" (The Capital of Salt Trade under the Ch'ing Dynasty), *Toyoshi Kenkyu*, XI, No. 1 (September, 1950), 51-61, and XI, No. 2 (March, 1951), 128-40. Kitamura Hirotada, "Chugoku no jinushi to Nippon no jinushi" (Landlords in China and Japan), *Rekishi hyoron*, IV, No. 2 (February, 1950), 19-25. N. Niida, "Shina kinsei no ichiden ryoshu kanko to sono seiritsu" (The Practice of Having Two Kinds of Owners of One Field in Molern China), *Hogaku kyokai zasshi* (Tokyo: Tokyo University), LXIV, No. 3 (March, 1946), and LXIV, No. 4 (April, 1946). T'ao Meng-ho, *Meng-ho wen-ts'un* (Shanghai: Ya-Tung t'u-shu-kuan, 1926), pp. 9-20.

R. H. Tawney, *Land and Labour in China* (London: George Allen & Unwin, 1932), pp. 54-77; Sun Yüeh-T'ang, "Cultivated Area in China in the last 370 Years," *Ta Kung Pao* (Shanghai, June 29, 1951). Chang Chung-li, *The Gentry of* 19th *Century China: Their Economic Position as Evidenced by Their Share of the National Product* (unpublished Ph.D. dissertation, University of Washington, Seattle, 1953).

CHAPTER IV

1. Cf. C. Martin Wilbur, *Slavery in China during the Former Han Dynasty*, 206 B.C.-25 A.D. (Chicago: Field Museum of Natural History, 1943), pp. 33-49; Yang Lien-sheng, "Powerful Families of the Eastern Han," in E-tu Zen Sun and J. De Francis (eds.), *Chinese Social History* (Washington, D. C.: American Council of Learned Societies, 1956), pp. 103-34; Mitsuo Moriya, *Rokucho monbatsu no kenkyu* (A Study of the Clan Institute in the Six-Dynasties Period) (Tokyo: Nihon shupan kyodo Pub. Co., 1951); Wang Yi-t'ung, *Wu-ch'ao men-ti* and *Kao-men shih-hsi hun-yin piao* (The Social, Political, and Economic Aspects of the Influential Clans of the Southern Dynasties, Appended with 69 Genealogical Tables of Imperial Families of the Period) (Nanking: Chin-ling University, 1943), 2 vols.; Wang Yi-t'ung, "Slaves and Other Comparable Social Groups during the Northern Dynasties, 386-618," *Harvard Journal of Asiatic Studies*, XVI (December, 1953), 293-364; W. Eberhard, *Das Toba-Reich Nordchinas* (Leiden: E. J. Brill, 1949); K. A. Wittfogel, *New Light on Chinese Society* (New York: International Secretariat, Institute of Pacific Relations, 1938); E. A. Kracke, Jr., "Family vs. Merit in the Civil Service Examinations under the Empire," *Harvard Journal of Asiatic Studies*, X (1947) 103-23; Meng Ssu-ming, *Yüan-tai she-hui chieh-chi chih-tu* (Social Class System in Yuan Dynasty) (Peiping: Harvard-Yenching Institute Publications, 1938); F. L. K. Hsu, "Social Mobility in China," *American Sociological Review*, XIV (1949), 764-71.

2. See interpretative studies of Pai-lien Chiao (White Lotus Society), Nien-fei, Taiping, Boxer, and other rebellions, as in Sano, *op. cit.*, Vol. III; Li Kuang-pi (ed.), *Ming-Ch'ing shih lun-ts'ung* (Collected Essays in Ming and Ch'ing History) (Wuhan: Hupei Jen-min ch'u-pan she, 1957); Li Hsün, *Ming-Ch'ing shih* (Ming and Ch'ing History) (Peking: Jen-min ch'u-pan she, 1957); Li Kuang-pi and Ch'ien Chün-i (eds.), *Chung-kuo li-shih jen-wu lun-chi* (Collected Essays on Chinese Historical Personages) (Peking: San-lien shu-tien, 1957); Chia Chih-fang, *Chin-tai Chung-kuo ching-chi she-hui* (Modern Chinese Society in Its Economic Aspects) (Shanghai: T'ang-ti ch'u-pan she, 1949). See also the review article, by H. S. Levy, of Chang Hui and Hsi Chih-pien, *Journal of Asian Studies*, XVI (August, 1957), 612-17.

CHAPTER V

1. Especially Li Huan, *Kuo-ch'ao ch'i-hsien lei-cheng* (Ch'ing Dynasty Biographies Arranged by Categories) (Hunan: Hsiang-yin, 1890); Ch'ien I-chi, *Pei Chuan Chi* (Kiangsu shu-chü ed., 1893); Miao Ch'üan-sun,

Hsü Pei Chuan Chi (Kiangsu shu-chu ed., 1893); Min Erh-ch'ang, *Pei Chuan Chi Pu* (Peiping: Yenching University, 1931).

2. For enlightening discussions of Chinese biographical genre, see Liang Ch'i-ch'ao, *Chung-kuo li-shih yen-chiu fa (pu-pien)* (Research Methods in Chinese History, Supplementary) (Taipei: Chung-hua shu-chü, 1956), pp. 37-41; Herbert Franke, "Some Remarks on the Interpretation of Chinese Dynastic Histories," *Oriens*, III, 113-22; T. D. Twitchett, "Chinese Biographical Writing" (unpublished ms., c/o Hugh Borton, East Asiatic Library, Columbia University); Ch'en Shih-hsiang, "An Innovation in Chinese Biographical Writing," *Far Eastern Quarterly*, XIII, No. 1 (November, 1953), 49-62; G. H. Kennedy, *ZH Guide: An Introduction to Sinology*, "Biographies" (New Haven: Yale University Press, 1953).

3. For this discussion of the complication of biographies, I am indebted to Twitchett, *op. cit.*

4. *United States Quarterly Book List*, I, No. 1 (March 1945), 60-61; Hu Shih, "Preface" to ECCP, pp. iii-vii.

5. It was decided to code the following as having official careers, and to include them in our sample: (1) "Expectant officials" (*hou-hsüan*), because they had official status even before appointment to a substantive post; (2) Bannermen and Imperial Clansmen (*tsung-shih*) because of their special privileges; (3) Holders of literary posts in the Hanlin Academy or the State Historiographical Board, providing that these posts carried official ranks (*p'in*), e.g., the editorial staff of the *Ssu-k'u ch'üan-shu;* (4) The controversial group of "unclassed" officials, below 9B rank (*wei-ju-liu*). Although the *Ta Ch'ing Lü Li* states that clerks and others below the 9B rank were not considered as permanently distinguished from commoners (cf. Staunton, *op. cit.*, note, pp. 10-11), we have nevertheless coded them as officials because many students (*chien-sheng*) in the Kuo Tzu Chien purchased this *wei-ju-liu* rank as an entrance to officialdom; (5) Sub-directors of Schools (Studies), for they held both rank and post; (6) Secretaries in the Office of the Provincial Governor and above (i.e., in the Courts and Boards, the Imperial Study, or *Nan shu-fang,* all in Peking). Those coded as not officials, and not included in our sample, were: (1) Secretaries below the level of the Provincial Governor's Office, e.g., magistrates' secretaries; (2) salaried or senior licentiates in district schools; (3) those engaged by a magistrate to take charge of an academy (*shu-yüan*); (4) Nobles of the Imperial lineage not in substantive posts in the nine-rank official hierarchy.

6. The biographical collections are: *Ming Shih, Ch'ing Shih Kao, Ch'ing Shih Lieh Chuan, Kuo-ch'ao ch'i-hsien lei-cheng ch'u-pien, Pei Chuan Chi, Hsü Pei Chuan-chi,* and *Pei Chuan Chi Pu*. For full bibliographic citation, see Fang Chao-ying and Tu Lien-che, *Tseng-chiao Ch'ing-ch'ao chin-shih t'i-ming pei-lu fu yin-te* (Peiping: Harvard-Yenching Institute, 1941), p. ii.

7. See *Huang-ch'ao T'ung-tien,* 40/1a-3b.

8. For guidance in differentiating these terms, the writer is greatly indebted to Professor Ho Ping-ti. Other coding decisions as to whether ancestors or relatives had themselves been officials, etc., followed the same lines as above, in the definition of our sample.

CHAPTER VII

1. Shimizu Morimitsu, *Chugoku zokusan seido ko* (A Study of Clan or JJoint-Family Property in China) (Iwanami Shoten, 1949), has clearly shown that there was lineage—or clan-held property (*tsu-ch'an*) separate from the patrimony of a single branch family.

2. Ritual purposes were in connection with sacrifices for the ancestors, maintenance of ritual fields (*chi-t'ien*), tombs (*mu*), and shrines (*tz'u*). Relief purposes were for lineage families beset by crop failure, floods, etc.

3. Chu Shih, 1665-1736, one of the officials in our sample from a commoner family, established a school for the poor of his lineage in Kao-an, Kiangsi. Pupils from the lineage over twelve years old who had already had their elementary education were eligible. "Children of exceptional intelligence were admitted free of charge" (Chu Shih, *Chu-wen-tuan-kung wen-chi*, 1/60a-61a, quoted in Hu Hsien-chin, *op. cit.*, p. 71). Hu lists several other lineages which also subsidized good students.

Makino Tatsumi has shown that the "joint family" shrines (*ho-tsu tz'u*) were centers of the inter-village activities of lineages and that they played a vital role in relation to the examination system. "Kanton no gozokushi to gozakufu," in *Kindai chugoku Kenkyu* (Kogakusha, 1948), pp. 89-129.

4. *Ibid.*, pp. 41-50. See also Ch'ien Ch'ien-i, *Mu Chai yu-hsüeh chi*, "Ch'ien-shih i-chuang chi," 27/16a; Shao T'ing-ts'ai, *Ssu-fu t'ang wen-chi*, "Shao-shih yu-t'ien hsien chuang chi," 4/9a; Yuan Mei, *Hsiao-Ts'ang-shan fang wen-chi*, "T'ao-shih i-chuang pei-chi," 12/13a; Wang Chih-ch'ang, *Ch'ing-hsüeh chai chi*, "I-t'ien shan tsu shuo," 30/9b.

5. Ku Yen-wu, *Jih Chih-lu* (1795), 6/16, cites the *Chou Li* system of mutual help among people of the same clan or same locality (*Chou Li, Cheng-shih chu*, 3/66-67). Ku also cited Fan Chung-yen's system of clan land. See also Cheng Hsing-hsün, "A Study of the Economic Thoughts of Ku T'ing-lin," *Kuo-wen chou-pao*, chap. 7, No. 32, pp. 3 ff. I am indebted to Chang Chung-li (1953) for these references.

GLOSSARY

Beile	貝勒
Beise	貝子
Chang-sui	長隨
Chen	鎮
Chen-chieh	貞潔
Cheng i-p'in	正一品
Cheng-shih	正史
Cheng-tsung ssu-chiu p'in	正從四九品
Cheng-t'u	正途
Chi-pen-ti chia-t'ing	基本的家庭
Chi-t'ien	祭田
Ch'i-ch'in	妻親
Ch'i-i-chü-chu	起居注

Ch'i-min 齊民

Ch'i-tu-wei 騎都尉

Chia-ch'an-tzu 家產子

Chia-p'u 家譜

Chia-sheng-nu 家生奴

Chia-shih chia-k'o, ch'ing-pai hsiang-shan 家世甲科清白相嬗

Chia-shu ching yen shih chiao tzu 家塾競延師教子

Chia-t'ing nu-li 家庭奴隸

Chiang-ch'en 疆臣

Chiang-shuai 將帥

Chiao-yü 教諭

Chieh-chi 階級

Chien-ch'en 諫臣

Chien-ch'en 姦臣

Chien-jen 兼任

Chien-min 賤民

Chien-sheng 監生

Chien-ssu 監司

Ch'ien-tsung 千總

Chih 志

Chih-kuan 職官

Ch'ih-tz'u 敕賜

Chin-ch'i 衿耆

Chin-feng 晉封

Chin-shen 搢紳

Chin-shih 進士

Chin-tseng 晉贈

Chin-tse-shih, t'ui-tse-wu-nung 進則仕退則務農

Ch'in-shu 親屬

Ching-hsüeh 經學

Ch'ing-ch'e-tu-wei 輕車都尉

Ch'ing-erh 卿貳

Ch'ing-han 清寒

Ch'ing pai 清白

Chiu-hsing yü-hu 九姓漁户

Chiu-p'in 九品

Cho-hsing 卓行

Chou li 周禮

Chou ssu-ma 州司馬

Chu-chüan 硃卷

Chü-jen 舉人

Chu wang 諸王

Chuan 撰

Chüan 卷

Chuan chi 傳記

Chüan-na chih-tu 捐納制度

Chuang-yüan 狀元

Chung-chieh 忠節

Chung-i 忠義

En-ch'i-wei 恩騎尉

En kung-sheng 恩貢生

Erh-ch'en 貳臣

Fa-chia 法家

Fang 房

Feng-kao 封誥

Feng-mi 俸米

Feng-shui 風水

Feng-tseng i, erh, san tai 封贈一二三代

Feng-yin 俸銀

Fu 府

Fu	福
Fu-mu chih ming, mei-cho chih yen	父母之命媒妁之言
Han-chan	翰詹
Hao-tsu	豪族
Ho-ch'en	河臣
Ho-chi	合集
Ho-tsu-tz'u	合族祠
Hou	侯
Hou-hsüan	候選
Hsi-chüeh	襲爵
Hsiang	鄉
Hsiang-chün	湘軍
Hsiang-shen	鄉紳
Hsiao-fan	小販
Hsiao-hsing chia-t'ing	小型家庭
Hsiao-i	孝義
Hsien	縣
Hsien hsüeh-sheng	縣學生
Hsin-pan ta-ch'en	新辦大臣

Hsin-shui kao-huo 薪水膏火

Hsing-chuang 行狀

Hsing-fa 刑法

Hsing pu 刑部

Hsing-t'i sheng-shuai 興替盛衰

Hsing-yen 行鹽

Hsiu-ts'ai 秀才

Hsüan-chü 選舉

Hsüeh-shih 學士

Hsüeh t'ien 學田

Hsün-li 循吏

Hu 戶

Hu pu 戶部

Huai-chün 淮軍

Hui-kuan 會館

Hun-yin 婚姻

I-ch'in 議親

I-chuang chi 義莊記

I chün kung ch'i-chia 以軍功起家

I-feng 馳封

I-hsi	移徙
I-hsüeh	義學
I-hsüeh chuang chi	義學莊記
I-i	遺逸
I-kuei	議貴
I-min	逸民
I-shu t'ien	義塾田
I-t'ien-chi	義田記
I-tseng	馳贈
I yang-sheng	邑庠生
Jen-ts'ai	人才
Jih-li	日曆
Ju-hsing	儒行
Ju-lin	儒林
Kai-hu	丐户
Kao-feng	誥封
Kao-shou	誥授
Kao-tseng	誥贈
K'ao-kung-ssu	考功司
Ko-ch'en	閣臣

K'o-mu-t'u	科目途
K'o-t'u	科途
Ku-kung-jen	雇工人
Kuei	貴
Kung	公
Kung fei	公費
Kung-k'uan	公款
Kung-sheng	貢生
Kuo-shih	國史
Kuo Shih Kuan pen-chuan	國史館本傳
Kuo Tzu Chien	國子監
Lai kuei	來歸
Lang-chung	郎中
Lang-shu	郎署
Lao-hsin	勞心
Lao-li	勞力
Li	禮
Liang	良
Liao-tso	僚佐
Li Pu	吏部, 禮部

Li chien-sheng 例監生

Li-feng 例封

Li kung-sheng 例貢生

Li-shou 例授

Lieh-chuan 列傳

Ling shan sheng 廩膳生

Ling-sheng 廩生

Lu 祿

Lu-ying 綠營

Man 蠻

Miao-chi 苗籍

Min-chi 民籍

Mo-chüan 墨卷

Mou 畝

Mu 墓

Nan Shu-Fang 南書房

Nei-Ko chiu-ch'ing 內閣九卿

Ni-ch'en 逆臣

Nien-p'u 年譜

Nu-pi 奴婢

Pa-i	八議
Pa-ku wen	八股文
Pa-ta-chia	八大家
Pai-hsing	百姓
Pang-yen	榜眼
Pao-chia chih-tu	保甲制度
Pao chü	保舉
Pao-i	包衣
Pao-pien	褒貶
Pan-tang	伴當
Pen	本
P'eng-chi	棚籍
Pi-chi	筆記
Pien-ta	鞭撻
P'in-chi	品級
Ping	兵
P'ing-min	平民
Pi t'ieh-shih	筆帖式
Po	伯
Po-hsüeh hung-tzu	博學鴻詞

Pu ch'iu yu kung, tan ch'iu wu kuo 不求有功但求無過

Pu-i 布衣

Pu-pu ch'ing yün 步步青雲

Pu-Yüan ta-ch'en 部院大臣

San-tai ch'ing-pai yüan-tse 三代清白原則

Shang-chi 商籍

She-hsüeh 社學

Shen-chin 紳衿

Shen-shih shu-min 紳士庶民

Shen-tao pei-ming 神道碑銘

Sheng-yüan 生員

Shih-cheng-chi 時政記

Shih-hsiao-chuan-lu 識小傳錄

Shih-huan 仕宦

Shih-huo 食貨

Shih-lu 實錄

Shih nung kung shang 士農工商

Shih-ta-fu 士大夫

Shou 壽

Shou-ling 守令
Shu-jen 庶人
Shu-shen 贖身
Shu-yüan 書院
Ssu-min 四民
Ssu-shu 私塾
Ssu-tzu 私資
Ta ch'en 大臣
Ta-hsing chia-t'ing 大型家庭
Ta hu 大户
Ta yuan 大員
T'ai-p'u-ch'ing-ying-ping 太僕卿應聘
Tan-chia (Tanka) 蛋家
T'an hu 蛋户
T'an-hua 探花
Ti-chu 地主
T'ien-lien-ch'ien-mo 田連阡陌
To-min 墮民
Tsa-t'u 雜途
Tsai-fu 宰輔

Ts'ai-wu	材武
Tso ling	佐領
Tsu	族
Tsu-ch'an	族產
Tsu p'u	族譜
Tsung-ch'in	宗親
Tsung erh-p'in	從二品
Tsung-p'u	宗譜
Tsung-shih chüeh-hao	宗室爵號
Tsung-shih wang-kung	宗室王公
Tu-fu	督撫
T'u-chi	土籍
Tu-shu t'ien	讀書田
T'uan-lien	團練
T'ung-chü ch'in-shu	同居親屬
T'ung kuan lu	同官錄
T'ung-sheng	童生
T'ung-t'ang ta-chia-t'ing	同堂大家庭
Tzu	子
Tz'u	詞，祠

Tz'u-ch'en	詞臣
Wei-ch'in	外親
Wang	王
Wei-ju-liu	未入流
Wei-k'o	巍科
Wen-chi	文集
Wen-hsüeh	文學
Wen-i	文藝
Wen-kuan	文官
Wen-yüan	文苑
Wu Hsün	武訓
Wu-kuan	武官
Wu nung	務農
Wu-shih t'ung-chü, chia wu hsien-yen	五世同居家無閒言
Yang lien	養廉
Yao-chi	猺籍
Yao-i	徭役
Yin-i	隱逸
Yin-sheng	蔭生

Yüan-chi	原籍
Yüan-jen	原任
Yüeh-hu	樂戶
Yün-ch'i-wei	雲騎尉
Yung-fu-yin pu-kuan	用父蔭補官
Yung-p'ing-wei	永平衛

BIBLIOGRAPHY

I. Gazeteers (Biographical Sections)

Anhwei t'ung-chih, by Wu Lien-hsün, 1887. 安徽通志

Chang-chou fu-chih (Fukien), by Shen Ting-chün, 1878. 漳州府志

Chao-ch'ing fu-chih (Kwangtung), by T'u Ying, 1876. 肇慶府志

Chekiang t'ung-chih, by Chi Tseng-yün, 1735. 浙江通志

Ch'en-chou fu-chih (Hunan), by Hsi Shao-pao, 1765. 辰州府志

Ch'eng-tu hsien-chih (Szechwan), by Li Wu-hsüan, 1873. 成都縣志

Chi-mo hsien-chih (Shantung), by Li P'u, 1872. 即墨縣志

Chi-nan fu-chih (Shantung), 濟南府志
by Wang Tseng-fang, 1839.

Chia-hsing hsien-chih (Chekiang), 嘉興縣志
by Hsü Yao-kuang, 1878.

Chia-ting hsien-chih (Kiangsu), 嘉定縣志
by Ch'eng Ch'i'chüeh, 1880.

Chiang-hsia hsien-chih (Hupeh), 江夏縣志
by Wang T'ing-chen, 1869.

Chiang-shan hsien-chih (Chekiang), 江山縣志
by Wang Pin, 1873.

Chiang-tu hsien-chih (Kiangsu), 江都縣志
by Hsieh Yen-keng, 1883.

Ching-hsien-chih (Anhwei), 涇縣志
by Hung Liang-chi, 1806.

Ching-hai hsien-chih (Chihli), 靜海縣志
by Cheng Shih-hui, 1873.

Ch'ing-p'u hsien-chih (Kiangsu), 青浦縣志
by Ch'en Ch'i'yüan, 1877.

Chu-ch'eng hsien-chih (Shantung), 諸城縣志
by Kung Mou-jang, 1764.

Ch'üan-chou-chih (Kwangsi), 全州志
by Wen Chih-ch'eng, 1799.

Ch'üan-chou fu-chih (Fukien), 泉州府志
by Huai Yin-pu, 1689.

Feng-hsiang hsien-chih (Shensi), 鳳翔縣志
by Lo Ao, 1767.

Fo-shan chung-i hsiang-chih (Kwangtung), by Tai Tseng-mou, 1923. 佛山忠義鄉志

Fo-shan hsiang-chih (Kwangtung), by Wu Jung-kuang, 1830. 佛山鄉志

Fukien t'ung-chih, by Sun Erh-chun, 1867. 福建通志

Hai-ning chou-chih kao (Chekiang), by Chan Hsiao-tseng, 1776. 海寧州志稿

Hai-yen hsien-chih (Chekiang), by Wang Pin, 1876. 海鹽縣志

Han-yang hsien-chih (Hupeh), by Wang Shih-tu, 1868. 漢陽縣志

Hangchow fu-chih (Chekiang), by Lung Chia-chun, 1923. 杭州府志

Ho-fei hsien-chih (Anhwei), 1804. 合肥縣志

Honan t'ung-chih, by T'ien Wen-ching, 1830. 河南通志

Hsiang-shan hsien-chih (Kwangtung), by T'ien Ming-yao, 1879. 香山縣志

Hsiang-t'an hsien-chih (Hunan), by Wang K'ai-yün, 1889. 湘潭縣志

Hsiao-kan hsien-chih (Hupeh), by Chu Hsi-pai, 1882. 孝感縣志

Hsiao-shan hsien-chih (Chekiang), by Liu Yen, 1683. 蕭山縣志

Hsien-hsien-chih (Chihli), by Wan T'ing-lan, 1761. 獻縣志

Hsüan-ch'eng-chih (Anhwei), by Wu Ch'ao, 1888. 宣城志

Hu-chou fu-chih (Chekiang), by Sung Yüan-han, 1874. 湖州府志

Hua-t'ing hsien-chih (Kansu), by Chao Hsien-chia, 1796. 華亭縣志

Huai-an fu-chih (Kiangsu), by Wu K'un-t'ien, 1884. 淮安府志

I-ch'un hsien-chih (Kiangsi), by Lu Ch'ing-yün, 1871. 宜春縣志

I-tu hsien-chih (Shantung), by Ch'en Shih-hua, 1672. 益都縣志

Kan-ch'üan hsien-chih (Kiangsu), by Hsü Ch'eng-tien, 1885. 甘泉縣志

Kao-yu chou-chih (Kiangsu), by Kung Ting-ying, 1883. 高郵州志

Kuang-chou fu-chih (Kwangtung), by Tai Chao-ch'en, 1879. 廣州府志

Kuang-shan hsien-chih (Honan), by Yang Tien-hsin, 1785. 光山縣志

Kuei-an hsien-chih (Chekiang), by Lu Hsin-yüan, 1881. 歸安縣志

Kwangsi t'ung-chih chi-yao, by Yang Fu-li, 1889. 廣西通志輯要

Kwangtung t'ung-chih, by Yüan Yüan, 1822. 廣東通志

Lai-yang hsien-chih (Shantung), by Wan Pang-wei, 1678. 萊陽縣志

Li-p'ing fu-chih (Kweichow), by Yü Wei, 1892. 黎平府志

Li-yang hsien-chih (Kiangsu), by Wu Hsüeh-lien, 1743. 溧陽縣志

Lin-kuei hsien-chih (Kwangsi), by Ts'ai Ch'eng-shao, 1804. 臨桂縣志

Lou-hsien-chih (Kiangsu), by Lu Hsi-hsiung *et al*., 1788. 婁縣志

Nan-hai hsien-chih (Kwangtung), by Cheng Yung, 1910. 南海縣志

Nan-hsün-chih (Chekiang), by Chou Ch'ing-yün, 1922. 南潯志

Pao-te chou-chih (Shansi), by Wang K'o-ch'ang, 1710. 保德州志

P'ing-ho hsien-chih (Fukien), by Wang Hsiang, 1719. 平和縣志

P'ing-hu hsien-chih (Chekiang), by P'eng Jun-chang, 1886. 平湖縣志

Shantung t'ung-chih, by Yang Shih-hsiang, 1934. 山東通志

Shan-yang hsien-chih (Shensi), by Ho Shu-tzu, 1796. 山陽縣志

Shang-ch'iu hsien-chih (Honan), by Chang To-shou, 1885. 山陽縣志

Shanghai hsien-chih (Kiangsu), by Wang Ta-t'ung, 1813. 上海縣志

Shanghai-hsien hsü-chih (Kiangsu), by Wu Hsing-hsiu, 1918. 上海縣續志

Shao-chou fu-chih (Kwangtung), by O Che-yüan, 1873. 韶州府志

Shao-hsing fu-chih (Chekiang), by Chou Hsü-ts'ai, 1719. 紹興府志

Sheng-ching t'ung-chih (Liaotung), by Sung Yün, 1736. 盛京通志

Shensi t'ung-chih, by Liu Yü-i, 1735. 陝西通志

Shih-chu t'ing-chih (Szechwan), by Wang Huai-ling, 1843. 石砫廳志

Shou-ting hsien-chih (Kiangsu), by Ch'eng Ch'i-chüeh, 1882. 壽定縣志

Shun-te hsien-chih (Kwangtung), by Kuo Ju-ch'eng, 1853. 順德縣志

Shun-t'ien fu-chih (Chihli), by Chou Chia-mei, 1884. 順天府志

Su-chou fu-chih (Kiangsu), by Feng Kuei-fen, 1877. 蘇州府志

Sung-chiang fu-chih (Kiangsu), by Sung Ju-lin *et al.*, 1819. 松江府志

T'ai-hsing hsien-chih (Kiangsu), by Yang Chi-yün, 1886. 泰興縣志

T'ai-ts'ang chou-chih (Kiangsu), by Miu Chao-ch'üan, 1909. 太倉州志

Taiwan fu-chih, by Yü Wen-i, 1763. 台灣府志

Tan-t'u hsien-chih (Kiangsu), by Ho Shao-chang, 1879. 丹徒縣志

Tse-chou fu-chih (Shansi), by Chu Chang, 1735. 澤州府志

Tsou-p'ing hsien-chih (Shantung), by Lo Tsung-ying, 1836. 鄒平縣志

T'ung-an hsien-chih (Fukien), by Wu T'ang, 1885. 同安縣志

Wu-chiang hsien-chih (Kiangsu), by Chin Fu-tseng, 1877. 吳江縣志

Wu-hsi Chin-kuei hsien-chih (Kiangsu), by P'ei Ta-chung, 1881. 無錫金匱縣志

Wu-hsien-chih (Kiangsu), by Ts'ao Yün-yüan, 1933. 吳縣志

Yeh-hsien-chih (Shantung), by Chang Ssu-mien, 1758. 掖縣志

Yin-hsien-chih (Chekiang), by Chang Shu, 1877. 鄞縣志

Ying-shan hsien-chih (Hupeh), by Liu Tsung-yüan, 1871. 應山縣志

Yüan-chou fu-chih (Kiangsi), by Lo Min-hsiu, 1874. 袁州府志

Chu Shih-chia, "Chinese Local Histories at Columbia University," *Harvard Journal of Asiatic Studies*, VIII (1944), 187-95.

——— (comp.), *Chung-kuo ti-fang-chih tsung-lu*. Shanghai: Commercial Press, 1935. 中國地方志綜錄

———, *Kuo-hui t'u-shu-kuan ts'ang chung-kuo ti-fang-chih mu-lu*. Washington, D.C.: U. S. Government Printing Office, 1942. 國會圖書館藏中國地方志目錄

II. Other Chinese and Japanese Sources

A. Sources from which biographical information was obtained

Ch'ing-ch'ao kung-chü nien-piao, Hsiu-hai shan-fang ed. 清朝貢舉年表

Ch'ing-shih-kuan chuan lieh-chuan, Ch'ing-shih-kuan ed. Shanghai, 1928. 清史館傳列傳

Ch'ing shih-lu, 1937 ed. 清實錄

En-yin t'ung-nien ch'ih-lu, Tao Kuang ed. 恩蔭同年齒錄

Hsi-ch'ao tsai-fu lu, 2 vols. 熙朝宰輔錄

Hui-shih t'ung-nien ch'ih-lu, 1822, 1835, 1876, 1895, etc. 會試同年齒錄

Ko-sheng hsiang-shih ch'ih-lu, 1832, 1835, 1840, 1843, 1851, 1870, etc. 各省鄉試齒錄

Kuo-shih erh-ch'en piao (*Yen-hua tung-t'ang hsiao-p'in*, Vol. IV). 國史貳臣表 煙画東堂小品

Ming-Ch'ing wei-k'o hsing-shih lu (1372-1895). 明清巍科姓氏錄

Pa-ch'i hsüan-pa ming-ching t'ung-p'u. 八旗選拔明經通譜

Shun-K'ang-Yung san-ch'ao hui-shih t'i-ming. 順康雍三朝會試題名

Ta-Ch'ing chin-shen ch'üan-shu. Peking: Lien-ch'i-ko, 1792, and later eds. 大清搢紳全書

Ta-Ch'ing chung-shu pei-lan (Appendix to 1890 ed. of *Ta-ch'ing chin-shen ch'üan-shu*. Peking: Jung-lu-t'ang, 1890). 大清中樞備覽

T'ung-nien kuan-chih lu, for various years. 同年官職錄

Chang T'ing-yü, *et al.*, *Ming-shih*, 1903 Wu-chou t'ung-wen shu-chü ed. 張廷玉, 明史

Chao Erh-sun, *et al.*, *Ch'ing-shih kao*, 1927 edition. 趙爾巽, 清史稿

Chao I-ch'en, "Min-ch'ao tung-huan chi-shih," *Yu-man-lou ts'ung-shu*, 1925. 趙詒琛, 民抄董宦紀實, 又滿樓叢書

Chen Chün, *Kuo shu-jen chi-lüeh*, 1908. 震鈞, 國書人輯略

Ch'en-hu i-shih, *Ching-t'o i-shih*, Ch'ing ed. 陳湖逸士, 荆駝逸史

Ch'en Shou-ch'i (ed.), *Huang-chung-tuan-kung ch'üan-chi*, 1830. 陳壽祺, 黃忠端公全集

Ch'en Shou-ch'i, *Tso-hai ch'üan-chi*, 1830 and 1882. 陳壽祺, 左海全集

Ch'en T'ien, *Ming-shih chi-shih*, 1899. 陳田, 明詩紀事

Ch'en Ting, *Tung-lin lieh-chuan*, 1711. 陳鼎, 東林列傳

Ch'en Yüan, "Che-hsi Li Chih-tsao chuan," *Ch'ung-k'an pien-hsüeh i-tu*. 陳元, 浙西李之藻傳. 重刊辯學遺牘

Chi Liu-ch'i, *Ming-chi pei-lüeh*. Shanghai: Commercial Press, 1936. 計六奇, 明紀北略

Chi Yün, *et al.*, *Ch'in-ting sheng-ch'ao hsün-chi chu-ch'en lu*, 1896 ed. 紀昀, 欽定勝朝殉節諸臣錄

Chiang Liang-fu, *Li-tai ming-jen nien-li pei-chuan tsung-piao*. Shanghai: Commercial Press, 1937. 姜亮夫, 歷代名人年里碑傳總表

Ch'ien Ch'ien-i, "Ch'ien-shih i-chuang chi," *Mu-chai yu-hsüeh chi*, 27/16a. 錢謙益, 錢氏義莊記, 牧齋有學集

Ch'ien i-chi, *Pei-chuan chi*, 1893 Kiangsu shu-chu ed. 錢儀吉, 碑傳集

Chin Liang, *Chin-shih jen-wu chih*, 1934. 金梁, 近世人物志

Chu Fang-tseng, *Ts'ung-cheng kuan-fa-lu*, 1884 Ying-hsüeh-lu ed. 朱方增, 從政觀法錄

Chu Ju-chen, *Tz'u-lin chi-lüeh*, 11 vols., 1927. 朱汝珍, 詞林輯畧

Chu I-Tsun, *Ming shih-tsung*, K'ang-hsi ed. 朱彝尊, 明詩綜

Chung-hua shu-chü, *Ch'ing-shih lieh-chuan*. Shanghai: Chung-hua shu-chü, 1928. 中華書局, 清史列傳

Fang Chao-ying and Tu Lien-che, *Tseng-chiao Ch'ing-ch'ao chin-shih t'i-ming pei-lu fu yin-te*. Peiping: Harvard-Yenching Institute, 1941. 房兆楹, 杜聯喆, 增校清朝進士題名碑錄附引得

Fang Shu-mei, *Tien-nan pei-chuan-chi*, K'ai-ming shu-tien, 1940. 方樹梅, 滇南碑傳記

Hsü K'ai-chiang, *Ming ming-ch'en yen-hsing lu*, 1669. 徐開江, 明名臣言行錄

Hsü Ping-i, *Ming-mu chung-lieh chi-shih*. 徐秉義, 明末忠烈紀實

Hsü Ting, *Hsiao-t'ien chi-nien*, 1887 Chin-ling ed. 徐鼒, 小腆紀年

Jung Chao-tsu, "K'ung Shang-jen nien-p'u," *Ling-nan hsüeh-pao*, III, No. 2 (1934), 1-86. 容肇祖, 孔尚任年譜, 嶺南學報

Kao Ch'eng-yen, *Ch'ung-chen chung-chi lu*. 高承埏, 崇禎忠節錄

Ku-kung po-wu yüan, *Ch'ing-tai wen-tzu-yü tang*, 1931-34. 故宮博物院, 清代文字獄檔

Kuo-li pei-p'ing t'u-shu kuan, *Ch'ing-tai wen-chi p'ien-mu feng-lei suo-yin*, 1935. 國立北平圖書館, 清代文集篇目分類索引

K'ung Hsiang-hsi, *Shansi ming-hsien chi-yao*, 8 vols. Hankow: Chung-hua shu-chü, 1938. 孔祥熙，山西名賢輯要

Kwangsi sheng-cheng-fu t'ung-chi chü, *Ku-chin Kwangsi jen-ming chien*. Kweilin: Kwangsi sheng-cheng-fu t'ung-chi chü, 1934. 廣西省政府統計局，古今廣西人名鑑

Li Chou-wang (comp.), *Kuo-ch'ao li-k'o t'i-ming pei-lu* (7 *ts'e*), covering Shün-chih to T'ung-chih. 李周望，國朝歷科題名碑錄

Li Huan, *Kuo-ch'ao ch'i-hsien lei-cheng*, Hsiang-yin Li-shih ed. 李桓，國朝耆獻類徵

Li Kuang-pi and Ch'ien Chün-i, *Chung-kuo li-shih jen-wu lun-chi*. Peking: San-lien shu-tien, 1957. 李光璧，錢君曄，中國歷史人物論集

Li Yen, "Li Shan-lan nien-p'u," *Chung suan-shih lun-ts'ung*, 4 vols. Shanghai: Chung-hua hsüeh-i she, 1931-47. 李儼，李善蘭年譜，中算史論叢

Li Yao, *Nan-chiang i-shih chih-i*, Tao-kuang ed. 李瑶，南疆繹史摭遺

Li Yüan-tu, *Kuo-ch'ao hsien-cheng shih-lüeh*. Shanghai: Chung-hua shu-chü (*Ssu-pu pei-yao* ed.). 李元度，國朝先正事略

Liao T'ien-hsien and Chang Po-tsung, *Shang-yu lu*, 1666. 廖田賢，張伯琮，尚友錄

Ling T'i-an, *Ch'ing-tai Kweichow ming-hsien hsiang-chuan*. Shanghai: Commercial Press, 1946. 凌惕安，清代貴州名賢像傳

Liu Sheng-mu, *Ch'ing-fen lu* (in his *Chih-chieh-t'ang ts'ung-k'an*), 1929. 劉聲木,清芬錄,直介堂叢刊

"Ma tuan-min-kung nien-p'u," in Sun Meng-p'ing, *Sun hsien-sheng i-shu pen*. 馬端敏公年譜,孫孟平,孫先生遺書本

Min Erh-ch'ang, *Pei-chuan-chi pu*. Peiping: Yenching University Sinological Research Institute, 1931. 閔爾昌,碑傳集補

Miu Ch'üan-sun, *Hsü pei-chuan-chi*, 1893 Kiangsu shu-chü ed. 繆荃孫,續碑傳集

P'an Kuang-tan, *Ming-Ch'ing liang-tai Chia-hsiang ti wang-tsu*. Shanghai: Commercial Press, 1947. 潘光旦,明清兩代嘉興的望族

Shao T'ing-ts'ai, "Shao-shih yü-t'ien-hsien chuang chi," *Ssu-fu-t'ang wen-chi*, 4/9a. 邵廷燦,邵氏玉田縣莊記,思復堂文集

"Shih Yü-shan hsien-sheng nien-p'u," in *Shih Yü-shan hsien-sheng ch'üan-chi*, Ch'ing ed. 施愚山先生年譜,施愚山先生全集

T'an Cheng-pi, *Chung-kuo wen-hsüeh-chia ta-tz'u-tien*. Shanghai: Kuang-ming shu-chü, 1934. 譚正璧,中國文學家大辭典

Tou Chen, *Kuo-ch'ao shu-hua-chia pi-lu*, 1911 Wen-hsüeh shan-fang ed. 竇鎮,國朝書畫家筆錄

Ts'ai Kuan-lo, *Ch'ing-tai ch'i-pai ming-jen chuan*, 3 vols. Shanghai: World Book Company, 1937. 蔡冠洛,清代七百名人傳

Ts'ao Jung, *Ming-jen hsiao-chuan*. 曹溶,明人小傳

Tseng Kuo-fan, *Tseng wen-cheng-kung chia-shu*, 8 vols. 曾國藩，曾文正公家書

Wan Ssu-t'ung, *Ming shih*. 萬斯同，明史

Wang Chih-ch'ang, "I-t'ien shan-tsu shuo," in *Ch'ing-hsüeh-chai chi*, 30/9b. 汪之昌，義田贍族說，青學齋記

Wang Chung-min, *Ch'ing-tai wen-chi p'ien-mu fen-lei suo-yin*. Peiping: Kuo-li Peiping t'u-shu-kuan, 1935. 王重民，清代文集篇目分類索引

Wang Hsien-ch'ien, *Tung-hua hsü-lu* (Ch'ang-sha ed., 1884-90), Ch'ien-lung, 101/2b. 王先謙，東華續錄

Wang Hung-hsü, *Ming-shih kao*, Ching-shen-t'ang ed. 王鴻緒，明史稿

Wang Lan-yin, "Chi Hsiao-lan hsien-sheng nien-p'u," in *Shih-ta Yüeh-k'an* I, No. 6, 1933. 王蘭蔭，紀曉嵐先生年譜，師大月刊

"Wang wen-ching-kung tzu-chuan nien-p'u," in Wang Hsi, *Wang wen-ching-kung wen-chi*, 1707 ed. 王文靖公自撰年譜，王熙，王文靖公文集

Wang Yung, *Ch'un-jung-t'ang chi*, 1892 ed. 王昶，春融堂集

Wei Yüan, *Sheng-wu chi*, 1822. 魏源，聖武記

Wen Jui-lin, *Nan-chiang i-shih*, Pan-sung chü-shih ed. 温睿臨，南疆繹史

Yang Kuo-chen, *Yang Kuo-chen tzu-ting nien-p'u*. 楊國楨，楊國楨自訂年譜

Yao Ming-ta, *Liu Tsung-chou nien-p'u*. Shanghai, 1934.
姚名達, 劉宗周年譜

Yeh Kung-ch'o, *Ch'ing-tai hsüeh-che hsiang-chuan*, 1928 Yeh-shih ed.
葉恭綽, 清代學者象傳

Yen Mou-kung, *Ch'ing-tai cheng-hsien lei-pien*. Wusih, 1931.
嚴懋功, 清代徵獻類編

Ying Tzu, *Chung-kuo hsin hsüeh-shu jen-wu chih*. Hong Kong: Chih-ming shu-chü, 1956.
潁子, 中國新學術人物志

Yü Yüeh, *Ch'un-tsai-t'ang tsa-wen liu-pien*, in *Ch'un-tsai-t'ang ch'üan-shu*, 1899.
俞樾, 春在堂雜文六編, 春在堂全書

Yüan Mei, "T'ao-shih i-chuang pei-chi," *Hsiao-ts'ang-shan-fang wen-chi*, 12/13a.
袁枚, 陶氏義莊碑記, 小倉山房文集

B. Reference works and compendia

Ch'ing-ch'ao t'ung-chih, chüan 71 ("Chih-kuan lüeh").
清朝通志, 職官略

Ch'ing-ch'ao t'ung-tien. Wan-yu wen-k'u ed., Shanghai, 1937.
清朝通典

Ma Feng-ch'en (comp.), *Ch'ing-tai hsing-cheng chih-tu yen-chiu ts'an-k'ao shu-mu*. Peking: Peking University, 1935.
馬奉琛, 清代行政制度研究參考書目

Ta-Ch'ing hui-tien, 1690, 1727, 1764, 1813, and 1899 eds.
大清會典

Ta-Ch'ing hui-tien shih-li, "Li-pu," 1818 ed.; "Hu-pu," 1828 ed.
大清會典事例, 吏部, 户部

Yung Yung *et al.*, *Li-tai chih-kuan piao*. Shanghai: Commercial Press, 1936. 歷代職官表

C. Secondary sources

(Sources consulted but not cited in the text are preceded by an asterisk.)

*Chang Chin-chien, *Chung-kuo wen-kuan chih-tu shih*. Taipei: Chung-hua wen-hua ch'u-pan shih-yeh wei-yüan hui, 1955. 張金鑑.中國文官制度史

*Chang Chün-kuang, *Chung-kuo she-hui fa-chan shih-kang*. Shanghai: Chung-hua shu-chü, 1935. 張軍光.中國社會發展史綱

*Chang Chung-ju, *Ch'ing-tai k'ao-shih chih-tu*. N.p.: Li-ming Book Co., 1931. 章中如.清代考試制度

*Chao Chih-ch'ien, *Huang-ch'ao shih-fa k'ao*, 1864. 趙之謙.皇朝謚法考

*Ch'en Ku-yüan, *Chung-kuo fu-nü sheng-huo-shih*. Shanghai: Commercial Press, 1928. 陳顧遠.中國婦女生活史

Ch'en Ku-yüan, *Chung-kuo hun-yin shih*. Shanghai: Commercial Press, 1936. 陳顧遠.中國婚姻史

Cheng T'ien-t'ing, *Ch'ing-shih t'an-wei*. Chungking: Tu-li Press, 1946. 鄭天挺.清史探微

Ch'i Ju-shan, *Chung-kuo ti k'o-ming*. Taipei: Chung-kuo hsin-wen ch'u-pan kung-ssu, 1956. 齊如山.中國的科名

Chia Chih-fang, *Chin-tai Chung-kuo ching-chi she-hui*. Shanghai: T'ang-ti ch'u-pan she, 1949. 賈植芳, 近代中國經濟社會

*Ch'ü Hsüan-ying, *Chung-kuo she-hui shih-liao ts'ung-ch'ao chia-chi*. Shanghai: Commercial Press, 1937. 瞿宣穎, 中國社會史料叢鈔甲集

Ch'ü T'ung-tsu, *Chung-kuo fa-lü yü Chung-kuo she-hui*. Shanghai: Commercial Press, 1947. 瞿同祖, 中國法律與中國社會

Ch'ü T'ung-tsu, *Chung-kuo feng-chien she-hui*. Shanghai: Commercial Press, 1937. 瞿同祖, 中國封建社會

*Chung-kuo jen-min ta-hsüeh Chung-kuo li-shih chiao-ven shih (ed.), *Ming-Ch'ing she-hui ching-chi hsing-t'ai ti yen-chiu*. Shanghai: Jen-min ch'u-pan she, 1957. 中國人民大學中國歷史教研室, 明清社會經濟形態的研究

*Fan Wen-lan, *Chung-kuo chin-tai shih*, Part I, Vol. 1. Peking: Jen-min ch'u-pan she, 1952. 范文瀾, 中國近代史

*Fan Wen-lan *et al.*, *Chung-kuo t'ung-shih chien-pien*. Shanghai: Hsin-chih shu-tien, 1947. 范文瀾, 中國通史簡編

Fukutake Tadashi, *Chugoko noson shakai no kozo*. Tokyo: Yuhikaku, rev. ed., 1951. 福武直, 中國農村社會の構造

*Hatano Yoshihiro, "Chugoku kanryo no shogyo-kori kashiteki seikaka," *Toyoshi Kenkyu*, October, 1951, pp. 233-52. 波多野善大, 中國官僚の商業高利貸性格

Hsiao I-shan, *Ch'ing-tai t'ung-shih*, 2 vols. Shanghai: Commercial Press, 1927. 蕭一山，清代通史

*Hsiao I-shan, *Chin-tai pi-mi she-hui shih-liao*. Peiping: Kuo-li Peiping yen-chiu yüan, 1935. 蕭一山，近代秘密社會史料

*Hsieh Kuo-chen (ed.), *Ch'ing-ch'u nung-min ch'i-i tzu-liao chi-lu*. Shanghai: Hsin chih-shih ch'u-pan she, 1956. 謝國楨，清初農民起義資料輯錄

*Hsiung Te-shan, *Chung-kuo she-hui shih yen-chiu*. Shanghai: K'un-lun Book Co., 1929. 熊得山，中國社會史研究

Hsü Ta-ling, *Ch'ing-tai chüan-na chih-tu*. Peking: Harvard-Yenching Institute Publications, No. 22, June, 1950. 許大齡，清代捐納制度

Kanda Nobuo, "Manchu minzoku no suibo," *Kindai chugoku kenkyu*, Kogakusha, 1948, pp. 271-96. 神田信夫，満洲民族の衰亡

Kitamura Hirotada, "Chūgoku no jinushi to Nippon no jinushi," *Rekishi hyoron*, IV, No. 2 (February, 1950), 19-25. 北村敬直，中國の地主と日本の地主

*Kitamura Hirotada, "Shindai kaito no ichikōsatsu," *Shirin*, XXXIII, No. 1 (January, 1950), 64-77. 北村敬直，清代械鬪の一考察

Lee, F. C. H., *Ting-hsien she-hui k'ai-k'uang t'iao-ch'a*. Peiping: Chung-hua p'ing-min chiao-yü ts'u-chin hui, 1932. 李景漢，定縣社會概況調查

*Lei Yen-shou, *Ch'ing shih-fa k'ao*. Shanghai: Commercial Press, 1924. 雷延壽，清諡法考

Li Hsün, *Ming-Ch'ing shih*. Peking: Jen-min ch'u-pan she, 1957.
李洵, 明清史

*Li Kuang-pi (ed.), *Ming-Ch'ing shih lun-ts'ung*. Wuhan: Hupeh jen-min ch'u-pan she, 1957.
李光璧, 明清史論叢

Li Pao-chia, *Kuan-ch'ang hsien-hsing chi*. Shanghai: Ya-tung t'u-shu kuan, 1933.
李寶嘉, 官場現形記

*Li Shu-ch'ing, *T'ui-pien chung ti Chung-kuo she-hui*. Shanghai: Commercial Press, 1947.
李樹青, 蛻變中的中國社會

Liang Ch'i-ch'ao, *Chung-kuo li-shih yen-chiu fa (pu-pien)*. Taipei: Chung-hua shu-chü, 1956.
梁啟超, 中國歷史研究法(補編)

Liang Ch'i-ch'ao, *Chung-kuo wen-hua shih (she-hui tzu-chih p'ien)*. Taipei: Chung-hua shu-chü, 1956.
梁啟超, 中國文化史(社會組織篇)

Lü Ssu-mien, *Chung-kuo t'ung-shih*. Taipei: K'ai-ming shu-tien, 1954.
呂思勉, 中國通史

Makino Tatsumi, "Kanton no gozoku shi to gozoku fu," *Kindai Chūgoku Kenkyu*, Kōgakusha, 1948, pp. 89-129.
牧野巽, 廣東の合族祠と合族譜

*Makino Tatsumi, *Kinsesi Chūgoku sōzoku kenkyu*, Nikkō shoin, 1949.
牧野巽, 近世中國宗族研究

*Makino Tatsumi, *Shina ni okeru kazoku seido, Iwanami koza toyo shicho*, Series 10, 1935.
牧野巽, 支那に於ける家族制度, 岩波講座東洋思潮

*Makino Tatsumi, *Shina kazoku kenkyu*, Seikatsu, 1944.
牧野巽, 支那家族研究

*Makino Tatsumi, "Shinahō ni okeru gaiinshin no han-i no henka," *Kato hakushi kanreki kinen tōyōshi shusetsu*, Fuzamo, 1941.
牧野巽, 支那に於ける外姻親の範圍の變化. 加藤博士還曆紀念東洋史集說

*Makino Tatsumi, "Soshi to sono hattatus," *Tōhō gakuho*, Tokyo, IX (January, 1939), 173-250.
牧野巽, 宗祠と其の發達, 東方學報

Mao Tse-tung, *Mao Tse-tung hsüan-chi*. Peking: Jen-min ch'u-pan she, 1951.
毛澤東, 毛澤東選集

Mencius, T'eng-wen-kung. Shanghai: Commercial Press, 1929.
孟子, 滕文公

*Meng Ssu-ming, *Yüan-tai she-hui chieh-chi chih-tu*, Harvard-Yenching Publications, 1938.
蒙思明, 元代社會階級制度

Moriya Mitsuo, *Rokucho monbatsu no kenkyu*. Tokyo: Nihon shupan kyodo Pub. Co., 1951.
守屋美都雄, 六朝門閥の研究

Motomura Shōichi, "Shindai shakai ni okeru shinshi no sonzai," *Shien*, XXIV (November, 1940), 61-78.
本村正一, 清代社會に於ける紳士の存在

Niida Noburu, *Chūgoku no nosen kazoku*. Tokyo: Tokyo University Tōyō Bunka Kenkyujo, 1952.
仁井田陞, 中國の農村家族

Niida Noburu, "Shina kinsei no ichiden ryo-shu kanko to sono seiritsu," *Hōgaku kyokai zasshi*, LXIV, No. 3 (March, 1946) and LXIV, No. 4 (April, 1946). Tokyo: Tokyo University Press.
仁井田陞, 支那近世の一田兩主の慣行と其の成立

*Niida Noburu, *Shina mibunhoshi,* Zauhō Kankōkai, 1942.
仁井田陞，支那身分法

*P'an Kuang-tan, "Chung-kuo chia-p'u-hsüeh lüeh-shih," *Eastern Miscellany,* XXVI, No. 1 (January, 1929), 107-20.
潘光旦，中國家譜學略史，東方雜誌

P'an Kuang-tan and Fei Hsiao-t'ung, "K'o-chü yü shei-hui liu-tung," *She-hui k'o-hsüeh,* IV (1947), 1-21.
潘光旦，費孝通，科舉與社會流動，社會科學

Saeki Tomi, "Shindai ni okeru engyo shihon ni tsuite," *Toyoshi Kenkyu,* XI, No. 1 (September, 1950), 51-61, and XI, No. 2 (March, 1951), 128-40.
佐伯富，清代に於ける塩業資本について，東洋史研究

Sano Manabu, *Shincho shakai shi.* Tokyo: Bunkyōdo, 1947-48.
佐野學，清朝社會史

*Shen Te-fu, *Pi-chou-hsüan sheng-yü* (*Hsüeh-hai lei-pien* ed.).
沈德符，敝帚軒賸語

Shimizu Morimitsu, *Chūgoku zokusan seido ko,* Iwanami shoten, 1949.
清水盛光，中國族產制度考

Sun Pen-wen, *Hsien-tai Chung-kuo she-hui wen-t'i* (*Chia-tsu wen-t'i* Series, Vol. I). Shanghai: Commercial Press, 1943.
孫本文，現代中國社會問題

Sung Nien-tz'u, *Chung-kuo tsu-ch'an chih-tu k'ao* (translation of a Japanese work by Shimizu). Taipei: Chung-hua wen-hua ch'u-pan shih-yeh wei-yüan-hui, 1956.
宋念慈，中國族產制度考

T'ao Hsi-sheng, *Chung-kuo she-hui chih shih-ti fen-hsi.* Taipei: Ch'üan-min ch'u-pan she, 1954.
陶希聖，中國社會之史的分析

T'ao Hsi-sheng, *Hun-yin yü chia-t'ing*. Shanghai: Commercial Press, 1934. 陶希聖.婚姻與家庭

T'ao Meng-ho, "Chung-kuo ti jen-min ti fen-hsi," in *Meng-ho wen-ts'un*. Shanghai: Ya-tung t'u-shu-kuan, 1926. 陶孟和.中國的人民的分析.孟和文存

Teng Ssu-yü, *Chung-kuo k'ao-shih chih-tu shih*. Shanghai: Commercial Press, 1936. 鄧嗣禹.中國考試制度史

Tseng Fan-k'ang, *Chung-kuo cheng-chih chih-tu shih*. Taipei: Chung-hua wen-hua ch'u-pan shih-yeh wei-yüan-hui, 1953. 曾繁康.中國政治制度史

Ts'ui Shu, *Wu-fu i-t'ung hui-k'ao*, *Chi-fu ts'ung-shu* ed., *han* 32. 崔述.五服異同彙考.畿輔叢書

Wang Feng-chieh, *Chung-kuo chiao-yü shih*. Taipei: Chung-cheng shu-chü, 1954. 王鳳喈.中國教育史

Wang I-t'ung, *Wu-ch'ao men-ti, kao-men shih-hsi hun-yin piao*, 2 vols. Nanking: Chin-ling University, 1943. 王伊同.五朝門第高門世系婚姻表

Yü T'ing-ts'an, "Fu-min," in *Ching-shih wen-pien*, chap. 36. 余廷燦.富民.經世文編

III. Western Language Sources

ANONYMOUS, "Literary Examinations," *The Chinese Repository*, IV (July, 1835), 118-35.

BARBER, B., *Social Stratification: A Comparative Analysis of Structure and Process*. New York: Harcourt, Brace & Co., 1957.

BENDIX, REINHARD, AND LIPSET, SEYMOUR MARTIN (eds.), *Class, Status and Power: A Reader in Social Stratification*. Glencoe, Ill.: The Free Press, 1953.

BODDE, DERK, "Feudalism in China," in Rushton Coulborn (ed.),

Feudalism in History, pp. 49-92. Princeton, N. J.: Princeton University Press, 1956.

BRUNNERT, H. S., AND HAGELSTROM, V. V., *Present Day Political Organization of China*, a translation of the work by A. Beltchenko and E. E. Moran based upon the *Ta-Ch'ing hui-tien.* Shanghai: Kelly & Walsh, 1912.

BUCK, J. L., *Chinese Farm Economy.* Shanghai: Commercial Press, 1930.

———, *Land Utilization in China.* Chicago: University of Chicago Press, 1937.

CHANG CHUNG-LI, *The Chinese Gentry: Studies on Their Role in Nineteenth-Century Chinese Society.* Seattle: University of Washington Press, 1955.

———, *The Gentry in Nineteenth-Century China: Their Economic Position As Evidenced by Their Share of the National Product.* Unpublished Ph.D. dissertation, University of Washington, Seattle, 1953.

CH'EN SHIH-HSIANG, "An Innovation in Chinese Biographical Writing," *Far Eastern Quarterly*, XIII (November, 1953), 49-62.

CHI CH'AO-TING, *Key Economic Areas in Chinese History, As Revealed in the Development of Public Works for Water Controls.* London: George Allen & Unwin, Ltd., 1936.

CH'Ü T'UNG-TSU, "Chinese Class Structure and Its Ideology," in J. K. Fairbank (ed.), *Chinese Thought and Institutions.* Chicago: University of Chicago Press, 1957.

COMMEAUX, CHARLES, "De K'ang Hi à Kien Long, L'âge d'or des Ts'ing," *Annales de L'Université de Lyon*, 3d Series, Fasc. 29, 1957.

DAHRENDORF, RALF, *Class and Class Conflict in Industrial Society.* Stanford, Calif.: Stanford University Press, 1959.

DAVIES, A. F., "Prestige of Occupations," *British Journal of Sociology*, III (1952), 134-47.

DAVIS, K., *Human Society.* New York: Macmillan Co., 1949.

DAVIS, KINGSLEY, AND BLAKE, JUDITH, "Social Structure and Fertility: An Analytic Framework," in *Economic Development and Cultural Change*, IV (April, 1956), 211-35.

DIMOCK, M. E., AND HYDE, H. K., "Executive Appointment in Private and Public Bureaucracies," in R. K. Merton *et al.* (eds.), *Reader in Bureaucracy.*

DURKHEIM, E., *The Elementary Forms of Religious Life.* Glencoe, Ill.: The Free Press, 1954.

EBERHARD, WOLFRAM, *Conquerors and Rulers.* Leiden: E. J. Brill, 1952.

———, *Das Toba-Reich Nordchinas.* Leiden: E. J. Brill, 1949.

EISENSTADT, S. N., *From Generation to Generation: Age Group and Social Structure.* Glencoe, Ill.: The Free Press, 1956.

FAIRBANK, J. K., *The United States and China.* Cambridge, Mass.: Harvard University Press, 1948.

FAIRBANK, J. K., AND TENG, S. Y., "On the Transmission of Ch'ing Documents," *Harvard Journal of Asiatic Studies,* V (May, 1939), 12-46.

———, "On the Types and Uses of Ch'ing Documents," *Harvard Journal of Asiatic Studies,* VI (January, 1940), 1-71.

FEI HSIAO-T'UNG, *Peasant Life in China.* London: Routledge & Kegan Paul, Ltd., 1939.

———, "Peasantry and Gentry: An Interpretation of Chinese Social Structure and Its Changes," *American Journal of Sociology,* LII (1946), 1-17.

FEI HSIAO-T'UNG AND CHANG CHIH-I, *Earthbound China.* Chicago: University of Chicago Press, 1945.

FENG HAN-YI, *The Chinese Kinship System.* Cambridge, Mass.: Harvard University Press, 1948.

FENG HAN-YI AND SHRYOCK, J. S., "Marriage Customs in the Vicinity of I-Ch'ang", *Harvard Journal of Asiatic Studies,* XIII (1950), 362-430.

FEUERWERKER, ALBERT, *China's Early Industrialization, 1844-1916.* Cambridge, Mass.: Harvard University Press, 1958.

FRANKE, HERBERT, "Some Remarks on the Interpretation of Chinese Dynastic Histories," *Oriens,* III, 113-22.

GAMBLE, SIDNEY D., "Hsin Chuang, A Study of Chinese Village Finance," *Harvard Journal of Asiatic Studies,* VIII (1944), 1-33.

———, *Ting Hsien: A North China Rural Community.* New York: International Secretariat, Institute of Pacific Relations, 1954.

GILES, H. A., *China and the Manchus.* Cambridge: Cambridge University Press; New York: G. P. Putnam's Sons, 1912.

———, *Historic China and Other Sketches.* London: T. de La Rue, 1882.

GLASS, D. V. (ed.), *Social Mobility in Britain.* London: Routledge & Kegan Paul, Ltd.; Glencoe, Ill.: The Free Press, 1954.

GOODMAN, L., AND KRUSKAL, W., "Measures of Association for Cross-Classification," *Journal of the American Statistical Association* (Dec. 1954) 732-764.

GOODRICH, L. C., *The Literary Inquisition of Ch'ien-lung*. Baltimore: Waverly Press, 1935.

GORST, HAROLD, *China*. London: Sands & Co., 1899.

GÜTZLAFF, CHARLES, *China Opened*. 2 vols. London: Smith, Elder & Co., 1838.

HAGOOD, M. J., AND PRICE, D. O., *Statistics for Sociologists*. Rev. ed. New York: Henry Holt, 1952.

HAN YÜ-SHAN, *Elements of Chinese Historiography*. Hollywood, Calif.: W. M. Hawley, 1955.

HERSON, L. J. R., "China's Imperial Bureaucracy: Its Direction and Control," *Public Administration Review*, XVII (Winter, 1957), 44-53.

HO PING-TI, "The Salt Merchants of Yang-Chou: A Study of Commercial Capitalism in Eighteenth-Century China," *Harvard Journal of Asiatic Studies*, XVII (1954), 130-68.

———, "Social Mobility in China, 1368-1911," in *Comparative Studies in Society and History*, July, 1959.

HOBBES, THOMAS, *Leviathan*.

HOZUMI, FUMIO, "A Study of the Character of Current Chinese Economy," in *Kyoto University Economic Review*, XV (1940), 41-66.

HSIEH PAO-CHAO, *The Government of China, 1644-1911*. Baltimore: Johns Hopkins Press, 1925.

HSÜ F. L. K., "The Myth of Chinese Family Size," *American Journal of Sociology*, XLVIII (March, 1943), 555-62.

———, "Social Mobility in China," *American Sociological Review*, XIV (1949), 764-71.

———, "Social Research in China," *Quarterly Bulletin of Chinese Bibliography*, n.s., IV, Nos. 1-4 (March-December, 1944), 12-26.

———, *Under the Ancestors' Shadow*. New York: Columbia University Press, 1948.

HU SHIH, "Preface" to Arthur Hummel (ed.), *Eminent Chinese of the Ch'ing Period*.

HU HSIEN-CHIN, *The Common Descent Group in China and Its Functions*. New York: Viking Fund, Publications in Anthropology, No. 10, 1948.

HUMMEL, ARTHUR W. (ed.), *Eminent Chinese of the Ch'ing*

Period. Washington, D.C.: U. S. Government Printing Office, 1943.

———, Letter to R. M. Marsh, dated March 10, 1955.

INSTITUTE OF PACIFIC RELATIONS, *Agrarian China: Selected Source Materials from Chinese Authors.* London: George Allen & Unwin, Ltd., 1939.

JANOWITZ, M., "The Systematic Analysis of Political Biography," *World Politics,* VI (1954), 406-12.

JOHNSTON, R. F., *Lion and Dragon in North China.* London: John Murray, 1910.

KATO SHIGERU, "On the *Hang* or the Associations of Merchants in China," *Memoirs of the Research Department of the Toyo Bunko,* VIII (1936), 45-83.

KENNEDY, G. H., *ZH Guide: An Introduction to Sinology.* New Haven: Yale University Press, 1953.

KOLABINSKA, M., *La Circulation des Élites en France.* Lausanne, 1912.

KRACKE, E. A., JR., "Family vs. Merit in the Civil Service Examinations under the Empire," *Harvard Journal of Asiatic Studies,* X (1947), 103-23.

———, "Region, Family, and Individual in the Chinese Examination System," in J. K. Fairbank (ed.), *Chinese Thought and Institutions,* pp. 251-68. Chicago: University of Chicago Press, 1957.

LANE-POOLE, STANLEY, *The Life of Sir Harry Parkes.* New York: Macmillan Co., 1894.

LANG, OLGA, *Chinese Family and Society.* New Haven: Yale University Press, 1946.

LATOURETTE, K. S., *The Chinese, Their History and Culture.* New York: Macmillan Co., 1950.

LATTIMORE, OWEN, *Manchuria, Cradle of Conflict.* New York: Macmillan Co., 1935.

LEE, ROSE HUM, "Research on the Chinese Family," *American Journal of Sociology,* LIV (May, 1949), 497-504.

LEE, SHU-CHING, "Intelligentsia of China," *American Journal of Sociology,* LII (May, 1947), 489-497.

LEVY, H. S., Review article, *Journal of Asian Studies,* XVI (August, 1957), 612-17.

LEVY, MARION J., JR., "Contrasting Factors in the Modernization of China and Japan," in Simon Kuznets, Wilbert E. Moore, and Joseph J. Spengler (eds.), *Economic Growth: Brazil,*

India and Japan, pp. 496-536. Durham, N. C.: Duke University Press, 1955.

———, *The Family Revolution in Modern China*. Cambridge, Mass.: Harvard University Press, 1949.

Li Hsiung-fei, *Les Censeurs sous la dynastie Mandchoue, 1616-1911*. Paris: Presses Modernes, 1936.

Lipset, S. M., and Bendix, R., *Social Mobility in Industrial Society*. Berkeley: University of California Press, 1959.

———, "Social Status and Social Structure," *British Journal of Sociology*, Vol. II, 1951.

Luthy, H., "Dynasties familiales et mobilité social," *Preuves*, V, No. 50 (April, 1955), 22-30.

Ma Feng-ch'en, "Manchu-Chinese Social and Economic Conflicts In Early Ch'ing," in E-tu Zen Sun and J. De Francis (eds.), *Chinese Social History*, pp. 333-52. Washington, D.C.: American Council of Learned Societies, 1956.

Makino, Tatsumi, "The Family System in China," *Transactions of the Third World Congress of Sociology*, IV (1954), 208-14.

Mannheim, Karl, *Freedom, Power and Democratic Planning*. New York: Oxford University Press, 1950.

Mao Tse-tung, *Selected Works of Mao Tse-tung*. London: Lawrence & Wishhart, Ltd., 1954.

Martin, W. A. P., *A Cycle of Cathay*. 2d ed. London: Oliphant, Anderson & Ferrier, 1897.

———, *Hanlin Papers*. 2d Series. Shanghai: Kelly and Walsh, 1894.

Mayers, W. F., *The Chinese Government*. 3rd ed. rev. by Playfair. Shanghai, 1897.

Meadows, T. T., *The Chinese and Their Rebellions*. London: Smith, Elder and Co., 1856.

———, *Desultory Notes on the Government and People of China*. London, 1847.

Medhurst, W. H., "Marriage, Affinity and Inheritance in China," *Transactions*, Royal Asiatic Society, China Branch, 4.

Merton, R. K., *Social Theory and Social Structure*. Rev. ed. Glencoe, Ill.: The Free Press, 1957.

Merton, R. K., *et al.* (eds.), *Reader in Bureaucracy*. Glencoe, Ill.: The Free Press, 1952.

Merton, R. K., and Kitt, A. S., "Reference Group Theory and Social Mobility," in Bendix and Lipset (eds.), *Class, Status and Power*.

MICHAEL, FRANZ, *The Origin of Manchu Rule in China.* Baltimore: Johns Hopkins Press, 1942.

MILLER, JAMES MARTIN, *China: Ancient and Modern.*

MORRISON, R., A *View of China, for Philological Purposes.* Macao: East India Co. Press., 1817; London: Black, Parbury & Allen, 1817.

MOSCA, G., *The Ruling Class.* Translated by H. D. Hahn. New York: McGraw-Hill Book Co., 1923.

MURDOCK, G. P., *Social Structure.* New York: Macmillan Co., 1949.

NATIONAL OPINION RESEARCH CENTER, "Jobs and Occupations: A Popular Evaluation," in Bendix and Lipset (eds.), *Class, Status and Power,* pp. 411-26.

PARETO, V., *The Mind and Society,* Vol. III, "Elites." New York: Harcourt, Brace & Co., 1935.

PARSONS, T., *Essays in Sociological Theory.* Rev. ed. Glencoe, Ill.: The Free Press, 1954.

———, *The Social System.* Glencoe, Ill.: The Free Press, 1951.

———, *The Structure of Social Action.* Glencoe, Ill.: The Free Press, 1949.

PARSONS, T., AND BALES, R. F., *Family, Socialization and Interaction Process.* Glencoe, Ill.: The Free Press, 1955.

PARSONS, T., AND SHILS, E. A., *Toward A General Theory of Action.* Cambridge, Mass.: Harvard University Press, 1949.

POWELL, RALPH, *The Rise of Chinese Military Power, 1895-1912.* Princeton, N. J.: Princeton University Press, 1955.

PULLEYBLANK, E. G., Review article, *Bulletin of the School of Oriental and African Studies,* XV (1953), 588-97.

R. I. (Anonymous), "The Chinese Government and Constitution," *Chinese Repository,* 1836, pp. 11-17.

RICCI, MATTEO, *China in the Sixteenth Century: The Journals of Matteo Ricci, 1583-1610.* Translated by Gallagher, L. J., S. J. New York: Random House, 1953.

ROGOFF, NATALIE, *Recent Trends in Occupational Mobility.* Glencoe, Ill.: The Free Press, 1953.

ROUSIERS, PAUL DES, *L'élite dans La Societé Moderne.* Paris, 1914.

SCHNEIDER, L., AND LYSGAARD, S., "The Deferred Gratification Pattern: A Preliminary Study," *American Sociological Review,* XVIII (1953), 142-49.

SCHUMPETER, J., *Imperialism and Social Classes.* New York: Meridian Books, 1955.

SELZNICK, P., *TVA and the Grass Roots: A Study in the Sociology of Formal Organization.* Berkeley: University of California Press, 1949.

SHIROKOGOROFF, S. M., *Social Organization of the Manchus.* Shanghai, 1924.

SKINNER, G. W., "The New Sociology in China," *Far Eastern Quarterly*, X (August, 1951), 365-71.

SOROKIN, P. A., *Social Mobility.* New York: Harper & Bros., 1927; reprinted in *Social and Cultural Mobility*, The Free Press, Glencoe, Ill., 1959.

STAUNTON, SIR GEORGE T., *Ta Tsing Leu Lee,* being a translation of *The Fundamental Laws and Supplementary Statutes of the Penal Code of China* (*Ta-Ch'ing lü-li*). London: Bart. F.R.S., 1810.

STOUFFER, S. A., *et al.*, "Who Were the Most Critical of the Army's Promotion Opportunities?" in Merton *et al.* (eds.), *Reader in Bureaucracy.*

TAUSSIG, F. W., AND JOSLYN, C. S., *American Business Leaders.* New York: Macmillan, 1932.

TAWNEY, R. H., *Land and Labour in China.* London: George Allen & Unwin, Ltd., 1932.

TENG, SSU-YÜ, *New Light on the History of the Taiping Rebellion.* Cambridge, Mass.: Harvard University Press, 1950.

TENG, SSU-YÜ, AND BIGGERSTAFF, KNIGHT, *Annotated Bibliography of Chinese Reference Works.* Rev. ed. Cambridge, Mass.: Harvard University Press, 1950.

TENG, SSU-YÜ, AND FAIRBANK, J. K., *China's Response to the West: A Documentary Survey, 1839-1923.* Cambridge, Mass.: Harvard University Press, 1954.

TUMIN, M. M., AND FELDMAN, A. S., "Theory and Measurement of Occupational Mobility," *American Sociological Review*, XXII (June, 1957), 281-88.

TWITCHETT, T. D., "Chinese Biographical Writing." Unpublished ms., c/o Hugh Borton, East Asiatic Library, Columbia University.

VAN DER VALK, MARC, *An Outline of Modern Chinese Family Law.* Monograph II of Monumenta Serica.

WALEY, ARTHUR, *Chinese Poems.* London: George Allen & Unwin, Ltd., 1948.

———, *Yuan Mei, Eighteenth Century Chinese Poet.* New York: Grove Press, Inc., 1956.

WANG YU-CH'UAN, "The Rise of the Land Tax and the Fall of Dynasties in Chinese History," *Pacific Affairs*, IX (1936), 201-20.

WEBER, MAX, *From Max Weber: Essays in Sociology*. Translated and edited by Hans H. Gerth and C. Wright Mills. New York: Oxford University Press, 1946.

———, *The Religion of China*. Translated and edited by Hans H. Gerth. Glencoe, Ill.: The Free Press, 1951.

———, *The Theory of Social and Economic Organization*. Translated by A. M. Henderson and T. Parsons. New York: Oxford University Press, 1947.

WERNER, E. T. C., *Descriptive Sociology of the Chinese*. London, 1910.

WILBUR, C. MARTIN, *Slavery in China during the Former Han Dynasty*, 206 B.C.-25 A.D. Chicago: Field Museum of Natural History, 1943.

WILLIAMS, S. WELLS, *The Middle Kingdom*. 2 vols. New York: Wiley & Putnam, 1848.

WITTFOGEL, K. A., "The Foundation and Stages of Chinese Economic History," *Zeitschrift fur sozialforschung*, IV (1935), 26-58.

———, *New Light on Chinese Society*. New York: International Secretariat, IPR, 1938.

———, *Oriental Despotism: A Comparative Study of Total Power*. New Haven: Yale University Press, 1957.

———, "The Ruling Bureaucracy of Oriental Despotism: A Phenomenon That Paralyzed Marx," *Review of Politics*, XV (1953), 350-59.

WITTFOGEL, K. A., AND FENG, C. S., *History of Chinese Society, Liao*, 907-1125. Philadelphia: American Philosophical Society; New York: Macmillan Co., 1949.

WRIGHT, MARY C., *The Last Stand of Chinese Conservatism*. Stanford, Calif.: Stanford University Press, 1957.

YANG, C., *Statistics of China's Foreign Trade*. Nanking: National Research Institute of Social Sciences, Academia Sinica, Monograph IV, 1931.

YANG, LIEN-SHENG, "The Concept of *Pao* As A Basis for Social Relations in China," in J. K. Fairbank (ed.), *Chinese Thought and Institutions*.

———, *Money and Credit in China: A Short History*. Cambridge, Mass.: Harvard University Press, 1952.

———, "Powerful Families of Eastern Han," in E-tu Zen Sun and J. De Francis (eds.), *Chinese Social History*. Washington, D.C.: American Council of Learned Societies, 1956.

Zi, Etienne, *Pratique des Examens Litteraires en Chine. Varietées Sinologiques*, No. 5, 1894.

———, *Pratique des Examens Militaires en Chine. Varietées Sinologiques*, No. 9, 1896.

INDEX

Abahai, 95
Abegglen, J. C., 107
Absentee landlordism, 61; and examination candidates, 77; in Kiangsu, 77
Achievement factors, 142
Adaptive mechanisms, 179
Adaptive structures, 190
Administration, "patrimonial-praebendal," 185
Advancement, 115; based on extraordinary promotions, 173; bureaucratic determinants of, 118, 183, 184, 191, 192; bureaucratic norms of, 28; determinants of, 116, 154; ethnic and stratum differences in, 124, 133, 135, 137, 142, 152; extra-bureaucratic determinants of, 28, 31, 32, 118, 136, 143, 154, 169, 174, 175, 183, 184, 191; and family economic status, 175; and family stratum position, 132, 135, 136, 141, 142, 144, 154, 155, 156, 164, 174, 175; to high military posts, 141; and recruitment paths taken, 139, 140, 141, 144, 146, 149, 164, 173, 174; and seniority, 154, 173, 174; and strength of official tradition in family, 154, 155, 156, 157; through military career, 151
Advancement pattern, of Chinese Bannermen, 121; of Manchu Bannermen, 121
Advancement patterns, 159
A-k'o-tun, 119
Asitan, 112

Banner families, Chinese, 119, 120; Manchu, 119, 120
Banner military organization, 120
Bannerman, Chinese, 54, 120, 121, 122; 123; Manchu, 54, 75, 120, 121, 122, 123; Mongol, 54

Banners, Manchu, 60
Barber, B., 177
Bendix, R., 30, 61
Biggerstaff, K., 95
Board of Civil Office (*Li-pu*), 91, 111, 112, 165, 171, 173
Board of Civil Service; *see* Board of Civil Office
Board of Punishments (*Hsing-pu*), 112
Board of Revenue (*Hu-pu*), 112
Board of Rites (*Li-pu*), 112
Boggodo, 53
Bourgeoisie, 24
Buck, J. L., 16
Bureaucracy, formal organization of the Chinese Imperial, 84; informal structure of, 124
Bureaucratic determinants, of official recruitment and advancement, 31, 32, 152; *see also* Recruitment, Advancement
Bureaucratic elite, Chinese, 185; *see also* Elite
Burschen, German, 6

Campaigns, in Annam, 149; in Burma, 149; in the Ili Valley, 149; in Taiwan, 149; in Turkestan, 149
Caste system, 3, 4
Censorate (*Tu ch'a yüan*), 134
Chang Chin-wu, 100
Chang Chung-li, 14, 35, 37, 56, 62-67, 79-82, 140, 175, 179, 188
Chang Hai-p'eng, 100
Ch'ang-ling, 98
Chang Yin-huan, 150
Chao Chih-ch'ien, 100
Chao I-ch'ing, 100
Chen (Towns), 77
Ch'en Hung-mou, 181
Ch'en Ta-shou, 173
Ch'en Yin-k'o, 12
Ch'eng Chin-fang, 100
Cheng-shih (Dynastic histories), 85
Ch'eng-shih (Cities), 77
Chi Ch'ao-ting, 35
Chi Chen-i, 100
Ch'i-min (Commoners), 57
Ch'i-tu-wei, 53, 54
Chia-hsing, prominent clans in, 75
Chiang Kuang-hsu, 100
Chiao Hung, 100
Chia-p'u, 108
Chien (Mean people), 50, 57, 58, 59, 60
Chien-jen, 112
Ch'ien Lung Emperor, 47; literary inquisition under the, 95
Chien-min (People of "mean" occupations), 42
Chien-sheng (Imperial collegians), 38, 55, 56, 131
Ch'ien T'ai-chi, 100
Ch'ih-tz'u, 110
Chin-ch'i, 55
Chin Dynasty (A.D. 1115-1234), 44
Chinese culture, core values of, 2
Chin-feng, 110
Chin-shen (Officials), 54
Chin-shih degree, 3, 13, 15, 31, 38, 55, 56, 65, 72, 74, 75, 82, 113, 114, 115, 117, 124, 125, 126, 127, 131, 140, 151, 152, 173, 187; age at attainment, 126, 127, 128; influence of wealth upon the attainment of, 130; and intellectual family background, 128, 129
Chin-shih examinations, 3, 49, 81; as a Chinese channel of advancement, 125, 127

Chin-shih "graduates," 81; family background of, 78, 126, 127, 128, 129
Chin-tseng, 110
Ch'ing-ch'e-tu-wei, 53, 54
Ch'ing Dynasty, histories of the, 85; institutional changes in the, 72, 73; institutional practices of the, 109; institutional reforms in the, 88
Ch'ing-pai ("Pure"), 58
Ch'ing period, 75
Ch'ing-shih kao, 85, 87
Chiu-p'in hierarchy ("Nine-rank"), 54
Ch'ou Chao-ao, 100
Chou Li, 179
Chu-chüan, 77
Chu I-tsun, 100, 124
Chü-jen, 15, 38, 55, 56, 65, 72, 82, 130, 131, 140
Ch'ü T'ung-tsu, 35, 51
Chu Yün, 100
Chuan-chi (Biographies), 90, 91
Chuang-yüan, 74
Chung Ho Tien, 141
Chung-to, 57
Class, the concept of, 23, 24
Commoners, extra tax burden of the, 68
Common lineage property (*tsu-ch'an*), 178
Conformity, 6, 7, 9
Confucian clichés, in biographies, 89
Confucian scholar-general, the tradition of the, 141
Confucian view of the individual, 88
Co-optation, 49
Corvée, 42

Daisan, 53
Deferred gratification pattern, 182, 183
Degree-holders, 54, 55; legal privileges of, 56
Deviant groups, social control of, 58, 59
Diplomats to Western nations, 150
Dodo, 53
Dorgon, 53
Dynastic cycle, 33, 34, 43, 44, 160, 162; and upward mobility into officialdom, 163, 164, 188

Eberhard, W., 35
Economic status, and social status, 38, 39
Education, as a means of mobility, 125; stratum differentials in, 125
Educational subsidies, lineage pooling in, 177-180; non-kin sources of, 180, 181, 182
E-le-teng-pao, 119
Elite, alienation of the Chinese, 46; American, 185; career patterns of, 14; fertility rates of, 10, 16; income of the, 66, 67; the industrial, 21; "irregular," 65; local or "lower," 15, 65; the Nazi, 21; the power, 21; professional services of the, 66; "regular," 65; size of the, 10, 14; tax evasion of the, 67; the upper, 65; and the upper class, 21
Elite demand, 10, 15, 16
Elite mobility, definition of, 9; *see also* Mobility
Elite of the Realm, 51, 52, 53, 54, 186; hereditary positions of the, 52, 53
En-ch'i-wei, 53, 54
Endogamy, 25
Examination, the 1721 *Chin-*

shih, 6; the 1738 *Chin-shih*, 8; *po-hsüeh hung-tz'u*, 140

Examination candidates, social background of, 77, 78

Examination path (*K'o-t'u, k'o-mu-t'u*), 73, 140, 189

Examination system, the, 2, 3, 5, 6, 28, 40, 73, 80, 124, 125, 128, 130; decline of social mobility in the, 81; ideological indoctrination of the, 39; and later official advancement, 82; Manchu Bannermen in the, 48, 49; as means of elite recruitment, 73, 82, 103; as a mechanism for upward mobility, 78; as a mobility channel, 76, 144, 151, 187; as the preferred path, 13, 31, 117; satires and attacks on, 8; in the T'ang Dynasty, 12

Examinations, *hsien* (District), 4; metropolitan, 4, 49, 55, 181, 182; palace, 4, 55; special, 124; prefectural (*fu*), 4, 55; provincial, 4, 55

Extra-bureaucratic determinants, of official recruitment and advancement, 146, 152, 153, 175, 183; *see also* Recruitment, Advancment

Fa (Law), 50

Fa-chia (Legalists), 50

Fairbank, J. K., 116

Family background, 30, 116; as a determinant of advancement, 170

Family of procreation, 25

Family size, and socio-economic status, 17

Family stratum position, 10, 113, 114, 117, 118, 124, 126, 131, 158, 190; and length of incumbency, 137, 152; and official advancement, 146, 149; and rank reached, 152; and rate of promotion, 134; and recruitment path taken, 146; and upward mobility, 160

Fan Chung-yen (989-1052), 179

Fang (Branches of a lineage), 177

Fa-shih-shan, 100

Fei Hsiao-t'ung, 76, 77, 78, 82, 150, 177

Feng-kao, 109

Feng-mi, 112

Feng-shen-chi-lun (1763-1807), 49

Feng-shui (Geomancy), as an explanation of lineage mobility, 76

Feng-yin, 112

Fertility, class differences in, 16; and economic status, 16, 17

Feudalism, 36, 50, 57

Foreign affairs, 150, 151

Free-school fields (*I-shu t'ien, i-t'ien*), 178

Free schools, 183

Freedman, Maurice, 179

Fu-lin, 95

Functional alternatives, 177, 194

Functional prerequisites of bureaucracy, 190

Gentry, 35, 40, 186; the English, 40; functions, 15, 38, 62, 65; lower, 80, 188; upper, 80, 188

Goldhamer, H., 192

Goodman, L., 113

Grand Secretary (*Ko-ch'en*), 140

Gross National product, 67

Guilds, merchant, 33

Hai-lan-ch'a, 119

Hanlin Academy, 160

Haoge, 53

Hao-tsu (Influential families), 3
Historiography, the "praise and blame" school of, 87
Ho-chi, 108
Ho Ch'o, 100
Ho Ping-ti, on mobility, 72, 78, 81, 82, 179
Ho-shen (1750-99), 65
Honors bestowed posthumously, 110
Horatio Alger myth, the, 2
Hou (Marquises), 53, 54
Hsi-chüeh (Office by inheritance), 73
Hsiang, 77
Hsiang-shen, 55
Hsiao Yung-tsao, 98
Hsieh Pao-chao, 112, 171
Hsien (District), 36, 37; magistrate, 36, 63
Hsing-chuang (Account of conduct), 91
Hsü Ch'ien-hsüeh, 100
Hsu, Francis L. K., on social mobility, 78, 79, 82
Hsü Shu-k'uei, 100
Hsü Wen-ching, 100
Hsün-tzu, 3
Hu (Households), 14
Hu Hsien-chin, 180
Hu Shih, 85, 86
Huang P'ei-lieh, 100
Hummel, Arthur W., 94, 97
Hun-yin (Marriage), as a factor in vertical mobility, 75
Hydraulic control, 36
Hypergamy, 25, 30
Hypogamy, 25, 30

I-ch'in (Those of Imperial blood), 52
I-chuang, 178
I-feng, 109, 110
I-hsi (Residential mobility), as a factor in vertical mobility, 75
I-hsin, 119
I-hsüeh (Free schools), 180, 181
I-huan, 119
I-kuei (Those of nobility), 52, 53
I-t'ien, 178
I-tseng, 110
I-tsung, 119
Imperial Academy, 55
Income distribution, disparity of, in China, 68
Incumbency, extra-bureaucratic influence on, 138
Incumbency in high-rank posts, family background and, 143, 147; and recruitment path, 147; Manchus, 147
Inheritance patterns, 10, 27, 28, 30
Innovation, 6, 7
Intellectual family background, influence of, 128
Intelligence, 29, 30
Intermarriage, Manchu-Chinese, 47
Irregular path (*tsa-t'u*), 130, 131, 139-143; and high mobility, 147-148

Jen-ts'ai (Men of talent), 3
Jirgalang, 53
Joslyn, C. S., 77, 105
Jung Hung, 150

Kao-feng, 110
K'ao-kung ssu (Department of Merit Assessment), 91
Kao-shou, 110
Kao-tseng, 110
Kao-tsung, Emperor, 49
Kinship solidarity, and social mobility, 177
Kinship units, effective, 23
Kracke, E. A., on Sung officials, 155, 187

Kruskal, William H., 113
Ku Kuang-ch'i, 100
Ku Yen-wu, 179
Kuei ("Elite"), 50
K'uei-lun, 47
Kung (Artisan), 34
Kung (Dukes), 53, 54
Kung-sheng (Senior licentiate), 15, 38, 55, 56, 65, 82, 130, 131
Kuo Hsiu, 173
Kuo Shih Kuan (History Office), 91
Kuo Shih Kuan pen-chuan, 91

Lamson, H., 16, 17
Landownership, 33
Land tenure, 62, 68, 69
Lang, O., 116
Lao-hsin (Mental work), 34
Lao-li (Manual labor), 34
Latourette, K. S., 116
Le-pao, 98
Lekedehun, 53
Levy, Marion J., 116
Li (Propriety), 50
Li Ch'eng-liang, 94
Li chien-sheng, 131
Li-feng, 110
Li kung-sheng (Imperial students through purchase), 65, 131
Li Pao-chia, 8
Li-shou, 110
Li Wen-t'ien, 182
Liang (Commoners), 50, 57, 60
Liang Shih-cheng, 110
Licentiate, 130, 131; *see also Sheng-yüan*
Lieh-chuan, 90, 91
Ling-sheng, 140
Lipset, S. M., 30, 61
Literati, 41, 55
Liu E, 8
Liu Jui-fen, 150
Liu Lun (1711-73), 140
Liu Ming-ch'uan (1836-96), 151
Liu Ting, 94
Liu T'ung-hsun, 49
Local elite, 40, 41, 51, 54, 82, 186; income of, 66, 67; special legal privilege of, 51
Local leadership roles, and economic status, 38; and social status and prestige, 38, 39
Lower degrees, attainment of, 130-132
Lü Kung, 173
Lü Ssu-mien, 60

Ma Yüeh-kuang, 100
Maci, 98
Manchu Dynasty, the origin of the, 44, 45
Manchu rule, impact of, 34
Manchus, early economic and political acculturation of the, 46; feudalism of the, 46; irregular-path, 148; regular-path, 148; sinicization of the, 46-49; tribal despotism of the, 46
Mandate of Heaven, 43
Mannheim, Karl, 11
Mao Chin, 100
Marx, Karl, the concept of class of, 24
Meadows, T. T., 48
Means of seeking office, permitted, 4, 5; preferred, 4, 5; proscribed, 4-7
Mencius, 34
Merit, 28, 29, 30
Merton, Robert K., 6, 9, 183
Metropolitan graduates, 3; *see also Chin-shih*
Miao people, 181
Mien-k'ai, 119
Military bureaucracy, career in, 149, 150
Military career, in the Republican

period, 150; and upward mobility, 150
Miller, William, 107
Mills, C. W., 107
Ming-Ch'ing struggle (Ming-Manchu struggle), 171, 189
Ming Dynasty, 44, 45, 75, 85; institutional changes in the, 72, 73; institutional practices of the, 109
Ming-liang, 98
Ming-shih (History of the Ming), 85
Miscellaneous path (*tsa-t'u*), 170
Mo Yu-chih, 100
Mobility, 20, 21, 26, 70, 116, 184, 192; American studies of, 107; biographies as sources on, 84; and bureaucratic career, 72, 108; bureaucratic determinants of, 11, 115, 116; of Chinese elite, 71; comparative analysis of social, 192; consequences of, 11; determinants of social, 9, 10, 14, 29, 30, 75; determinants of the amount of, 13; downward, 25-27; and dynastic cycle, 12; earlier research on Ch'ing, 71-83, 183; extra-bureaucratic determinants of, 11, 115, 116, 160; by extraordinary promotion, 180, 183; and familv, 21; horizontal, 20; inter-generational, 9, 13, 14, 21, 27, 79, 154, 159, 160; intra-generational, 13, 14, 25, 83, 154; mass, 20; occupational, 192; patterns of, 11, 78, 83, 188; recent Chinese Marxist studies of, 73, 74; as a reward for virtue, 76; by seniority, 180; socio-historical sources on, 84; a theory of comparative, 194; upward, 29; values and norms affecting, 10, 30; vertical, 20, 23, 25, 26, 29; Western elite, 71
Mobility processes, 154, 176-183; functional alternatives to American, 194; pooling of lineage resources as, 177-180; post-recruitment career, 183; pre-career, 176; and pre-career recruitment, 183
Mo-chüan, 77
Monopolies, government, 33
Motivation, 29, 30

Nan (Barons), 53, 54
Nei Ko, 141
Nepotism, 114, 116, 171; alternatives to overt, 184; restraints on, 184; versus seniority principle, 189
Nien-p'u, 90, 108
Ning Wan-wo, 150
Nü-chen, 44
Nung (Farmers), 34
Nurhaci (Emperor Hsien-tsu), 47, 52, 95

Occupational opportunity structure, 10, 193
Occupational roles, differential ranking of, 34; low, 40
Occupational structure, intersocietal differences in, 192; the demand factor in, 192, 194; social distance factor in, 193
Official career, definition of, 99; and intellectual attainment, 75
Official Directories (*T'ung-kuan lu*), 191
Officialdom, "patrimonial-praebendal," 184, 185; satires and attacks on, 8; social composition of, 45, 81

Official-family tradition, strength of, 158, 187
Officials, examination-path (or regular-path), 117, 118, 145, 146, 148, 172-174, 187; in the highest-rank posts, 104, 105; humanistic education of, 103; irregular-path, 117, 118, 146, 148, 149, 172; legal and extra-legal income of, 61, 63; lower-level, 104, 105; military-path, 173, 174; non-examination-path, 150, 151, 173, 174, 189; special legal privileges of, 51
Omutu, 119, 141

Pa-i (Eight privileged groups), 52
Pai-hsing (Commoners), 57
Pa-ku wen ("Eight-legged essay"), 4
P'an Kuang-tan, 75-78, 82, 177
Pang-yen, 74
Pao-i (Bondservants), 59
Pao T'ing-po, 100
Parsons, T., 21, 22; on seniority and advancement, 165
Pa-ta-chia (Eight Great Families), 52
Perpetual inheritance, the right of, 53
Pi-chi (Miscellaneous notes), 90
Ping (Soldiers), 34
P'ing-min (Commoners), 57
Pi-t'ieh-shih (Clerks), 134
Plato, 26
Po (Earls), 53, 54
Pooling of resources, within the kinship system, 183, 194
Prefect, duties of the, 37; the post of, 73
Preferred path. 142, 143; *see also* Examination path
Primogeniture, 40
Proletariat, 24
Promotions (Bureaucratic), 112; for extraordinary performance, 176; by favoritism, 171; by merit, 171; rate of, 115, 134; by seniority, 171-173, 176; sources of, 173; standardized, 172, 173; "unusual," 173
Provincial inns (*Hui-kuan*), 181, 183, 194
Public Funds, misappropriation of, 33
Pulleyblank, E., 73
Purchase system (*Chüan-na chih-tu*), 5, 13, 64, 124, 131; as means of recruitment, 73

Rank (*P'in-chi*), 112
Rebellion, 5, 6, 8
Recommendation system (*Pao-chü*), 171, 184
Recruitment, determinants of official, 116
Recruitment path, 83, 114, 115; ethnic differences in, 132, 152; and family stratum position, 131, 142, 152; and incumbency in high-rank posts, 139, 143; and later career, 117, 146; the preferred, 117; and rank reached, 152; and stratum position among Chinese, 132
Reference group, 182
Regular path (*Cheng-t'u, k'o-t'u*), 124, 130, 132, 139-142, 187
Retreatism, 6, 8
Ritualism, 6, 7
Rogoff, N., 20, 192, 193
Roles, differentiation of, 18, 19; integrative and highly valued (administrative), 35, 36
Role-models, of Classical China, 26

Sacrificial land (*Chi-t'ien*), 178

Salt Controller (*Yen-yün-shih, yen-fa-tao*), 58
Salt merchants, as aristocracy of the merchants, 57, 58
Schumpeter, J., 158
Secret societies, 33, 45
Seniority, 28, 29, 31, 32, 115, 117, 118, 175, 184, 185, 188, 189; and family stratum position, 165-169; and incumbency in high-rank posts, 170; the nature of, 164; and (official) advancement, 154, 164-170; and rank reached, 166
Shang (Merchants), 34
Shang-chi (Merchant status), 57, 58
Shao T'ing-ts'ai, 100
Shen-chin, 55, 56
Shen Chin-ssu, 181
Shen-shih (Degree-holders), 40, 54-56, 80, 186
Sheng-yüan (Hsiu-ts'ai, licentiates), 15, 55, 56, 65
Shih (Scholars), 34
Shih-huan (Offiicals), 54
Shih I-chih, 98
Shih-ta-fu position, the, 55
Shih-tzu, 55
Shou (Longevity), as a factor in vertical mobility, 75
Shu-jen (Commoners), 57
Shu-yüan (Academies), 38
Six Boards (*Liu-pu*), 112
Six Ministries, 161, 162; *see also* Six Boards
Social distance mobility, definition of, 193, 194
Social structure, nature of Chinese, 72
Ssu-min ("Four peoples"), 34
Status ascription, 109, 159, 160; versus bureaucratic rules, 21, 22, 190
Staunton, Sir George, 52
Stratification, 22, 33, 43, 70, 116; of authority, 43, 46, 158; a comparative theory of, 18-20, 24, 194; discrepancy between legal and social, 56, 57; economic, 19, 20, 34, 38, 60, 61, 69, 70, 154, 176; and elite legal status, 54, 55; empirical studies on Chinese, 82, 118, 183; ethnic factors in, 44; historical dynamics of, 20, 33, 70; legal criteria of, 19, 20, 34, 42, 50, 53, 56, 158; Manchu impact on Chinese, 49; among Manchus, 119; occupational, 34, 39; within officialdom, 54; of power and authority, 20; recent Chinese Marxist studies of, 60, 61, 73, 74; social, 6, 18-20, 42, 158; and social roles, 44; social-evaluational, 34; socio-historical sources on, 84
Stratum, the concept of, 23, 24
Stratum position of family of orientation, 107, 108, 109, 117, 118, 123; *see also* Family stratum position
Sub-chancellor (*Hsüeh-shih*), 141
Sumptuary law, Ch'ing Dynasty, 51, 52
Sung-yün, 98

Ta-Ch'ing hui-tien shih-li, 59
Ta-Ch'ing lü-li, 51
Ta-yüan (Great officials), 111
Tai Ming-shih, 98
T'ai Tsung (Abahai), Emperor, 46
Taiping Rebellion (1850-64), 8, 46, 149, 150, 171, 189
T'ang Hsien-tsu, 94, 105
T'an-hua, 74
Tao-kuang Emperor, 64

Tartar conquest dynasties, 47
Taussig, F. W., 77, 105
Tawney, R. H., 40, 69
Te-hsing-a, 119
Tenancy, 33, 62
Teng Ssu-yü, 95
T'ien Wen-ching, 124
Ting Jih-ch'ang, 150
Ting Ping, 100
To-min (Fallen people), 59
Tsu (Lineage, "Common descent group"), 177
Tsu-p'u, 108
Ts'ui Shu, 150
Tsung-p'u, 108
Tsung-shih chüeh-hao (Imperial titles), 53
Tu-shu t'ien (Study field), 178
Tulisen, 119
T'ung-sheng (Junior students), 55
Tzu (Viscounts), 53, 54

Uprisings, of the Chahar Mongols, 149; of Miao, 149; of Moslems, 149; of Nien Fei, 149; of Pai Lien Chiao, 149

Value-systems, of Chinese and American societies, 5, 29; and social roles, 19
"Veritable Records" (*Shih-lu*), 85, 86, 91, 95

Wang (Princes of the Blood), 52
Wang Chien, 98
Wang Ch'i-shu, 124
Wang Feng-chieh, 180
Wang Hsiang-ch'ien, 94
Warner, W. L., 23, 24, 107
Wealth, in Confucian system, 177
Weber, Max, 41, 74, 184, 185
Wei-k'o, 75
Wen (Civil), 54
Wen-chi, 103, 108
Wen-kuan (Civil officials), 103
Westernizers in China, 150, 151
Wittfogel, K. A., 35, 81, 82, 106
Wu (Military), 54
Wu Chien-chang, 150
Wu Ching-tzu, 8
Wu Ch'ung-yüeh, 99
Wu Hsün, 181
Wu Wo-yao, 8

Yang Kuang-hsien, 98
Yang-lien, 61, 63, 64
Yang Lien-sheng, 182
Yao Ch'i-sheng, 173
Yin-hsiang, 119
Yin privilege, 73
Yin-sheng (Government student by inheritance), 55, 130, 131
Yoto, 53
Yüan Dynasty, 47
Yüan-jen, 110
Yüan Mei, 8, 37, 47
Yü-ch'ien, 106
Yün-ch'i-wei, 53, 54
Yung-cheng Emperor (1723-35), the reign of the, 60
Yung, Prince, 6

Zi, Etienne, 74, 75, 82, 133